The PGA
Manual
of Golf

The PGA Manual of Golf

REVISED AND UPDATED

The Professional's Way to Learn and Play Better Golf

Rick Martino

with Don Wade

WARNER BOOKS

An AOL Time Warner Company

Warner Books, Inc., 1271 Avenue of the Americas, New York, NY 10020
Visit our Web site at www.twbookmark.com.

 An AOL Time Warner Company

Printed in the United States of America
First Printing: May 2002
10 9 8 7 6 5 4 3 2 1

ISBN: 0-446-52653-3
LCCN: 2002101114

Photo Credits
All photos by Montana Pritchard/PGA OF AMERICA with the exception of the
following contributors:

PGA of America: pp. ix, 3, 4, (top and bottom), 5, 6 (middle), 7 (bottom), 9 (bottom),
10 (top and middle), 11 (bottom), 15, 16, 17 (left, right, bottom)

Professional Golfer: pp. 7 (top), 8, 9 (top), 10 (bottom), 11 (top), 12, 13,
14 (full page and top right), 18 (bottom)

Walter Hagen Estate: p. 6 (top)

Paramount News: p. 6 (bottom)

Illustration on p. xii by Lydia Dardi/The PGA of America.

Illustration on p. 37 (top and bottom) from PGA Teaching Manual: The Art and Science of Golf
Instruction, Professional Golfers' Association of America, 1990.

Book design by H. Roberts Design

Dedication

On January 17, 1916, Rodman Wanamaker, the son of department store owner John Wanamaker and the managing director of Wanamaker's New York store hosted a luncheon for New York area golf professionals and a number of prominent amateur golfers. The purpose was to discuss the formation of an organization similar to the Professional Golfers Association of Britain and to establish a trophy and purse for a national match play championship for professionals. At the conclusion of the luncheon, James Hepburn, a former British PGA secretary, had been named to chair a seven-member organizing committee. Approximately three months later, on April 10, 1916, The Professional Golfers' Association of America was founded by 35 charter members.

What they launched, in just over 85 years, has grown into the world's largest working sports organization comprised of more than 26,000 men and women PGA Professionals who are recognized as the game's teaching authorities.

A celebration of their vision and commitment to the game, *The PGA Manual of Golf* is proudly dedicated to our 35 Founding Fathers.

Carl H. Anderson	P. J. Gaudin	Tom McNamara	Gordon Smith
Bert Battell	William Gourlay	Joseph Mitchell	David Stevens
Frank Belwood	W. G. Green	Gilbert Nicholls	Walter Stoddard
Willie Collins	Jack Hagan	Frank Noble	Herbert Strong
J. Crabbe	Walter Hagen	F. N. Noble	Harry Vinall
James Crossan	James Hepburn	Alex Pirie	Robert White
John D. Dunn	John Hobens	Jack Pirie	T. B. Whitehead
W. G. Fotheringham	Jack Mackie	C. W. Singleton	Jack Williams
Edward Galligan	Dan Mackie	Tom Skipper	

Acknowledgments

The information presented in *The PGA Manual of Golf* is based on the teaching curriculum that has been developed for the PGA Learning Center in Port St. Lucie, Fla. The PGA of America would like to acknowledge the outstanding performance of our Teaching Department and their contributions to the development of the Learning Center as well as *The PGA Manual of Golf.* However, to acknowledge each PGA Professional who over the course of time has made a significant contribution to that curriculum, this book and the many theories of instruction for the game would be impossible.

Teaching is an integral part of the history of The PGA, which was founded by English and Scottish golf professionals who had emigrated to the U.S. Their purpose in forming the Association was to create greater interest in the game and encourage people to learn how to play golf.

As technology began to change how America lived and conducted business, PGA Professionals were among the first to adapt technical concepts to teaching the game. In 1919, reigning PGA Champion Jim Barnes authored the book, *Picture Analysis of Golf Strokes,* which was the first golf book to use high-speed sequence photography and immediately became the leading instructional manual of the day.

As the manufacture of equipment became more streamlined and the game became more popular, new methods of teaching began to evolve. In the 1930s, PGA Professional Irv Schoss began using high-speed cameras to film his students' golf swing. Eventually he was filming and analyzing the swings of hundreds of professional golfers. Today, video technology enables PGA Professionals to provide their students with instant analysis.

To spread the word, the pages of *The Professional Golfer,* today's PGA

Magazine, became an excellent vehicle for displaying swing sequences of the game's top players, graphically showing how different shots should be executed and discussing the variety of teaching methods and programs that were being employed throughout the U.S.

As scientific disciplines matured and researchers began to learn more about the human body and how we function, PGA Professionals were eager to embrace that knowledge as well. The concept of how a student learns and the biomechanics involved in the golf swing became just as important to any instruction program as teaching a proper grip.

In 1986, The PGA established the Teacher of the Year Award to recognize the outstanding performance of some its most dedicated members. The first recipient of this national award was Manuel de la Torre of Milwaukee, Wisconsin, Country Club. Each of The PGA's 41 Sections also honors their own PGA Teacher of the Year.

Today, PGA Professionals teach everybody how to play golf. Juniors, Seniors, Inner City Youths with limited access to golf courses, Special Olympians, the Physically Disabled, High-Handicappers, Heads of State, Royalty, Scratch Golfers, Tour Players and you.

The PGA Manual of Golf is the product of an evolutionary process that has been taking place throughout the golf industry since the late 19th century. Every PGA Professional who ever gave a golf lesson or showed someone how to improve their game has contributed in some way or another to this teaching body of knowledge.

We will always be thankful for their commitment and their contributions.

The Professional Golfers' Association of America

Contents

Introduction

Welcome to *The PGA Manual of Golf.*

This book is designed to provide you with an overview of the game of golf, and the skills that are necessary to play the game. *The PGA Manual of Golf* also mirrors the training techniques that are taught at the national PGA Learning Center in Port St. Lucie, Fla.

An integral part of the teaching program developed at the PGA Learning Center is the Player Evaluation Analysis Kit (PEAK) System. The core section of this manual follows the principles that were developed for instruction at the PGA Learning Center.

The first principle is the player's level of fitness and biomechanics. These determine the type of swing that best matches your physical makeup. Your fitness determines the type of golf skills you may develop.

The next principle, equipment, is one aspect of golf that many players find fascinating. It is necessary that your equipment not only *fits* you, but also *fits* your game.

The third principle addresses the mental aspects that complement your physical skills. Developing this area includes the management of your shots, how you develop and improve those shots, and how you use those shots when you compete with the golf course or other players.

The five scoring skill areas are putting, chipping and pitching, bunker play, iron play and wood play. As you master these shotmaking skills, you will see lower and lower scores.

The manual contains a chapter on the history of golf, outlining the events that brought the game to where it is today, and a chapter on golf course etiquette.

We also review what a day at the course is like, the best ways to start youngsters playing golf, how you can be a good guest when you're invited to play at another course and a glossary of the terms used in golf.

The PGA Manual of Golf is your guide to understanding the game of golf, and how to enjoy the golf experience. I encourage you to further enhance that experience by taking advantage of the expertise of the PGA Professional at the club or course where you play.

Rick Martino
Director of Instruction
The PGA of America

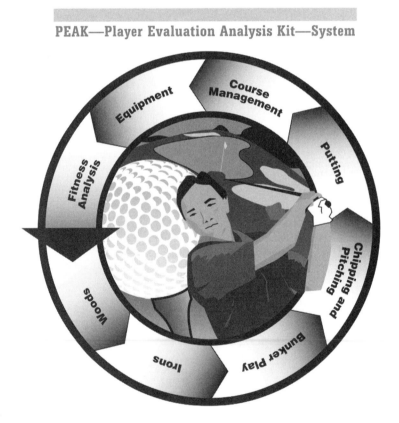

PEAK—Player Evaluation Analysis Kit—System

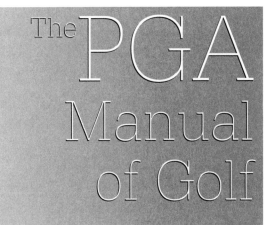

The PGA
Manual
of Golf

The History of Golf

While golf's traditions are firmly rooted in early Scotland, there is ample evidence based on written references and artwork that early variations of the game involving hitting a stone with a stick to a specific target were played in Asia and even parts of what is now known as South America. There's even a persuasive school of thought that argues some early form of a golflike game was played by Roman legionnaires who occupied Europe. Their game, "Paganica," consisted of hitting feather-stuffed leather balls with clublike sticks.

But the strongest case for the true foundation of the game can be made for Holland, where the Dutch made references to golflike games dating back to the 13th century. In fact, the best evidence lies in the works of Dutch artists that depict people hitting balls with rudimentary forms of golf clubs, as well as a description of a game where teams of four men played across the countryside, hitting balls with clubs. The winners were the first team to hit the doors on four buildings. The description was written in 1297 and notes that the winners received a barrel of beer.

So how then did golf arrive in Scotland? Almost certainly as a result of trade between the Scots and Dutch, which grew substantially during the Middle Ages as the construction of improved sailing vessels made the passage both safer and faster. Dutch sea merchants would often find themselves in ports along the east coast of Scotland, waiting for their ships to be either loaded or unloaded or waiting for bad weather to end or favorable winds to arrive. With all this time on their hands, it's reasonable to assume that they would spend hours playing their early forms of golf. And it's also reasonable to assume that the Scots would be fascinated by the game and take it up themselves, particularly on the public links land that was ill suited to farming.

The first artistic evidence of the game's existence in what would become the British Isles consisted of a stained-glass window in Gloucester Cathedral depicting a man swinging a club at a ball. But the most infamous evidence of the game's impact in Scotland was a 1457 Act of Parliament banning the playing of golf by order of King James. It seems too many of the king's subjects were neglecting archery practice in favor of golf.

Regardless of the game's varied origins, it is safe to say that the game of golf, as it is played today—with an assortment of clubs designed to help players get a ball into a series of holes in the fewest number of strokes—emerged in Scotland and spread throughout what we now call Great Britain.

While essentially democratic in nature, particularly in places like St. Andrews, where, in 1553 the Archbishop of St. Andrews confirmed the right of the townspeople to play golf over the links, the rigors of life for the working class and the relatively high cost of equipment—especially balls—ensured that it would become a pastime for the wealthy and titled. The most famous of these was Mary Queen of Scots, who was passionate about the game. Perhaps just a bit too passionate for her own good, the queen was seen playing golf within two weeks of her husband Darnley's death. This evidence of insufficient mourning led, at least in part, to her execution.

Golf enjoyed a remarkable growth in Scotland during the latter half of the 18th century. In 1744, the Honourable Company of Edinburgh Golfers held the first meeting of what is believed to be the first golf club in the world. That same year, the 13 Leith Code of Rules were established and were generally adopted across Scotland within the decade.

In 1754, the St. Andrews Club was founded and hosted its first tournament, attracting a field of 22. The winner was Bailie William Landale, a local merchant. In 1764, a round of golf at St. Andrews was reduced from 22 to 18 holes and, in 1834, King William IV bestowed the title Royal and Ancient Golf Club of St. Andrews upon the club.

As the British extended their empire to the far reaches of the globe, British expatriates transplanted the game wherever they went. In 1829, the Calcutta Golf Club, now Royal Calcutta, became the first golf club outside Britain. In 1870 (Royal) Adelaide Golf Club became the first such club in Australia and the following year Dunedin Golf Club opened in New Zealand. In 1873, (Royal) Montreal Golf Club was founded, becoming the first golf club in North America, and in 1885 the Royal Cape Club opened in South Africa, becoming the first club in Africa.

In 1858 Allan Robertson, a ballmaker by trade who is generally considered the first great player, died from jaundice at age 44. Robertson's death prefaced the beginning of championship golf. The first (British) Open Championship was played in 1860 at Prestwick. Willie Park Sr. became the first "Champion Golfer," beating a field of eight professionals. In 1861, the championship was opened "to all the world."

Young Tom Morris of St. Andrews won the Open Championship in 1869,

'70 and '71 and retired the red Moroccan championship belt. No championship was held in 1872 and in 1873 a silver claret jug was first presented to the Open Champion—Young Tom Morris. Two years later, on Christmas Eve, Young Tom died at age 24, three months after the death of his wife and infant son. Upon his death, a plaque was placed in St. Andrews Cathedral, where it remains today. The inscription reads:

"Deeply regretted by numerous friends and all golfers, he thrice in succession won the championship belt and held it without rivalry and yet without envy, his many amiable qualities being no less acknowledged than his golfing techniques."

He was golf's first great hero and remains a hero to this day.

Golf Comes to America

Historically, the game of golf's popularity in the United States is thought to date to 1888 with the founding of the St. Andrews Golf Club in Yonkers, N.Y., just north of New York City. In a sense this is true, since St. Andrews is the oldest club in continual operation today. But there is ample evidence that golf was played elsewhere. For example, in 1743 a shipment of some 100 clubs and several hundred balls arrived in Charleston, S.C., from Leith, Scotland. A club was formed in Charleston in 1786 and another in Savannah, Ga., in 1795. Indeed, newspaper accounts indicate that golf was played in varying degrees as far west as California and as far south as Texas prior to 1888.

Certainly, to some extent the early growth of golf in North America can be attributed to the British colonial influence, but to a larger extent, the growth was owed to the arrival of many top Scottish professionals in the States. Immigrants such as Willie Dunn Jr., Jim and Dave Foulis, Alex Taylor, Jock Hutchison and Laurie Auchterlonie of the famous St. Andrews family were not only skilled players, but also clubmakers, teachers and even golf course designers and builders. This explains why so many old courses, particularly along the East Coast, are so reminiscent of the courses in Scotland. It's also worth noting that a great number of Scottish immigrants may not have been professionals when they left their mother country, but assumed the title when they saw the seemingly endless possibilities open to a decent Scottish player when he arrived in America.

Old Tom Morris, left, won four British Opens from 1861 to 1867. His son, Young Tom, right, won four Opens of his own before his tragic death in 1875 at age 24.

The United States Golf Association, which is the governing body of the game in America, was established following a meeting of representatives from five clubs: the Newport (R.I.) Country Club, Shinnecock Hills Golf Club in Southampton, N.Y., The Country Club in Brookline, Mass., St. Andrews Golf Club in Hastings-on-Hudson, N.Y., and the Chicago Golf Club. The Dec. 22, 1894, meeting was held to resolve a debate over how to determine the national amateur champion. To that end, the first U.S. Amateur was played the following year at Newport, drawing a field of 32, and the first Open was played the following day, almost as an afterthought.

The Great Triumvirate

By 1900, there were 1,000 courses dotting America, but even allowing for immigration, most of the great players still resided in the British Isles and none were more dominant than Harry Vardon, John Henry Taylor and James Braid—The Great Triumvirate.

The three men were born within a year of each other and went on to dominate championship golf. From 1894, until the beginning of World War I in 1914, there were just five years in which the British Open was not won by one of the three. Harry Vardon won six times, while Taylor and Braid captured the Old Claret Jug five times each. In addition, Vardon won the U.S. Open.

Vardon was of particular importance; not just for his record, but also for the impact he had on the game and the way it was perceived by the public. While he did not, as many claim, invent the overlapping grip that bears his name, he certainly popularized it. More importantly, he almost single-handedly elevated the status of golf professionals, especially in the class-bound society in prewar England. He was also the first golfer to make considerable sums of money for his endorsements and exhibitions. The Vardon Flyer ball was enormously popular, and Vardon's public appearances in the United States invariably sold out and did much to foster the game's growth on this side of the Atlantic.

James Braid won five British Opens in the early 1900s, a total exceeded only by Harry Vardon and equaled by Peter Thomson and Tom Watson.

Harry Vardon and Ted Ray were dominant players in the late 1800s and early 1900s.

Francis Ouimet and the Great Upset of 1913

The U.S. Open came to The Country Club in Brookline, Mass., in 1913, and two of the favorites were naturally Vardon and Ray. They were in the country for a series of lucrative exhibitions. At the end of 72 holes they were tied for the lead by the most unlikely of players in the field, a 20-year-old amateur named Francis Ouimet.

Ouimet grew up across the street from The Country Club and learned the game there as a caddie. He had a local reputation as a fine player but had yet to distinguish himself nationally. That he made it into the playoff with the formidable Vardon and Ray was a remarkable accomplishment, but even his most fervent admirers didn't expect him to prevail.

But in the rainy, overcast conditions, Ray struggled on his way to a 78. Vardon, however, dueled with Ouimet until a gamble on the par-4 17th failed, leading to a 77. Ouimet, displaying virtually no nervousness, calmly shot an even-par 72 and was carried off the course on the shoulders of adoring fellow Bostonians.

Ouimet's victory marked the first time an American-born player—and an amateur, for good measure—had won the Open. It made front-page headlines across the country. But just as important as Ouimet's victory was his character. He was instinctively a sportsman and a gentleman and possessed an appealing, modest nature. In short, he was the perfect man for the perfect occasion. Ouimet would go on to win two U.S. Amateurs and was the first American to serve as captain of the Royal and Ancient Golf Club of St. Andrews.

Ouimet's victory symbolized the emergence of Americans as the golfing equals of their British cousins, and led to the formation of two team competitions that have deepened the golfing ties on both sides of the Atlantic.

When Francis Ouimet beat Harry Vardon and Ted Ray in a playoff for the 1913 U.S. Open, it helped popularize golf in America.

The first was the Walker Cup, a biennial match between teams of amateurs from the United States and Great Britain/Ireland, which began in 1922. The cup itself was donated by then-USGA President George Herbert Walker, the grandfather of President George W. Bush.

Then, in 1927, the first Ryder Cup Matches were played between teams of professionals from the United States and Great Britain/Ireland. A wealthy English seed merchant, Samuel Ryder, sponsored the early matches, which have evolved into one of the most popular events in all of sports.

Lost in all the excitement surrounding Ouimet's victory was the per-

Walter Hagen was enormously popular on both sides of the Atlantic.

Walter Hagen was brilliant in match play competitions, winning five PGA Championships, four of them in succession.

Walter Hagen was also a master of links-style golf, winning four British Opens.

formance turned in by another player making his Open debut. Walter Hagen, also 20, was a brash, hugely talented professional from Rochester, N.Y., who was in contention until he was felled by a case of shellfish poisoning on the final day.

Hagen was the game's first great showman. The press adored him and so did the public, on both sides of the Atlantic. He had an instinctive genius for publicity and a carefree, devil-may-care attitude that fostered comparisons with Babe Ruth.

But Hagen's showmanship would have been meaningless if he hadn't backed it up with a remarkable talent. He was a brilliant putter and had a gift for scrambling out of trouble, which was helpful since he was far from the most accurate player who ever lived.

How good was Hagen? In total, he won two U.S. Opens, four British Opens and five PGA Championships, four of them in succession, back in the days when the PGA Championship was contested at match play. He also played on every American Ryder Cup team from its inception in 1927 until 1937.

Like Vardon, Hagen used his popularity as a wedge to literally open the clubhouse doors for professionals. In 1920, when the Inverness Club in Toledo, Ohio, welcomed professionals into the clubhouse during the U.S. Open, Hagen passed the hat among his fellow professionals and presented the club with an elegant grandfather's clock in appreciation. At the 1923 British Open, where he finished second, Hagen refused to enter the clubhouse for the awards presentation because professionals had been banned from the clubhouse during the championship. Instead, he invited the gallery to join him at a local pub. They happily obliged him.

On the heels of the success enjoyed by the likes of Hagen and others, The Professional Golfers' Association of

America was formed in 1916 following a meeting of New York City area professionals and prominent amateurs. The goals of The PGA of America were the promotion of golf and improvement in the vocational lot of golf professionals.

Bobby Jones and the Grand Slam

The 1920s are known as "The Golden Age of Sports" in America, and with good reason. This decade produced legends like Babe Ruth, tennis great Bill Tilden, football star Red Grange and heavyweight champion Jack Dempsey. But in this remarkable era, no athlete eclipsed Bobby Jones.

People can and will debate who is the greatest golfer of all time, and that can never be resolved, which is the beauty of the exercise. But it is hard to imagine any ranking of the top five—maybe even the top three—that doesn't include Bob Jones.

Jones won 13 major championships: four U.S. Opens, three British Opens, five U.S. Amateurs and the 1930 British Amateur. His epic achievement came in 1930 when he won the U.S. and British Opens and U.S. and British Amateur Championships. He then retired from competitive golf at the age of 28.

If his record alone weren't remarkable enough, consider that he competed as an amateur and was really not much more than a weekend golfer. In the winter months, when there were no championships to prepare for, he rarely touched a club. He had degrees from Georgia Tech (engineering) and Harvard (literature) and was admitted to the Georgia bar after just one year of law school.

Following his retirement from competitive golf, Jones and a friend, Wall Street financier Clifford Roberts, founded the Augusta National Golf Club. Jones, who greatly admired the work of Dr. Alister Mackenzie, collaborated with Mackenzie on the design of the course. Upon

Bobby Jones was one of the greatest golfers in history, winning 13 major championships before retiring from competitive golf in 1930 at age 28.

Bobby Jones putting with "Calamity Jane," his favorite old blade. It is on display at the United States Golf Association Museum at the Golf House in Far Hills, New Jersey.

When Gene Sarazen made a double eagle on the par-5 15th hole during the 1935 Augusta National tournament, it helped put the Masters on the sporting map.

the course's completion, Jones and Roberts decided to host a tournament to help publicize the club. The field was comprised of the best players in the game and attracted newspapermen who were returning north following baseball's spring training in Florida. The Augusta National Invitation Tournament was first played in 1934 and was immediately perceived as something special by the players, press and public, owing largely to Jones's involvement. The name was changed to The Masters the following year, and when Gene Sarazen holed a 4-wood approach to the par-5 15th for a double eagle and then defeated Craig Wood in a playoff the following day, the headlines around the world ensured the success of the tournament and, eventually, the club itself. It soon came to be recognized as one of the four major professional championships, along with the PGA Championship, the British Open and the U.S. Open. It's worth noting that the first Senior PGA Championship was played at Augusta in 1937 and again the following year.

After his military service in World War II, Jones was afflicted with syringomyelia, a degenerative disease of the nervous system that ravaged his body. It was a particularly cruel disease for a person who had been such a magnificent athlete, but he bore it with courage.

When he died in 1971, *The New York Times* noted, "with dignity, he quit the memorable scene on which he nothing common did, or mean."

But it was left to the respected writer Herbert Warren Wind to capture the pure essence of the great Bobby Jones:

"As a young man he was able to stand up to just about the best that life has to offer, which is not easy, and later he stood up, with equal grace, to just about the worst."

To this day, Jones remains the standard against which all golfers are measured, both as players and as sportsmen.

The American Triumvirate

Golf is fortunate in that its eras seem to flow together so seamlessly, and that was certainly the case following the retirement of Bobby Jones. While Hagen and Sarazen and other of Jones's contemporaries continued to compete in the major championships, there was a void waiting to be filled by the next dominant player. That player's name was John Byron Nelson.

It is a coincidence—a historical fluke, actually—that Byron Nelson was born in 1912, the same year as Ben Hogan and Sam Snead. What are the odds on three of the greatest players in the history of the game being born in the same year? In fact, Nelson and Hogan were born just miles apart and caddied together as boys at Fort Worth's Glen Garden Country Club.

Of the three, Nelson made his mark first, winning the 1937 Masters. He would follow it with victories in four other major championships and would win 54 PGA Tour events in all before retiring at age 34 to run a cattle ranch in Texas.

Nelson is generally credited with the development of the modern swing. He emerged just as steel shafts were beginning to replace traditional hickory shafts. One clear advantage to steel was that it allowed players to practice longer without fear of breaking a shaft. But as Nelson was the first to realize, steel required a swing that was less handsy and more dominated by the large muscles of the torso and the legs.

Nelson was phenomenally accurate but also very powerful. It is no exaggeration to state that he would go round after round without missing a fairway. And his quiet demeanor masked a fierce competitiveness. The whole package came together in 1945 when he won 11 tournaments in a row and 18 overall. It is one record that almost certainly will never be equaled.

Beyond his record, however, Byron Nelson is widely respected for his character, sportsmanship and simple decency as a human being.

Byron Nelson won five major championships and a total of 54 PGA Tour events before retiring to his Texas ranch at age 34.

Byron Nelson is widely regarded as one of the greatest gentlemen in the history of the game.

"People can always argue who was the greatest player, but Byron is the greatest gentlemen the game has ever known," says 1964 U.S. Open Champion Ken Venturi, who honed his game under Nelson's tutelage.

Nelson's domination of the game got its first real challenge when Samuel Jackson Snead came out of the Virginia mountains and joined the Tour in 1936. He won four times in 1937 and eight times in 1938. He was the supreme athlete. A writer once described him as being "strong as a bull and as graceful as a panther."

Snead's swing is, if not the best in history, certainly the most beautiful and widely admired. He was a tremendously long driver, particularly into the wind. He could hit every shot in the bag.

Many people believe Sam Snead is the purest shotmaker to ever play the game.

Even when he was practicing his putting, Sam Snead could always draw a crowd.

When it came to power and grace, there was never a better or more beautiful swing than Sam Snead's.

"Sam could hit shots that other people never even dreamed of," said the late Dave Marr, the 1965 PGA Champion. "People talk about natural players, but Sam was supernatural."

Snead also had a sublime short game, was brilliant from bunkers, could finesse a 1-iron as though the club had been invented just for him, and was a ferocious competitor with an insatiable will to win.

"Desire to win is the most important thing in sports," he once said. "No one ever had more than I did."

That desire resulted in a record official 81 Tour victories (he claims more), the last coming in 1965 when he was 52 years and 10 months old. He won three PGA Championships, three Masters and the 1946 British Open. He never won the U.S. Open, but once figured that if he'd shot 69 or better in the final round he would have won seven Opens.

On top of that, he was a showman in the Hagen mold. The writers loved him and he loved center stage.

Ben Hogan was fascinated by every facet of the golf swing and shared his knowledge in some of the finest instruction books ever written.

"You can't overestimate how important Sam has been to the growth of golf and the Tour," Byron Nelson once explained. "Players like Ben (Hogan) and me loved to play but didn't much care for doing radio shows and the like. Sam would talk to a chimpanzee if it had a notebook and a press badge. And I don't think there's a place on earth he hasn't done a clinic or an exhibition."

Five-time British Open Champion Peter Thomson once praised Sam Snead when he said, "Sam is like the classic symphonies. He is timeless."

Ben Hogan's shotmaking and course management were a model for generations of players that admired his skill and courage.

Unlike Snead and Nelson, who won early and often, Ben Hogan struggled mightily before emerging as one of the game's greatest champions. He went broke twice and was on the verge of quitting altogether when he finished second and won $380 in the 1938 Oakland Open.

He finally broke through following World War II with victories in the 1946 and 1948 PGA Championships and the 1948 U.S. Open. But in February 1949 he and his wife, Valerie, were returning to Texas when a bus hit their car. Hogan instinctively threw himself across his wife to protect her and, in doing so, saved his own life, as the steering column would have almost certainly impaled him. Still, his injuries were so severe few people expected him to ever play golf again, let alone win at a championship level.

But Hogan came back and won the 1950 U.S. Open in a playoff at Merion. In 1953, he won the Masters, U.S. Open and British Open. In all, he won nine major championships and 63 Tour events, before retiring to run the golf equipment company that bears his name.

Ben Hogan's legacy rests on his courage, determination and willingness to work excruciatingly hard, first to succeed, then to overcome massive injuries and rebuild a game that came as close to perfection from tee to green as anyone has ever come.

Babe Zaharias was a brilliant all-around athlete who helped found the Ladies Professional Golf Association.

The Ladies' Game

Golf had long been popular among women, although in the years prior to World War II, it was largely restricted to those women who had the time and wealth to be able to indulge themselves in the sport. But following the war, life began to change for women, particularly in the United States. The country enjoyed a period of prosperity and Americans—both men and women—began to find themselves with additional time for recreation.

This reality wasn't lost on the manufacturers of golf equipment, particularly at Wilson Sporting Goods, which encouraged the founding of the Ladies Professional Golf Association. A fledgling Women's Professional Golf Association had been founded in 1944 but it had all but faded away by 1948 when Wilson stepped in and hired sports agent and promoter Fred Corcoran as its marketing director. Corcoran, who represented Babe Didrikson Zaharias, worked wonders. The new organization boasted some fine players: Patty Berg, Peggy Kirk, Louise Suggs, Marilynn Smith and Betsy Rawls, but their marquee name was Babe Zaharias, arguably the greatest female athlete in history. After winning two gold medals and a silver medal in track and field at the 1932 Olympics, she turned to golf, first as an amateur and then as a professional.

Like Walter Hagen, the Babe loved the limelight and seeing her name in the headlines. People who knew nothing about golf would flock to LPGA tournaments just to watch her in action. In all, she won 31 tournaments including three U.S. Women's Opens, before her death from cancer in 1956. By that time, the LPGA was well on its way to a sound footing.

The LPGA enjoyed a phenomenal growth in popularity when rookie Nancy Lopez won five tournaments in a row and nine in all in 1978. Lopez's arrival coincided with an influx of talented young players like Amy Alcott, Hollis Stacy, Pat Bradley, Jan Stephenson and Beth Daniel, just to name a few.

The increased media exposure, coupled with the effects of Title IX, the federal legislation designed to encourage female participation in collegiate sports, led to a growth in golf among women in every aspect of the game.

Today, with international stars such as Sweden's Annika Sorenstam, Australia's Karrie Webb and South Korea's Se Ri Pak, the LPGA can rightfully claim to be the most successful women's sports organization in history.

Patty Berg's infectious charm and enthusiasm helped attract millions of new golfers to the game.

Arnie

In 1954, a strong, handsome kid from Pennsylvania won the U.S. Amateur by beating Bob Sweeny on the final hole. His name was Arnold Palmer and he was something to behold. He slashed at the ball with enormous power, and constantly attacked the course. He was a bold, often brilliant putter and delighted in competition. Still, not everyone was convinced he would become the player to fill the void left as Hogan and Snead wound down their careers.

"Wilson asked me to go look at this kid but I never thought he'd amount to a hill of beans," said Gene Sarazen. "He hit it all over the lot but made enough putts from all over the place to win the championship. I told Wilson to forget it. Shows you how much I know."

The kid turned professional in 1956 and became the most popular player in the game's history. As millions of new golfers took up the game—in no small part because of the growth of television—they may have believed they had a swing like Sam Snead's but, in their heart of hearts, knew they played with Arnie's singular confidence and abandon.

Palmer went on to win 60 tournaments on the PGA Tour. He won the 1960 U.S. Open with one of the most famous final-round charges of his career. He won four Masters, helping to solidify its vast popularity among the masses. He won the 1961 and 1962 British Opens and is generally credited with reviving the game's oldest championship. That he, the son of a PGA Professional, never won the PGA Championship is one of the few regrets in his remarkable life.

Arnold Palmer's sheer power and charisma were two keys to his popularity.

There was never a golfer who took more joy in playing the game or who was more beloved by millions of fans than Arnold Palmer.

When Arnold Palmer turned 50 and joined the Senior PGA Tour, he assured its remarkable success.

It is a testimonial to Palmer's popularity that while his last Tour victory came in 1973, he remains to this day one of the biggest draws in the game. When he joined the Senior PGA Tour in 1980—where he would win 10 tournaments—he made it vastly more popular among fans, the press, sponsors and television networks.

It's fair to say that if Arnold Palmer hadn't come along, professional golf would be a very different game today.

Jack Nicklaus and His Challengers

The 1962 U.S. Open at Oakmont was one of the moments when the face of golf changed dramatically. The clear favorite going into the championship was Arnold Palmer, then at the height of his game and playing in his own backyard in front of a huge and adoring gallery.

But at the end of 72 holes, Palmer was tied with a 23-year-old Tour rookie named Jack Nicklaus, who had won two U.S. Amateurs and had finished second to Palmer in the 1960 Open. By the end of the playoff, Nicklaus had his first Open title and golf had a new dominant player.

On his record alone, a case can be made that Jack Nicklaus is the greatest player in history. Besides his two victories in the U.S. Amateur, he won four U.S. Opens, three British Opens, six masters and five PGA Championships. He won 70 PGA Tour events and 10 events on the Senior Tour.

But just as important, Nicklaus is the supreme sportsman. His father, Charlie, worshipped Bobby Jones and young Jack was no different. It's often been said that as gracious as Nicklaus is in victory, he is even more generous in defeat, no matter how painful. Like Jones, Berg, Nelson, Snead, Palmer, Zaharias, and so many others before and after him, Jack Nicklaus helped sustain the spirit of the game.

No one ever made more crucial putts than Jack Nicklaus, who many historians regard as the greatest player of all time.

Equally impressive is the number of truly great players he has successfully dueled with throughout his career. In the three decades it can be said that he dominated the game, he faced down challenges from South Africa's Gary Player, Billy Casper, Ray Floyd, Hale Irwin, Johnny Miller, England's Nick Faldo, Spain's Seve Ballesteros and, perhaps most memorably, Lee Trevino and Tom Watson—just to name the players elected to the World Golf Hall of Fame.

From the time that Jack Nicklaus's greatness began to become obvious, people have talked about the "next Jack Nicklaus" emerging. Tom Weiskopf was the first and Tiger Woods is the latest. But the true measure of the man isn't whether or not he is the greatest player of all time. The simple reality is that there will never be another Jack Nicklaus.

Lee Trevino always played his best when he was going toe-to-toe against Jack Nicklaus.

Tom Watson won 34 PGA Tour events, including five British Opens, two Masters and the 1982 U.S. Open.

Raymond Floyd has been one of the game's toughest competitors, both on the PGA Tour and the Senior PGA Tour.

17

Tiger Woods has brought a new level of
excitement and popularity to professional
golf around the world. He won two PGA
Championships in just six attempts, to go
along with his two Masters titles and victories in the U.S. and British Opens—all
by the age of 26.

South Africa's Gary Player has been an
inspiration for international players
around the world.

And Into the Future . . .

Late in his life, Ben Hogan was asked if today's players are better than the players of his generation. Hogan didn't mince any words.

"Of course they are," he said. "Every part of the game is better—the golf courses, the equipment, the players—everything. Good night, I'd feel like the players of my era had failed if the game wasn't better today."

And indeed it is. The changes in course design and maintenance are breathtaking. Equipment is light-years better than it was even a generation ago. The players are bigger and stronger and in much better shape. Teaching and coaching are assuming increased importance among players looking for every edge in improving their skills. Increasingly, the game of golf is being exposed to a wider audience and that is reflected in the emerging diversity of the golf population—which is also experiencing a phenomenal growth around the world.

But for all the improvements and changes, what remain constant are the very nature of the game, the challenge posed by the golf course, and the spirit of camaraderie and sportsmanship in which it's played. We'll give the last word to Sam Snead:

"Golf's the greatest game of them all," he said. "No one's ever been able to beat it, and no one ever will."

2

A Matter
of Etiquette

Golf is unique in sports in that the importance of etiquette is so paramount that its fundamentals are spelled out in the first section of the Rules of Golf. Indeed, it is etiquette that is both the heart and soul of golf and what separates the game from almost all other sports. Without knowledge of proper etiquette, a player's understanding of the nature of the game is only shallow at best.

What follows is a summation of Section I of the Rules of Golf, but we urge you to take the time to read the exact wording in the Rules of Golf. Copies of the Rules of Golf can be obtained from your local PGA Professional, major bookstore, or from the United States Golf Association in Far Hills, N.J.

The first topic addressed in Section I is titled **Courtesy on the Course** and its first subsection deals with Safety.

SAFETY—A player's first responsibility prior to making a stroke or practice swing is to make sure no one is standing close enough to be hit by the club, the ball or anything else which could cause injury or damage, such as sticks, dirt, or rocks.

CONSIDERATION OF OTHERS—The player who has the honor on the tee should be allowed to play before any other player tees his or her ball.

No one should move, talk, stand near the hole or near a player or otherwise distract a fellow player. In fairness to all, golfers should play without delay. In addition, no one should play until any other players are clearly out of range. If a player or players are searching for a ball that they have reason to believe may not be readily found, they should signal golfers behind them to play through, even if this action is taken in advance of the five-minute limit stipulated for the search. The party searching for the ball should not play until the group they wave through is clearly out of range. Finally, when a group finishes putting out on a green, they should immediately vacate that green so as not to hold up play.

SUMMARY—Before you make a swing or hit a shot, ensure no one is standing where they might be in danger. Treat everyone with the same courtesy you'd appreciate. Play as quickly as is reasonably possible. If you are holding up a group behind you, invite them to play through. Leave the green as soon as everyone in your group has putted out.

PRIORITY ON THE COURSE—The next subject addressed in Section I is which groups or matches have priority on the course. The Rules state that unless specified by local rules, two-ball matches have priority. In truth, this is a carry-over from the game's Scottish roots, where two-ball matches refer to an alternate-shot match between two teams within a foursome. This format, while very popular in the British Isles, is rarely played in the United States or Canada.

Section I also states that a single player has no standing and should give way to a match of any kind. In other words, a single player has no expectation that he or she should be allowed to play through a foursome, although the Rules do not prohibit this. Also, a group playing an 18-hole match is entitled to play through a group playing fewer than 18 holes.

Finally, etiquette requires that any group that fails to maintain its pace of play and falls more than one clear hole behind the preceding group should invite the group behind it to play through.

SUMMARY—Alternate-shot matches have precedence on the course. Foursomes are under no requirement to let smaller groups of golfers play through, including single players. A group playing 18 holes should be invited to play through by a group playing fewer than 18 holes. A match that is playing so slowly that it has fallen one clear hole behind the group in front must allow the foursome behind it to play through.

CARE FOR THE COURSE—Finally, Section I concerns itself with the proper respect a golfer owes to the course. This respect is deeply embedded in the spirit of the game. Witness this story about Old Tom Morris, the longtime professional at the Old Course at St. Andrews in the 1800s:

One Sunday, a man came to St. Andrews and was told that the Old Course was closed for the day. The man grew indignant, which had absolutely no impact on Old Tom.

"Sir," he said. "You may not need a day of rest but the Old Course does."

Section I specifies that prior to leaving a bunker, a player must smooth over any holes or footprints he or she produced. Players should repair and replace divots, as well as ball marks or spike marks on the putting surface.

The section specifies that spike marks should be replaced following completion of the hole. The Rules stress that players and their caddies should ensure that no damage is done to the hole by standing too close or by carelessly replacing the flagstick. Neither should players lean on their putters, since this could damage the green. The Rules specify that anyone using a golf car should carefully observe all local rules and that players should carefully avoid damaging any part of the course—with particular attention to the tees—when taking practice swings.

SUMMARY—In short, this segment lays down the common sense responsibilities a player has for the care of the course.

While not specified in Section I, there is one other area of etiquette that bears mentioning, and that is the responsibility a spectator has when watching a competition. While it is perfectly appropriate to reward a well-played shot with applause or cheering, it goes against the spirit of the game to cheer when a player hits a poor shot or gets a bad break.

In short, Section I—like so much of the Rules of Golf—comes down to a matter of fairness and common sense: Simply treat your fellow players and the course with courtesy and respect and you'll be treated that way as well.

Beyond the areas discussed in Section I of the Rules of Golf, no section on etiquette these days would be complete without a discussion of the proper use of a golf car.

Even if a course doesn't post these guidelines, they are important to follow.

First, whenever possible stay on cart paths, and if cars are allowed on the fairways, travel to and from your ball on a 90-degree angle. Never drive golf cars near greens, and if the course requires you to remain on cart paths, either as a general rule or because of wet conditions, always bring a selection of clubs with you prior to the shot. There's nothing that slows down play—and is more frustrating for fellow-players—than a golfer who walks back and forth from their golf car in search of the proper club.

3

Health, Fitness and You

One of the enduring misconceptions about golf and golfers—especially among those whose sole knowledge of the game comes from watching the classic movie *Caddyshack*—is that golfers are overweight, out-of-shape buffoons whose idea of strenuous weight lifting is a freshly opened can of beer.

In truth, golf, particularly at the highest levels of competition, is an athletic activity that requires hand-eye coordination, strength, concentration, discipline and, in many cases, sheer endurance. Even players with the most technically perfect swings and proficient short games will not play to their potential if they are not physically fit.

A person can commit to all the lessons in the world, but if they aren't willing to make even the minimal sacrifices needed to get into shape, then it's likely all the professional's efforts will be for naught in the long haul.

To gauge just how important health and fitness is in golf, all you have to do is take a look at the players on the PGA Tour, Senior PGA Tour or LPGA tour. Week in and week out, they flock to the fitness trailers that are available at the site of tournaments. Many even have their own personal fitness trainers to oversee their workout routines and diets. Not only does this help them improve or maintain their strength and flexibility, but it also helps prevent or mend injuries.

All this focus on health and fitness validates the example set by PGA Hall of Fame member Gary Player, who has long been a vocal and passionate advocate of fitness, whether by exercising and lifting weights, or in following a strict diet and nutrition regimen.

"For years and years, players kidded me about my weight lifting and my insistence on a healthy diet," said Player. "But isn't it a marvelous thing now to see so many people who are dedicated to just such behavior? And not just young players, mind you, but also my fellow seniors. I will tell you this: There are many reasons players like Tiger Woods and Annika Sorenstam are shooting these wonderful low scores, but I believe that you cannot overestimate the role that exercise and a proper diet play in all this."

Both professional and amateur golfers are keenly aware of the importance of health and fitness.

Just as there is no one correct club or set of clubs for everyone, there is no one fitness and nutrition discipline that will work best for every individual. For example, one person might need to do significant strength training to improve their distance and accuracy, while another person may need extensive work to improve their flexibility.

Our best advice, therefore, is to find a doctor or a group of doctors who specialize in sports medicine, or a fitness facility that employs certified specialists. If possible, these should be people who have specific knowledge and training concerning the golf swing. Poor advice about health and fitness, however well intended, can be just as damaging as taking advice about your golf game from people who don't have the training and experience of a PGA Professional. For example, HealthSouth, the Official Sports Medicine Provider for The PGA of America, maintains a facility as part of the PGA Learning Center.

In the pages that follow, we'll discuss the health and fitness elements that you need to be aware of if you are determined to get in optimum condition—and shoot your lowest possible scores.

In terms of physical conditioning, there are four areas of concentration: strength, flexibility, muscular stamina and cardiovascular fitness.

Strength is obviously important in terms of producing swing speed and control, but sheer muscular bulk alone won't get the job done. For years, people cautioned against weight lifting because of the common belief that large, bulky muscles actually retarded swing speed. We now know that weight training can be beneficial—if it is the proper type of training.

A skilled trainer can make all the difference when working out.

Exercising can help maintain muscular stamina as players grow older.

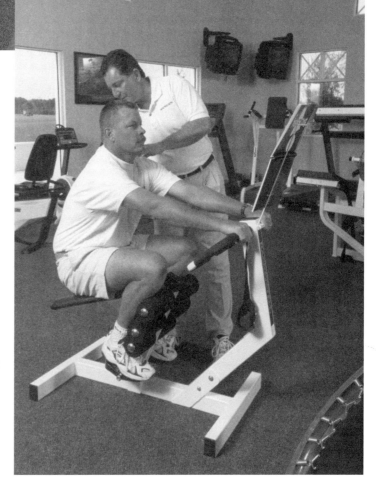

Flexibility is every bit as important as strength, since the golf swing requires that the body assume certain positions—a full turn of the upper body in the backswing, for example—that are difficult, if not impossible, without significant flexibility. This is particularly important for senior players, since our bodies tend to lose flexibility as we grow older. If you are losing distance off the tee, the answer might not be a new type of ball or the latest, state-of-the-art driver. It may be some serious physical training.

Muscular stamina is the measure of physical endurance that, like flexibility, tends to diminish with age. Obviously, if your legs or arms begin to tire after just nine holes, the chances of you scoring well on the back nine are going to fade rapidly. People who doubt that golf is an athletic competition have never faced four days of play under tournament pressure.

Cardiovascular fitness is of the utmost importance in the overall scheme of things, which is to say that if your cardiovascular system isn't functioning properly, a poor score may well turn out to be the least of your problems. It is in everyone's interest—golfers and nongolfers alike—to ensure that this category is well taken care of.

Now that we've outlined the four elements of physical fitness, we can discuss each category in more specific detail. Bear in mind our strong advice that you consult with qualified experts before beginning any exercise routine, particularly if you are 50 years old or older.

STRENGTH TRAINING—There are two keys to successful weight training. The first is that you continually make the muscles work harder than they are accustomed to, whether by increasing the *amount* of weight or resistance they must work against or the *number of repetitions*. The second is that you remember to give your muscles time to rest and rebuild tissue. The usual recommendation is to work out one day and relax the next.

It's vitally important to make a critical assessment of your physical condition before you begin any weight-training program. If you've been relatively sedentary for a number of years, beginning demanding, punishing workouts is an invitation to injury, and possibly serious injury at that. Slowly but surely may be a cliché, but it is also very good advice. While it is important to increase the intensity of your workouts, you should do this in a steady, incremental manner, focusing on the large muscle groups such as the legs, arms, abdomen and, perhaps most importantly, the lower back.

BECOMING MORE FLEXIBLE—Generalities are often misleading, but studies indicate that men are more likely to lose flexibility as they age than are women. For that reason, stretching is a particularly important element of an exercise routine for men as they approach middle age. Stretching will not only help maintain flexibility, but will also help guard against wear, tear and injuries. Bear in mind that, just as in weight training, stretching exercises should be done under supervision and gradually increased in intensity.

MUSCULAR STAMINA—Want to improve your muscular stamina? It's simple. Play and practice more often, since the more you play and practice, the stronger your muscles will become and the more endurance they will have. Of course, for the maximum benefit, avoid taking golf cars and walk when you play. If your schedule doesn't allow for as much golf as you'd like, however, walking at a fairly brisk pace during your lunch break or after dinner can certainly help build up the strength in your legs. Jogging and swimming are also recommended.

CARDIOVASCULAR FITNESS—By now, most people know what they need to do to maintain or improve their cardiovascular fitness. Maintain a proper weight for your height and frame. Don't smoke. Avoid fatty foods. Limit your alcohol intake. Engage in moderate exercise at least three times a week. Get regular physical exams and pay particular attention to your blood pressure and cholesterol readings. Again, when it comes to this area, consulting with your physician is vitally important—not only for your golf but also for the quality of your life.

Preventing and Dealing with Injuries

People who do not believe that golf is an athletic exercise are often hard-pressed to explain why the game can produce such a wide variety of nagging injuries. No one is comparing it to, say, football, where you can easily blow out a knee or receive a concussion. Still, there's no discounting the incidence of injuries to the neck, lower back, shoulders, waist, hands and other parts of the body.

Injuries are particularly damaging to players who compete regularly, either as amateurs or as world-class professionals. First, in the short term, injuries severely reduce effectiveness. Long-term problems, however, can be more debilitating.

One of the saddest—and most instructive—stories in sports history concerns the great St. Louis Cardinals pitcher Dizzy Dean. Dean was a brilliant pitcher but at one point in his career, he suffered a nagging injury. Rather than sit out his turns in the Cardinals' pitching rotation and let the injury heal, he continued to pitch, altering his pitching motion in an attempt to alleviate the pain. Eventually, his motion had been irreparably altered and he was never again as effective as he was before the injury.

The history of golf has many similar examples. Jack Nicklaus—who has been remarkably injury-free for most of his career—suffered persistent hip pain in the years leading up to his 60th birthday. When he finally had replacement surgery, he was astonished to realize how the hip pain had caused him to alter his swing.

The lesson in all this, for all golfers, is to pay close attention to your physical condition. "Playing through the pain," while admirable in concept, can be a recipe for long-term debilitating injuries that can easily hurt not only your golf game but your quality of life.

Protecting Your Back

Perhaps no other part of the body is more prone to injury for golfers than the back, and particularly the lower back, which is especially vulnerable to the twisting, turning and bending that is a part of the game.

While some of the causes of lower-back pain are congenital, owing to minor birth defects, or the long-term results of injuries, a great many back problems are avoidable if people take the proper precautions.

Two of the best things you can do to guard against back problems are simple functions of staying in shape. If you are overweight, and the weight tends to gather around your abdominal region, you should know that this is a significant cause of lower back problems. Also, if you don't work at keeping your abdominal muscles in shape, they cannot support your weight and poor posture ensues. This, in turn, increases pressure on the vertebrae and the inevitable result is back pain and even injury.

Another potential cause of lower-back pain is faulty swing technique coupled with inadequate flexibility. As noted before, this is a particular problem as we age. If you try and make a full 90-degree upper body turn, but are not sufficiently supple, the chances are pretty good that you will suffer some degree of back pain. In addition, if you try to make this type of full turn, but do not support the motion with your lower body, you are again inviting trouble.

If you look at photos of players like Jerry Pate or Dr. Cary Middlecoff in their prime, you'll see textbook examples of another cause of lower-back pain: the classic reverse "C" position at the finish of the swing. This arching of the back is unnatural at best, and potentially damaging at worst. How damaging? Enough that Tom Kite, for one, altered his swing at a very successful point in his career to avoid this sort of finish.

In addition to poor physical condition and the potential damage caused by the golf swing, there are some simple, everyday actions people can take to guard against back injury and pain.

1. Before any potentially strenuous activity, stretch slowly but fully, in small increments. This is particularly important before you begin hitting, particularly shots that require a full swing. It is equally important to stretch during and after your round or practice session.
2. When warming up before your round or when practicing, begin by hitting soft, partial shots with a wedge or short iron and proceed through the bag gradually.
3. Avoid riding in golf cars. Walking helps strengthen the muscle groups that support your back. Also, walking helps keep your back muscles loose between shots.
4. If you elect to ride a car, pay attention to the terrain. If that car goes over a bump or hits a depression at too great a speed, the jarring that results can do serious damage to your back. And do not, under any circumstances, dangle a foot outside the car. Your spikes can easily catch the turf, resulting in pulled muscles or worse.
5. Carry an extra sweater or jacket in your bag in case the temperature drops. Cold weather can cause muscles to tighten or contract, leading to potential injury.
6. Avoid lifting heavy objects. Even the simple act of lifting a golf bag from the trunk of your car can have a debilitating effect on your back.
7. Whenever you must lift an object, use your legs. If your bag, for example, is on the ground, bend from your knees and lift with your legs. Don't bend from your waist and lift with your back.
8. When sitting at work or at home, try to maintain proper posture by sitting at a straight-backed chair and, if you must sit for a long period of time, make a point of getting up and walking around briefly to prevent your back muscles from tightening.
9. If you must stand for a long period of time, make sure to shift your weight from one foot to the other, and pause to stretch occasionally. This is particularly true if you are practicing putting and your back is curved.

10. If you are opening windows, particularly windows that are snug or jammed, stand as close to the windows as possible and push with your legs.

11. If your back is sore or if you have been exercising, elevate your feet when resting or sleeping. This will help alleviate stress on your lower back.

12. Whenever exercising, keep the motions in balance. For example, if you swing a weighted club (which is an excellent way to develop your golf muscles), make sure you swing an equal number of times in both directions in order to maintain physiological balance. By the same token, if you are lifting hand weights, make sure to do an equal number of repetitions with each arm.

If you do experience frequent or repeated back pain, our strongest recommendation is to see a physician immediately. A qualified doctor can diagnose your problem, and provide a course of treatment that may include exercise, preventive measures, and possibly a combination of medicines.

If, on the other hand, the pain is infrequent, very often some combination of bed rest, over-the-counter pain relievers, heat (a hot bath can work wonders) and manipulation by a fitness trainer or doctor can ease the pain and discomfort.

The Role of Proper Nutrition and Diet

Like a finely tuned car, the human body can look great, and have all the parts in place and be ready to go at top performance. However, if it is lacking in fuel—or has the wrong sort of fuel—you'll be in for a short and unpleasant journey.

One very simple reason to watch your diet is to avoid becoming overweight. It's no secret that this is particularly important for Americans who, by virtue of our bountiful food supply and our relatively sedentary lifestyles, have a tendency toward weight gain that is not only unhealthy, but also has a derogatory effect on athletic performance—and make no mistake about it, playing your best golf requires you to be in reasonable, if not excellent, condition.

If you are overweight and find yourself tiring and hitting poor shots in the closing holes of a round, losing the extra weight may have tremendous benefits for your golf game.

While there is no shortage of often-conflicting diets and diet books on the market, we recommend a common sense approach to reasonable weight loss. If you are severely overweight, it's a good idea to consult with your physician. Otherwise, these ideas should help get the job done.

1. To lose weight, you must burn more calories than you consume. It's that simple and it doesn't take a rocket scientist to figure it out.

Either you need to reduce the number of calories you consume or you need to increase your exercise levels.

2. Most doctors and nutritionists agree that reducing the amount of fatty, red meat we consume will not only help lower weight, but also has numerous other health benefits. Lean meats, fish and chicken are suggested replacements. It's also a good idea to reduce the amount of high-fat items you consume, and check the packaging for content and calories. Not all yogurts, for example, are low-fat or low-calorie foods.

3. Whenever possible, reduce your consumption of processed foods, replacing them with fresh fruits, vegetables and meats. The problem with processed foods is that they often contain sodium, sugars or other additives.

4. Reduce your consumption of alcoholic beverages. Alcohol accounts for enormous amounts of calories and, if you combine it with mixers, you're adding even more calories. Common sense alone should tell you that drinking even a small amount of alcohol before or during a round cannot be helpful for either your coordination or your ability to think clearly.

5. It's also a good idea to stick with fruit juices, sports drinks or, better yet, water, since they contain no artificial sweeteners or ingredients.

6. Avoid salted foods and heavily sugared foods. If you feel the need for a bit of energy during a round, have some fruit. You'll not only reduce your caloric intake, but eliminating the sugar jolt will help your nerves.

7. Add to the amount of carbohydrates in your diet by eating more pasta, whole grain breads and cereals.

8. Change your eating habits. Instead of eating three large meals a day, eat only when you feel hungry, and then satisfy your hunger with small, healthy meals. If you are going to eat just one big meal per day, it should be breakfast, which will provide your body with the fuel to get a good start, and also gives your body time to burn off those calories. Eating a big meal at dinnertime and then going to sleep a few hours later is not an effective way to lose weight.

9. When you are playing golf, remember to keep yourself hydrated, especially if you play in hot or humid conditions. Don't wait until you feel thirsty to drink some fluid. By that time, your body is already feeling the effects of dehydration—hence, your thirst. Instead, try to drink small amounts of water or other liquids frequently, as often as every hole.

10. Try to avoid large swings in weight. Set a realistic target figure and work methodically toward achieving it. Work with your doctor or fitness expert to find a goal that works for you based on your body size and your family history.

By lowering your weight and getting yourself into better shape, you not only improve your physical skills, but also increase your confidence and self-image, reduce your chances of injury and extend the number of years you can compete at a satisfying level. Add to this the improvement in your quality of life, and you have every incentive to commit—and it will require a significant, long-term commitment—to improving your nutrition and fitness.

The rewards will far outweigh the sacrifices.

4

Laws, Principles and Preferences

There are many people teaching or playing golf, in a variety of ways. In itself that is not wrong. Confusing, maybe, but not necessarily wrong. It has been like this for most of the game's history. We have had proponents of one style or another, either as teachers or players, who have drawn battle lines against all approaches that differ from their own. That is wrong! Even a casual study of the game's greatest performers should firmly convince the most stubborn advocate of a single swing style that individual differences do exist. The only absolute statement you can make about the swings of great golfers is that they are all different. Some look familiar, yes. Several around which you could build a system of generalizations, definitely. All sharing common ground in principle, absolutely. But none actually the same.

These practitioners of a certain method usually offer a stable of stars as final evidence that their way is the best way, or maybe even the *only way*. To support their contentions and reinforce their beliefs, they argue that their method has worked for them and their pupils, particularly those who were successful and came back. (Failures have a convenient way of disappearing.) This type of logic leads to the conviction that anyone who arrives at a different conclusion through another approach has to be wrong . . . or, at least, must have an inferior method.

This conviction isn't hard to understand. It's a human failing. We can only subscribe to what we know, and we can only know what we have experienced. No one can live long enough to have experienced everything, nor can they place themselves in another's body and mind so as to appreciate fully what the other person is experiencing. Consequently, there will always be divergent views on what constitutes "rightness" in an activity such as the golf swing where "right" is measured only by result, not by style.

The following teaching model offers an overview of the cause-and-effect problem facing all golfers and then encourages the development of methods which can minimize or eliminate those problems. Three levels of priority in understanding the golf swing are presented:

- LAWS
- PRINCIPLES
- PREFERENCES

Each is defined for use here in the following manner:

- LAW is a statement of an order or relation of phenomena that so far as is known is invariable under given conditions.
- PRINCIPLE is a first cause, or force. It is a fundamental of high order which must be dealt with and which in this model has direct relation to and influence on LAW.
- PREFERENCE is the choice one makes based upon liking some particular approach, method, device, etc., better than all others. To be valid in this model, it must relate to PRINCIPLE.

Laws

When we speak of Law in the model, don't infer that Law deals directly with the golf swing. It doesn't. Law here refers to the physical forces which are absolutes in influencing the flight of the ball. *There are no absolutes in the golf swing, only Principles. Absolutes are reserved for ball flight, that's why they are called Laws.* The following five factors are the Laws in this model. The Ball Flight Laws (assessed at the moment of impact) are:

1. SPEED The velocity with which the clubhead is traveling. Speed influences the distance the ball will be propelled, as well as the trajectory and shape of the resulting shot.
2. CENTEREDNESS The exactness with which the ball makes contact on the face of the club relative to the percussion point or "sweet spot." Contact could be either on the center, fore (toe), aft (heel), above or below that "sweet spot."
3. PATH The direction of the arc described by the clubhead in its travel away from then back toward the target. Its line of travel at impact is one of the primary factors influencing direction for a full shot.
4. FACE The degree at which the leading edge of the clubface is at right angles to the swing path. It will determine the accuracy of the ball's flight along that line, or produce a left or right curve away from that line.

5. ANGLE OF APPROACH The angle formed by the descending or ascending arc of the clubhead on the forward swing in relation to the slope of the ground. Due to its influence on the ball's spin rate, the trajectory and the distance the ball travels will be affected by this angle.

Obviously, there are equipment factors such as clubface loft, construction of the ball, material of the hitting surface, etc., which will influence the distance and direction of the ball's flight. Environmental conditions such as temperature, humidity, wind, terrain and altitude also have an effect. There are also psychological elements which can influence all five laws. But in this model, consideration is given only to the human physical factors, and specifically those over which we have some control.

Ball Flight Laws rank as the first priority because they are absolute rather than arbitrary. They work every time without fail. The ball is not concerned with swing style. It responds to being struck without any prejudice toward the striker. It doesn't ask what particular swing method is being used, nor does it care about one's handicap, club affiliation, sex or age. The ball follows the basic Ball Flight Laws, whether the player uses an open or square stance, has a fast or slow backswing, an overlapping or tenderfingered grip, a firm or cupped wrist, or emphasizes leverage or centrifugal force as the primary source of power. Yet, all these could have an important influence on the flight of the ball.

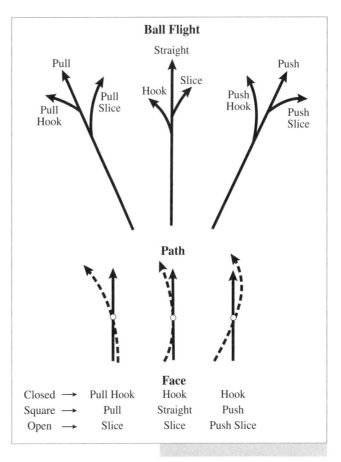

Before you can correct an undesirable ball flight, it helps to understand what causes the ball to travel in the direction it does.

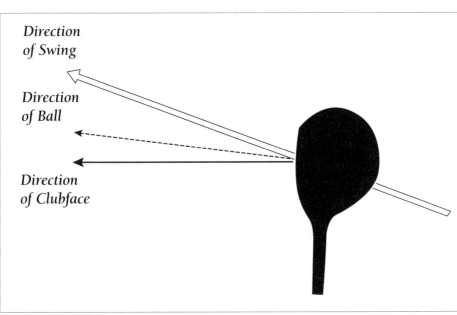

Understanding the role the Direction of Swing and Direction of Clubface play in the Direction of the Ball is crucial.

Principles

There are fundamental considerations in the swing which have a direct bearing on a player's application of the Laws. In this model they are labeled "Principles" . . . Principles of the Swing. Whereas the Laws are irrefutable and absolute, principles reflect some subjective judgment on the mechanics of the swing.

Listing these elements does no mean the list is all-inclusive. The reader may feel there are additional items needed to improve the model. The principle is listed, followed by a description of the principle, its primary influence on distance or direction, its effect on one or more of the Laws, and the goals of the principle. They are:

1. **GRIP** (Placement, positioning, pressure and precision related to applying the hands to the club.)

Primary Influence—Direction

Effect—Grip has the greatest influence upon clubface position.

Placement (how far up or down the shaft the hands are placed) can alter the club's effective length.

Positioning (the clockwise or counterclockwise rotation of the hands on the grip) by altering the hands a half inch counterclockwise from normal on the grip can cause the face to open enough for a 30-yard slice.

Grip pressure (the amount of squeezing) influences timing, speed and control.

Precision (taking the same grip each time) is critical for consistency.

Goals—Clubface alignment square to hand position.

Shoulder, elbow and wrist joint alignment square to clubface position.

2. **AIM** (The Alignment of the clubface in relation to the target.)

Primary Influence—Direction

Effect—Aim is one of the most influential principles. Aim influences clubface position at impact which influences ball flight.

Goals—Clubface at 90 degrees (right angle) to target line.

3. **ALIGNMENT** (The position of the joints of the body in relation to the club and target.)

Primary Influence—Direction

Effect—The position of the joints strongly influences the club path.

Goals—Shoulder joints and arms should be parallel to the target line.

Hips and legs should be set so shoulders can be parallel to the target line.

Eye line needs to be parallel to the target line.

4. **SETUP** (A player's posture, ball position, stance, weight distribution and muscular readiness.)

Primary Influence—Distance and Direction

Effect—Setup can influence *all five laws.*

Goals—Skeletal balance

>Ankles under shoulder joints

>Base of sternum points at ball

>Forward spine tilt from hips

>Spine tilt to trail side

>Set center of rotation

5. **SWING PLANE** (The tilt and direction of travel of the inclined plane made by the clubshaft.)

Primary Influence—Direction

Effect—The swing plane is determined by the angle of the club shaft relative to the ball and to the ground. The swing is on plane when, during the backswing, an extension of the clubhead points to the target line or is parallel to it, and in the forward swing the butt end of the club would intersect a line drawn through the ball to the target. Plane determines *path.*

Goals—Return the club on a chosen path to a position where the shaft lie angle is at or close to the club's lie angle with the shaft tilt in the desired direction.

6. **WIDTH OF ARC** (The distance the grip end travels in the backswing and the forward swing.)

Primary Influence—Distance

Effect—If the lead arm is noticeably bent at impact, clubhead speed is reduced due to a shortened lever. This is similar to the way the middle portion of a spoke on a wheel travels slower than the far end of the spoke although the force from the center is equal.

Goals—Maintain the angle or length set between the shoulders, wrist and shaft at address.

>Return to impact the same swing center to ball length.

7. **LENGTH OF ARC** (The distance the clubhead travels in the backswing and forward swing.)

Primary Influence—Distance

Effect—A short putt needs only a short backswing. A 20-yard pitch shot requires a longer swing than does a putt but not a full swing. Length of backswing is a contributing factor to swing pace or speed and, therefore, distance. If the arc length is shortened in the follow-through, that's a good indication of deceleration at impact.

Goals—Reach the point of maximum leverage at the top of the backswing. Maintaining swing center, have levers fully extended through impact.

8. **LEVER SYSTEM** (The combination of levers formed by the lead arm and club during the backswing and forward swing.)

Primary Influence—Distance

Effect—The hinging of the wrists in the backswing and forward swing allowing the player to conserve and release momentum.

Goals—Hinge the wrist in the backswing so as to reach the point of maximum leverage and maintain the desired wrist hinge until impact.

9. **TIMING** (The proper sequence of body and club movement which produces the most efficient result.)

Primary Influence—Distance and Direction

Effect—Timing creates a sequential link action that summates and maximizes the forces for the desired *speed* and power. The timing of the swing sequence also influences the *path* the clubhead takes to the ball.

Goals—Allow the body part to function so the desired speed is applied to the shaft.

10. **RELEASE** (Allowing the arms, hands, body and club to return to and through the correct impact position while directing the power created in the backswing.)

Primary Influence—Distance

Effect—The momentum exerted on the club will cause the arms and hands and body to extend through impact.

Goals—Full extension of the trail arm past impact.

11. **DYNAMIC BALANCE** (Body movement creating transfer of weight—downward pressure—during the swing to increase force.)

Primary Influence—Distance and Direction

Effect—Good players utilize the motion common to all striking and throwing actions: moving from the trail foot (rear foot) to the target foot (forward foot) in delivering the blow. Staying on the trail foot reduces power delivered to the ball and alters the path and arc of the swing.

Goals—Move mass so transfer of weight to rear foot (center) and transfer to front foot (center) through impact with finish on the center of the front foot.

12. **SWING CENTER (ROTATIONAL)** (A point located in the upper spine around which the upper-body rotation and swing of the arms takes place.)

Primary Influence—Distance and Direction

Effect—When the center of rotation moves, the arc of the circle made by the clubhead also moves, and striking the ball consistently in the center of the clubface becomes more difficult. The shorter the shot, the more constant the swing center should stay. Additional lateral freedom can be allowed as greater power is sought, but movements that are up and down, away from or toward the ball are discouraged. The motion the spine makes during the swing controls the center point.

Goals—Maintain the forward tilt angle of the spine and allow the pivot point (swing center) to be in the upper back.

13. CONNECTION (Establishing and maintaining the various body parts in their appropriate relation to one another in the setup and during the swing.)

Primary Influence—Distance

Effect—To produce an effective, properly timed link action, the body parts must maintain their correct positions relative to each other. They must fire in sequence to stay connected.

Goals—Use joints correctly (hips and shoulders rotary; wrists, elbows, knees and ankles hinged) so that no joint is past its range of motion and the lever system stays in front of the trunk.

14. IMPACT (The position of the body, clubshaft and clubhead at the moment energy is delivered to the ball.)

Primary Influence—Distance and Direction

Effect—There is only one moment of truth in the Swing . . . Impact! The clubface should be squaring at this moment while the path is to the target. It is the moment when the maximum speed should be reached and the center of the clubface is contacting the ball from the desired angle.

Goals—Shaft returned (as close as possible) to lie angle and tilted at angle for desired shot.

Clubface strikes the desired section of the ball and squares through separation.

Preferences

The third and final of priorities after Laws and Principles is Preferences, the choice of swing fundamentals that constitute style. Select the *Preference* that works best which relates to the *Principle* that influences the *Law*.

Limitless Preferences

When one gets into the Preference category, which determines one's style, the possibilities are limitless. Consider for a moment which of the following is correct: shoulders aimed left, toward or to the right of the target? Stance open, square or closed? Weight back on the heels or forward at address? Favoring the target or trail side? Ball position, variable or standard? Address, relaxed or taut? Flat, medium or upright swing plane? Bent left arm or straight at the top of the backswing? Short or long backswing? Left wrist cupped flat or bowed?

Face open, square or closed to the tangent of the arc? Forward swing initiated with feet, knees, legs, hips, arms, hands? Is the hip movement lateral, circular or both? Do the forearms rotate to provide release or is it the wrists, both or neither? Where is the weight distributed during the swing? Does the left knee straighten on the downswing or stay flexed? Does the head move laterally? Does it move up or down? These are Preference choices.

Whereas the Laws are fixed in number (five) and the Principles reasonably limited (fourteen), the Preferences could reach a staggering total. The point is, there are a great many techniques and combinations of techniques which can work. Ben Hogan could employ a particular grip, stance and swing quite different from Lee Trevino's, yet produce a ball flight that looked almost identical.

Preference Variety and Compatibility

This is the key—compatibility. Mixing preference styles when applied to certain principles doesn't work. A player can't use Paul Azinger's grip coupled with Tom Watson's release. This is one reason we sometimes note a strong difference of opinion among experts on the golf swing over what appear to be clear-cut fundamentals. Because once the player adopts a particular grip style or position at the top, it will dictate several of the moves on the way down and through the shot. The conclusion is, when comparing widely varying styles, each may be right. The test is, *what works for you?*

Above all, recognize that the swing may be simple in theory but the machine which performs it, the human being, is very complicated.

The Complete Model

The complete listing of the three levels follows:

BALL FLIGHT LAWS
1. Clubhead speed
2. Centeredness of contact
3. Clubhead path
4. Position of clubface
5. Angle of approach

PRINCIPLES
1. Grip
2. Aim
3. Alignment
4. Setup
5. Swing plane
6. Width of arc
7. Length of arc
8. Lever system
9. Timing

10. Release
11. Dynamic balance
12. Swing center (Rotational)
13. Connection
14. Impact

PREFERENCES (EXAMPLES)

Early wrist hinge
Two-knuckle grip
Outside takeaway
Flat backswing
Cupped left wrist
Left toe out
Fixed center
High hands
Slow back
Open stance
Lateral slide
Light pressure
Bent left knee
Extended arms
Chin behind
Weight forward
Shoulders closed
Etc., etc., etc.

5

Pre-swing Fundamentals

Ben Hogan once observed that if you have proper fundamentals and a good pre-shot routine, once you've addressed the ball the shot is 90 percent over. This explanation captures the importance of developing and maintaining sound fundamentals.

An Overview

As we have in other chapters, we begin this chapter of Pre-swing Fundamentals with an overview that covers the basics we believe are important for you to understand if you are going to achieve your goals of building a solid, repeating swing. We will go into greater detail in the pages that follow.

The least complicated method we've discovered to grip the club properly is to stand erect with your ankle

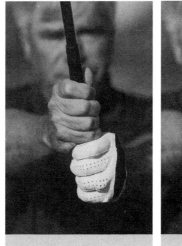
A 10-finger or baseball grip

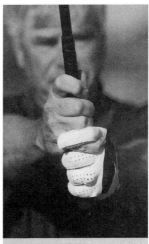
Interlocking grip

45

Grip sequence

joints under your shoulders, holding the club in front of you at a 45-degree angle with your trail hand (right hand for right-handed golfers). Place the club diagonally across the base of the fingers of your target hand (left hand for right-handers). Next, simply slide your trail hand down the shaft until the thumb of the target hand fits into the lifeline of the trail hand. At this point, the thumb of the target hand is covered with the thumb pad of the trail hand and the little finger of the trail hand rests on top of the first two fingers of the target hand.

A proper stance helps you create and maintain balance in the golf swing. Stand up to the ball with your ankle joints under your shoulder joints and your weight evenly distributed between the heels and balls of the feet and between your left and right foot. Once you assume a proper stance, push your hips back and tilt forward from the bottom of your hips until your sternum points to the ball. Finally, tilt your torso until the trail shoulder (right shoulder for right-handed players) is lower than the target shoulder.

To align yourself properly, begin by standing behind the ball and visualizing a line drawn from the target to the ball. Then pick a spot six to 12 inches on this line from the ball as a target. Once you have done that, walk into position and place the clubface behind the ball, aiming at your intermediate target. Make sure that you keep your eyes on the target as you walk into position and assume your stance.

Of all the fundamentals we will discuss in this chapter, the grip is first—simply because without a good grip the rest of the swing becomes an attempt to compensate for that central flaw.

The Keys to a Good Grip

A writer once asked Sam Snead what was the most common flaw he saw among the tens of thousands of amateurs he's seen over his long career. He didn't hesitate for a second.

"It's the grip, no question," Sam said. "Most folks, if they gripped a knife and fork as badly as they gripped a golf club, they'd starve to death. It's a funny thing, but you hardly ever see a bad player with a good grip or a good player with a bad grip. Every now and then one or the other will come along, but they're as rare as hen's teeth."

So what is a good grip?

Simply put, it's a grip that allows the hands to work together to produce the best combination of power and accuracy as well as allowing a skilled player to produce the greatest variety of shots.

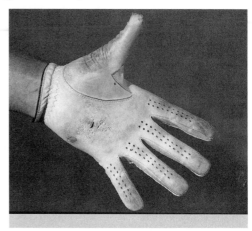

Worn spots on your golf glove show where the pressure is in your grip.

*Proper fundamentals
begin with individual
instruction.*

Developing a proper grip is so important that when beginners go to a PGA Professional for instruction, it is the first fundamental that they will work on together. The reason is twofold: first, everything in the swing flows from the grip, and second, if a person has a poor grip he will invariably revert to it under pressure—even the best players. Witness this story from Byron Nelson.

"When Ben [Hogan] and I were caddies at Glen Garden Country Club, all the boys used to have driving contests while we were waiting for our loops, and the short hitter had to go out and pick up everyone's balls. Well Ben was pretty small for his age, so he developed a real strong grip that would

A sound swing flows from a good grip.

help him hook the ball. That worked fine for the caddie games, but when he turned pro he really struggled with a hook. He'd go along fine for a round or two and then that old hook would jump up and get him. He compared it to a rattlesnake jumping out and biting him. To his credit, he worked real hard and figured out how to fix his grip and make it more neutral, but it took him a long time to get where he could trust it. He'd get in the hunt on the last day and you could see those hands turning to the right and, of course, a hook would just kill him. Once he finally got to where he could trust his new grip, well then he became the Ben Hogan everyone remembers today."

While the grip is clearly a crucial fundamental, it's important to note here that what follows are general guidelines that will help develop a sound grip. The actual positioning of the hands that works best for you will be determined by your physical build, the size and strength of your hands, and other variables such as the shape of your swing. For that reason we strongly recommend working with your PGA Professional to develop the grip that works best for your swing.

PLACING THE HANDS ON THE CLUB—Notice we use the word "placing" your hands on the club. This is important because it connotes a far more gentle

A player's view of the overlapping grip

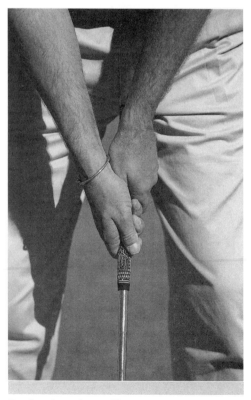

Overlapping grip at address

action than "gripping" a club. Watch a player with a beautiful grip—Ben Crenshaw is a perfect example—and you will notice how gently he places his hands on the club. There's no sense that he is trying to adjust his hands to any contrived or awkward positions.

If you stand naturally, you'll notice that your hands will turn slightly inward. They should do the same thing when you grip a club.

GRIP THE CLUB IN THE FINGERS—Golf is essentially a game of feel, so simple common sense dictates that when you grip the club you want to do it in a manner that will provide you with the maximum amount of feel. To do this, you want to place your hands on the club so that the grip rests largely in your fingers.

When you grip the club with your target hand, the grip should be held with the fingers, with the butt end of the club resting against the fleshy pad of the top of the palm. The thumb should be positioned to the trail side of the grip's center, so that it feels as if you are shaking hands with the club.

A good test to check if your target hand is positioned properly is to grip the club with just your target hand and then slowly swing the club back to the top of your backswing. If your grip is correct (assuming that your club is in roughly the correct position at the top of your swing), your target thumb should be under the shaft, supporting the weight of the club.

If you have your target hand positioned properly, the rest is easy. Grip the club in your target hand and hold it vertically in front of you. Then, with your trail hand opened, gently position it against the target hand and the grip so that the club rests in the first three fingers. Then close the thumb over the club so it barely touches the forefinger. The lowest knuckle of the trail hand should be behind the shaft pointed toward the target.

HOLD THE CLUB GENTLY—"How tightly should I grip the club?" is a question PGA Professionals are often asked by beginning golfers. If you think about it, a better way to phrase the question would be "How lightly should I hold the club?"

"More often than not, when I play with amateurs, the first thing I tell them is to lighten up that grip pressure," says Sam Snead. "They get to grinding the rubber right out of those grips and they don't have a prayer. You've got to be gentle with that grip, just like you were holding a pretty girl's hand at the senior prom. You want to hold the club as though it were a little baby bird. You don't want to hold it so tight you'll crush it, but just tight enough so it won't fly away on you."

Another way to think about it is to imagine that the grip is a tube of toothpaste without a top. You don't want to squeeze it so tightly that the toothpaste comes shooting out all over your shoes.

Also, keep in mind that your hands will naturally tighten on the club in the course of your swing as a reaction to the combination of the club's weight plus the force generated by the swing. It will also lighten. In truth, your grip pressure is constantly fluctuating.

WHICH GRIP IS RIGHT FOR YOU?—There are three basic types of grips—the Vardon or overlapping grip, the interlocking, and the 10-finger or baseball grip. Choosing which grip is right for you is largely a matter of personal preference based upon experimentation and consultation with your PGA Professional. There are, however, some general rules of thumb you can follow to help guide your decision.

The overlapping grip was popularized by Harry Vardon, the great British champion at the turn of the 20th century. With this grip, the little finger of the trail hand rests along the indentation formed between the forefinger and middle finger of the target hand. It is by far the grip used by the largest number of golfers because it is easy to learn and allows the hands to work together as a unit.

Historically, the interlocking grip has been used by players with smaller hands or shorter fingers, although this isn't always the case. Among the great players who have an interlocking grip are Jack Nicklaus, Tom Kite, Amy Alcott and Tiger Woods. In Woods's case, while he has large hands, it is the grip he learned as a child and remains what he is comfortable with today. A warning: If using the interlocking grip, don't squeeze with the interlocked fingers.

The baseball or 10-finger grip is really a throwback to the game's Scottish roots. It is rarely used and seldom even taught today because, of the three grips mentioned, it does the least to encourage the hands to work as one. Still, Bob Rosburg, the 1959 PGA Champion, used it with great success and it is sometimes a good grip for people who suffer from arthritis in their hands.

Questions and Answers

Q: *My friend suggested I buy one of those devices that are molded to help place your hands in a proper grip. Do they work?*

A: They can be a good reminder and training aids can be useful, but it's still a good idea to work with a PGA Professional to ensure that you get a grip that is best suited to you and your game.

Q: *I went to my Professional and he straightened out my grip, moving the club out of the palms of my hands and into my fingers. This works great on the practice tee but when I get out on the course, I fall back into my old habits. Any suggestions?*

A: As long as you're just playing a casual round and not in competition or playing for a score, have your professional draw a line on your glove indicating where the club should be placed. This will help you grip the club properly in your hands.

Q: *I have a good grip but should I adjust it to hit a draw or a fade?*

A: A good grip is one that will allow you to hit both those shots by adjusting your setup. It is dangerous to change your grip from shot to shot.

Occasionally, if players have to hit a big slice or hook, they may alter their grip accordingly, but that is very rare and not recommended.

Q: *Is there anything I can do at home or the office to improve my grip?*

A: Absolutely. Get your PGA Professional or a member of his staff to place a grip on a piece of shaft that is just long enough to accommodate the grip, say a piece about 18 inches long. When you are watching television or talking on the phone, practice placing your hands on the club. This will help you become more comfortable and confident when you play.

Aiming Properly

Of the two primary considerations in golf, distance and direction, direction is by far the most important since the secret to scoring successfully lies in minimizing mistakes—and one of the most common mistakes is aiming the clubface and/or aligning the body incorrectly. The simple reality is that the best swing in the world will still produce errant shots if the clubface or the player is aimed or aligned wide of the target.

Your clubface will tell you if you're hitting the sweet spot.

Aiming and setting up to the ball with correct body alignment are complicated since they involve the clubface, eyes, shoulders, hips, knees and feet. If any one element is misaligned to the target, either the player will have to compensate with his or her swing, or the shot will likely be off line.

Logic properly dictates that in order to aim properly, the clubface should be aligned to the starting point first, followed by the body. It is also crucial to understand that while the clubface must be aimed at the starting point—either directly or in the case of a fade/slice or draw/hook on a line where you want the shot to begin before it curves back to the ultimate target—your body is aligned to a point parallel left of the target (for right-handed golfers).

Here's an image that is helpful when trying to understand this fundamental of proper aiming and alignment: If you are hitting a straight shot, try to visualize a railroad track running from the ball to the target. The clubface and ball will rest on the outside rail, while you will be standing on the inside rail, your body actually aimed at a spot parallel to the target.

One of the most common faults among golfers (and for purposes of simplicity, we'll refer to right-handed golfers) is missing shots to the right of the target because the clubface is aimed to the right or the body is aligned to the right. This is caused, in part, because people misunderstand the concept explained in the previous paragraph. They mistakenly align their bodies to the target and, therefore, wind up with a swing path to the right. Another reason, however, is just the way our eyes work in the aiming process. People focus their eyes on the target and subconsciously align their shoulders to the target. The problem with this, however, becomes clear if you stand and address the ball: Notice that your eyes are actually positioned in a spot between the clubhead and your shoulders. If both shoulders are positioned correctly, it is almost anatomically impossible to misalign the trail shoulder, and if the shoulders are aligned properly it is much easier to align the hips, knees and feet as well. The position of the shoulders at address is also important because your body instinctively tries to return to the address position at impact and, therefore, the swing path—of both the arms and the club—is determined to a large degree by the alignment of the shoulders.

Here's one more thought to keep in mind when it comes to the role of the eyes in proper aim and alignment. Very often a player will address the ball properly but will work out of position by lifting his head to look at the target rather than rotating it. When you lift your head, there's a tendency to rotate your trail shoulder, which in turn misaligns your shoulders. So, to ensure you remain in a correct address position rotate, don't lift, your head to look at the target.

Aiming the Clubface

Of all the elements that go into proper aim and alignment, actually aiming the clubface is probably the easiest for most people—as long as you follow a routine.

It's just common sense to realize that it is easier to aim at a spot a few feet away than it is to aim at a target a hundred yards or more away. For that reason, the first step toward properly aiming the clubface is developing a pre-shot routine that will allow you to aim the club—and then align your body—to the target. As is so often the case in every part of the game, no one does this better than Jack Nicklaus.

If you watch him, he begins every shot by standing behind the ball and visualizing the shot he wants to play. Once he's done this, watch his eyes: He'll track a line from the target back to his ball, picking out a spot on that line a foot or two in front of his ball. This intermediate target can be an old divot or a discolored blade of grass.

As the tee gets taller, the ball is closer to your rotational center, so your stance needs to be adjusted.

Once he's visualized his shot and picked his intermediate target, he methodically approaches the ball and sets the clubhead down behind it, taking

Correct. Center of the clubface should be lined up with the inside edge of the ball.

Incorrect. Do not line up the center of the clubface with the center of the ball when the ball is on a tee.

great pains to ensure that the club is aimed at his intermediate target. Only after he's done this will he take his stance and align his body to the target.

The two important points to take away from the Jack Nicklaus example are the benefits of aiming at an intermediate target and the importance of building your address position only after you've aimed the clubhead to the target and not the other way around.

Aligning Your Body

If everyone were built exactly the same and had identical vision, then you could safely say that they should all address the ball in the same manner—with their feet, knees, hips, shoulders, and eyes all exactly parallel to the target line.

In truth, however a person's physical makeup and the way his or her eyes work often dictate minor—stress minor—variations from the parallel ideal. For example, Lee Trevino plays from a relatively open—that is, aimed to the left—address position while Arnold Palmer favors a slightly closed position. Why? Trevino prefers to fade the ball from left to right while Palmer favors a draw. It's important to note, however, that both men have enough talent to either fade or draw the ball at will.

For most people, however, and certainly for beginning golfers, the best idea is to begin with an address position where all the elements are parallel to the target line. If you find this isn't producing optimum results, work with your PGA Professional to find the modifications that are best for you . . . and keep in mind these words of wisdom from the late Harvey Penick: "An aspirin or two will probably cure what ails you, but taking a whole bottle will probably kill you."

Left wrist hinge position at the top of the swing.

Using target flags for aim and alignment: The clubface should be aimed at the target and the body aligned to a spot parallel to the target line.

Finding the Correct Ball Position

Ball position is one of those crucial fundamentals that require constant review. If you go to a professional tournament, you will notice that players often ask their fellow players or teachers to check their positions at address—and one of the elements they focus on closely is ball position.

When we talk about ball position, we're concerned with not only where the ball is placed relative to your stance, but also how far the ball is located from your body. In most cases, this will be largely determined by your body shape as well as the shape of your swing.

The great Byron Nelson, who helped form the games of players like Ken Venturi and Tom Watson, once famously said that "No one ever

Trail arm fold drill

stands too close to the ball." There are people who do, of course, but Byron's point was that the overwhelming majority of golfers err by standing too far from the ball, because it gives them a mistaken feeling of power.

Here's a good method that will help the vast majority of golfers determine how far the ball should be positioned from their body:

Assume your address position, with a 5-iron placed behind the ball. Now, take your lower hand off the grip and run it between the butt end of the club and your hips. Generally speaking, for most people the ball is correctly positioned if your hand can glide easily between the grip and your hips.

Addressing the Ball

Hitting a golf ball is an athletic exercise (despite what some nongolfers would have you believe) and therefore it has many things in common with other sports. For example, if you watch a batter waiting for a pitch, he will stay in motion, making practice swings until the pitcher is ready to begin his windup. The same is true for a basketball player at the foul line. She'll bounce the ball until the time comes to take her shot.

In golf, it's important to have a pre-shot routine that allows you to keep in motion, since this will help prevent tension from creeping into your swing. Please refer to the

This drill helps you set up with the correct spine angle and alignment.

"Overview" section at the beginning of this chapter for our recommended pre-shot routine. This is particularly crucial in golf, since hitting a golf ball is an "active" process as opposed to a "reactive" process. In other words, you are the only one who can decide when to begin your swing, unlike, say, a hitter in baseball who reacts to the pitch.

And just as in other sports, it's important that your beginning—or address—position provides both stability and strength. In other words, it should be an "athletic" position, similar to an infielder in baseball, a cornerback in football, or a tennis player preparing to receive serve. Your knees should be comfortably bent and should remain in that same flex throughout your swing. That's a very important but often overlooked point. If your knee flex changes throughout the swing, your body's position can't help but follow, and the result will be inconsistent ball striking.

For most shots your weight should be evenly balanced between both feet, although some Professionals prefer more weight on the trail foot for longer clubs versus on the target side for shorter clubs.

Questions and Answers

Q: *My favorite golfer is Fred Couples and I've noticed he has very little knee flex in his swing. When I try to copy his swing, I really lose a lot of distance. Could reduced knee flex be a reason?*

A: Because of Fred's extreme flexibility he can make a full shoulder turn with little or no leg movement. Not many people can do this.

View of aim and alignment aids from the target to the player.

Training aids can help you develop the proper aim and alignment.

Once you assume a proper stance you should tilt forward from the bottom of your hips until your sternum points at the ball.

The length and lie and shaft angle of your clubs determines ball position.

Q: *Why is a waggle so important?*

A: Two main reasons: First, it's a way of keeping in motion as you prepare to hit a shot, and that reduces tension. Second, think of it as a mini-swing. Use it to mirror how you want to take the club away from the ball and return it at impact.

Q: *I understand the difference between a closed stance and an open stance, but why does one help you hit a draw while the other makes you fade the ball?*

A: To a large extent, a fade or draw is determined by the path the clubhead is traveling upon contact, and by altering your stance, you alter your swing path and change your ball flight. For example, to hit a draw, you want the clubhead traveling from inside the target line and then squaring up at impact. A closed stance, with the back foot pulled away from the target line, helps you do just that. Conversely, an open stance does the opposite. Again, as with so many elements of the golf swing, it's a good idea to work with your PGA Professional to determine how open or closed your stance should be. And for a more detailed explanation of how to hit a fade or draw, see the chapter on "Shotmaking" that begins on page 119.

6

Full Swing Fundamentals

Now we get to what most people regard as the most glamorous part of the game, the full swing. But before we go any further, let's make one thing clear: While we strongly believe we can provide you with the fundamentals of a solid swing, we can't teach you the fundamentals of a perfect swing. Why? Because there is no such thing as a perfect swing.

Consider some of the players who are generally considered to have among the greatest swings in history.

Sam Snead: By virtual acclamation, the greatest swing of all time. But experts are quick to point out that he came over the top slightly on the downswing.

Jack Nicklaus: He won more major championships than any player in history but his so-called "flying" right elbow horrified purists, who preferred the traditional swing where the right elbow remained close to the body on the backswing.

Tom Weiskopf: Another long, rhythmic and powerful swing that his fellow players voted the Best Swing on Tour in 1977, but by his own admission, he shut the clubface at the top of his backswing, which could produce a hook for a player with lesser talent.

And so on.

The truth is you could find a technical flaw in the swing of virtually every member of the World Golf Hall of Fame, but they were all magnificent champions.

Everyone is unique, with strengths and weaknesses and varying physical characteristics. The swing that best fits your body type, temperament and innate athletic ability will, in the end, be the best swing for you. Our job is to help you find that swing.

The Importance of Balance

While certain elements of the full swing may vary from player to player, there are some important—even crucial—constants, and the first of these is balance. Why is balance so important? Because in the final analysis, golf is a game of control, and a swing that isn't balanced is a swing that will rarely produce solid, consistent shots.

Just as in almost every other sport, balance begins from the ground up, although beginning and high-handicap golfers frequently overlook the role of footwork in the golf swing. When you think about the golf swing, just consider how similar it is to the pitching motion in baseball or the serve in tennis. In all three, the athlete must first shift his or her weight away from the target and then return it toward the target. The difference is that in golf it is a far more subtle and rotational movement. A proper weight shift accomplishes two important things.

First, it supports and complements the rotation of the upper body and the swinging of the arms.

Next, it helps ensure that the club strikes the ball from the correct direction or path and angle of approach. This point is what made Byron Nelson's so-called "Modern" swing so revolutionary.

Prior to Nelson, players tended to have swings with very little lateral movement. Their swings were more rotational, the "Turn in a Barrel" swing that was designed to complement hickory-shafted clubs. But Nelson learned that the advent of steel shafts required a swing that would allow the club-head to travel along the target line for the longest possible period of time. Nelson went on to become one of the most accurate ball-strikers in history and the swing he developed is very much a model for today's players.

The late Jack Grout, who was one of the most respected PGA Professionals in our organization's history, was Jack Nicklaus's first teacher and they continued to work together throughout much of Nicklaus's career. One of the first fundamentals Grout stressed was that golf is played "between the inside of the left foot and the inside of the right foot."

The point Grout was stressing through this brilliantly simple observation was that while the weight must shift laterally during the full swing (to an increased degree as the clubs get longer), it must remain centered within the confines of the feet. In other words, it is a weight shift, not a sway. This weight shift should never cause either ankle to roll outward.

In fact, when Grout was teaching the young Nicklaus, one swing thought he used was that the left ankle rolled inward on the backswing, while the right ankle mirrored that motion on the forward swing.

In the earlier chapter on "Pre-Swing Fundamentals," we stressed the importance of flexing the knees at address and maintaining that flex throughout the swing. It's a point worth repeating here because a consistent knee flex will allow you to make a proper weight shift more easily.

To prove this to yourself, simply stand straight-legged and make a swinging motion as though you had a club in your hands. After doing this a few times, assume the athletic position we described in Chapter 5 and repeat the swinging motion. You should feel a world of difference.

While the legs play an important role in a good golf swing, it's important to note that they do not, as many people believe, produce the bulk of the power in the swing. To refer back again to Jack Nicklaus, many people credited his power to his enormously strong, 31-inch thighs (it's worth noting that in both of their primes, Nicklaus's thighs were the same size as Gary Player's waist) but in truth, his strength simply allowed his legs to support and complement the tremendous power and speed generated by his arms and upper body.

To prove this point, consider the story of Ernest Jones.

Jones was a fine player and respected teacher in England in the years just prior to World War I. When the war broke out, Jones enlisted in the British army and was badly wounded. Physicians had no choice but to amputate one of his legs just below the knee. No one seriously expected Jones to play golf again, but after four months in the hospital, he was released and promptly went out and shot an utterly remarkable 83.

Jones's stay in the hospital gave him plenty of time to think about the golf swing and that, plus his experiences following his release, convinced him that the primary role of the legs in the swing was to act as a base to support the force of the swing. To illustrate his point, he would sit in a chair and routinely hit drives of 200 yards and longer. This never failed to make believers of his students.

Sam Snead, Ernie Els and many other top-flight pros maintain great balance, which gives the impression of an easy golf swing resulting in a powerful ball flight. The body's dynamic movement occurs through its full range of movement in a very short period of time. Balance allows them to make long and accurate golf shots. When they are out of balance their ball striking is very inconsistent.

Balance is achieved when our bodies properly resist the forces which are pushing us away from the center of our feet. During a golf swing our muscles, joints and nervous system have to function in a coordinated fashion in order to resist the effects of gravity, the forces generated by swinging the club and the momentum generated by our trunk movements. Limitations in flexibility, poor muscular support—especially of the legs and trunk—and lack of awareness of proper balanced movement can result in compensations during the golf swing. The imbalanced swing not only looks bad but can result in inconsistencies and greater stress to the hips, lower back and shoulders.

In the medical field balance is evaluated with instrumentation measuring normal and compensated movement of the body's center of gravity (COG), a point generally behind the belt buckle and just in front of the spine where the body's weight is balanced. A well-balanced golf swing will result in smooth, controlled movement of the body's COG. Poor balance is indicated by excessive movement of the player's COG.

When addressing the ball, the body is supported over the legs with the weight evenly distributed between the balls and heels of the feet. Good posture alignment is important to allow maximum flexibility of our joints while allowing maximum efficiency of our muscles. Posture improvement will help maintain a stabilized swing in good balance. When using middle irons and short irons our body weight is equally distributed between the right and left feet. A very slight increase in weight through the trail leg frequently accompanies the use of longer clubs.

A biomechanically sound swing is one in which the golfer's spine and pelvis mainly rotate over the hip joints, which are larger and designed for more movement than the smaller joints of the lower back. Balanced rotation takes place over a stable base of support. Jack Nicklaus has written of anchoring his golf swing with his weight between the arches of his feet.

During the swing, golfers must learn to maintain a balanced rotation of their body so their COG moves within a balance zone between the balls of the feet and the inside of the heels. The PGA Learning Center in Port St. Lucie, Fla., uses a Dynamic Balance System that plots the movement of the body's COG during the swing and marks the location and direction of the COG at impact.

Turn drill at top of the swing away from the ball.

Tracing Movement

At address the golfer is balanced with his or her weight evenly distributed between the feet and on the middle of the arches.

The initiation of the backswing movement of the upper body to the trail side results in a weight transfer of the COG to the trail side. The proper back movement is accompanied by movement of the pelvis over the right hip, and the COG moves toward the trail heel.

At the top of the backswing, the body's weight should be no farther to the trail side than the inside of the heel.

The forward swing is initiated with movement of the hips, then the shoulders, which moves the COG toward the target side. In a perfectly balanced swing the COG line of the backswing and initial forward movement would be sandwiched on top of each other.

At ball contact, the COG is observed close to the initial balanced address position or slightly to the target side, indicating a stable base of support for the dynamic movement of the pelvis, spine, trunk, shoulders, arms and clubhead.

As the swing progresses, the golfer's body rotates over the target hip to a balanced finish and maintains good posture.

This is an idealized center-of-gravity motion. Every golfer will have their own "signature" swing pattern, which is predicated on their build, flexibility, tempo and a number of other factors. Your PGA Professional can help you learn the best-balanced swing pattern for you.

Coordinating the Weight Shift

As we've discussed, the golf swing is an athletic movement and, therefore, it's an action that is easier for some people to develop properly than others. PGA Professionals have discovered over the years that it is sometimes helpful to compare elements of the swing with other sports. In this case, where we are trying to coordinate the weight shift of the lower body with the rotation of the upper body and the swinging of the arms, a good analogy is the motion used to skip a flat stone across the water, something almost everyone has done at some time or another.

Close your eyes and try to visualize the throwing motion. Once you've done that, go ahead and make the throwing motion as you watch your reflection in a mirror. Pay careful attention to the sequence of motions that your body performs without any conscious thought.

First, you naturally stand at a right angle to the target, just as you do in the golf swing. As you draw your arm back, notice that your weight easily shifts to the back foot, coming to rest momentarily with a high percent of your weight over your back foot by the time your arm is fully hinged. It is at that point that your hips will slide forward, your throwing elbow will naturally tuck into the side of your body just above the hip, before extending as your arm accelerates toward the target. Also, notice at this point that your weight has almost fully shifted to the target foot and your hips and upper body have rotated to a point where your belt buckle will be facing either the target or to a point past that target. It is this rotation that clears the way for your arm to pick up speed. Finally, after you release the stone, notice how your arm naturally extends toward the target before *following* the rotation of your upper body. The point is that your arm has picked up speed and passed your body before releasing the stone.

Perform this exercise several times and then slowly lower your throwing hand until it is in the same position it would be at address in the golf swing. Now simply repeat the throwing motion, as if you were throwing to where the ball is sitting on the ground. With any luck at all, you not only will discover the proper weight shift we've been referring to in this section, but also will have established a very solid—yet incredibly simple—foundation to a good golf swing.

Understanding Swing Plane

The swing plane is an imaginary flat, thin surface which is used to describe the path and angle on which the club is swung. The plane has inclination or tilt, determined by the clubshaft, as well as direction: inside, down the line or outside.

The arc and path that the golf club draws around the golfer—from first motion to finish—creates the plane of the golf swing for that particular shot. The golfer's posture, length and lie of the shaft at address set up the swing plane. The goal of the swing is to return the club to impact position at or close to the club's original lie angle. The shaft should also be leaning as directed by the desired shot.

A logical question is why one person would develop a flat swing while another would have a more upright swing. There are many factors that influence the plane a player develops. The segmental lengths of a player's body parts determine the postural angle. This, combined with the club lie and length, are the starting points. How flexible a player is, and what the goals of the swing are, also are factors.

The swing plane also controls the path of the clubhead into the ball. A flatter swing will tend to deliver the clubhead on a more pronounced path from inside the target line to the ball and, therefore, will tend to promote a hooking or right-to-left ball flight. An upright swing, on the other hand, tends to deliver the clubhead to the ball more directly straight down the target line.

Ben Hogan had a very flat swing that he developed for a variety of reasons. First, he was relatively short, and the general rule is that taller players tend to develop more upright swings. Second, as a young caddie he used to participate in long, drive contests with the other caddies. He discovered by trial and error that a flat swing produced low, hard-running hooks that ran farther along the dry, hard ground in Forth Worth. Of course, the downside was that once he turned pro, this same swing would produce hooks that cost him valuable strokes, so he had to re-tool his swing from the grip up.

Jack Nicklaus, while of average height, learned to play at Scioto Country Club, a wonderful Donald Ross design in Columbus, Ohio. Scioto had small, well-bunkered greens that favored high, soft approach shots. Therefore, Nicklaus developed an upright swing that allowed him to hit these shots and, at the same time, allowed him to hit a fade which he found to be more accurate than a draw.

As a general rule, a flatter swing tends to be more repeatable and, therefore, more consistent, simply because the arms—and especially the right elbow—tend to remain closer to the body on the backswing. This led to the famous observation that "watching Ben Hogan hit balls is like watching a machine stamp out bottle caps."

One day Sam Snead was in a meeting with a panel of top teachers and players convened by *Golf Digest*. The conversation turned to the swing plane. Sam listened as all sorts of impressive theories were debated and then offered his simple, down-to-earth swing thought that he used throughout his career.

"If, at the top of your backswing, your left forearm is about halfway between your right ear and right shoulder, then you've got a pretty good swing plane going back," Sam said. "If your right forearm is between your left ear and left shoulder on your follow-through, then it means you pretty much stayed on plane for the whole swing and you've got one less thing to worry about."

We can't improve on that.

When and How the Wrists Hinge

One question that PGA Professionals are frequently asked by beginning and intermediate golfers is when the wrists should begin to hinge in the golf swing. It's a good question and the answer isn't as complicated as you might think.

The golf swing has evolved over the years as players on average have become taller and stronger and, more importantly, the equipment has changed.

Until the 1930s, clubs had hickory shafts that not only flexed during

Delivering the club through impact to finish

Drill to practice hinging the wrists

the swing but also twisted or torqued, causing the clubheads to open and close. As a result, swings from this period were designed to reduce or at least control the effects of this torque. This can be seen if we study swing sequences of players from that era. As they began their swings, they would literally drag the club back from the ball, so that their hands led the club-head. The wrists would then be completely hinged roughly at about the same time they were waist high. This dragging motion helped reduce torquing.

With the development of steel shafts in the 1930s, however, torque became less of a problem and the swing evolved to what became known as a "One-piece Takeaway," popularized by players such as Byron Nelson and Sam Snead. In this action, it's as if the hands rest on the grip as though they were in a holster. As the arms and upper body swing the club back, the wrists hinge naturally as the club reaches a more vertical position in the swing.

The wrists continue to hinge as the club reaches the top of the back-swing, but if you study sequence photos of some top players, something interesting becomes evident: The wrists continue to hinge as the arms begin the downswing. This "downward hinging" only adds to the power that a player can deliver to the ball at impact. This, along with proper body tilt, helps ensure that the club is routed on a proper path during the downswing.

As we have throughout this book, we'd like to suggest a drill that can help you develop a better feel for when and how your wrists should hinge during the swing.

Assume your address position. Now hinge your wrists so the club moves at an angle in line with your trail arm. Elevate your arms until your hands are shoulder high. The club will be pointing over your trail shoulder and your arms will have made their backswing motion. Now practice this from the address position. This is the arm motion that you will blend with your body turn. The hinging of your wrists will happen as your arms elevate and your trail elbow folds.

"Releasing" the Club on the Downswing

When people speak of releasing the club, what they are referring to is a release of the energy and power that has been stored in the process of making a backswing. As the body slides laterally and rotates toward the target on the downswing, there is an unhinging of the wrists, a rotation of the forearms and a straightening of the trail arm as the club moves through the hitting area. In short, your body is simply mirroring the movements it made on the backswing as you reach your impact position. The body at impact has more tilt to the trail side and the arms are extended past the ball.

Try this exercise. Place a golf ball on the ground. To feel the proper release in the downswing, put a golf ball in your trail hand and get in your address position. Swing back to the top of your swing and as you go forward throw the ball you are holding at the ball on the ground.

Timing and Tempo

The golf swing is a series of movements designed to do just one thing: deliver the clubhead to the ball in a manner that will produce the desired distance and direction with the most consistency. To do this, the movements must occur in a logical and repeatable order. Think of the swing as an automobile engine. If the cylinders are firing in the proper order, the engine runs smoothly and powerfully. But if they are out of order, the motor isn't nearly as efficient.

The timing of a golf swing is something very different from the tempo of the swing, although people often mistakenly use the terms interchangeably. Timing is the order of the swing, while tempo is the speed in which the timing occurs. And while the timing of the swing parts is generally agreed upon, tempo is a matter of individual preference. For example, players such as Fred Couples and Nancy Lopez have a slow, almost languid tempo in their swings—and games for that matter—while players such as Tom Watson and Sergio Garcia have tempos that are considerably faster, again both in the swings and games. If Tom and Sergio tried to copy Fred's tempo, their games would likely suffer. That's one reason faster players detest slow play. They know it wreaks havoc on their games.

While a good tempo is beneficial, timing is clearly the more important of the two. A good tempo can occasionally salvage a shot when a player's timing is out of sync, but it can only do it every so often. Eventually the odds will catch up with you.

Finding the "Slot"

Very often a simple image is all it takes for a golfer to grasp what seems to be a complicated element of the golf swing. One such image is getting your hands and club "into the slot" at the top of the backswing, just as the body begins its lateral slide toward the target, beginning the downswing.

You start the club forward by tilting your torso toward the target. The target hip effectively is withdrawn just as the trail hip was in the backswing. There is no weight shift, only a transfer of pressure to the lead foot. And, in the earliest stage of the forward swing, the arms come down more than they move forward. Only the left hip is active at this point. The trail hip more or less stays back. It does not rotate yet, storing power for the time when it does rotate through impact. As a result, early in the forward swing there will be more tilt of the trail side than there was at address. This is slotting the club.

The Width and Length of the Swing

Basically, if you trace the path the clubhead travels in the course of a swing, you'll see that it is fundamentally circular, although the path does flatten by necessity as the club passes through the hitting area. It stands to reason, therefore, that the longer and wider the swing arc, the more power can be generated in the swing, assuming that the ball is struck squarely.

Here's a very simple analogy: If you attached a weight to a length of string and swung it at a controlled pace around a fixed center, the weight would achieve a sustainable maximum speed. But if you changed the equation by lengthening the string, centrifugal force would cause the weight to have more power at impact. However, the reality of diminishing returns comes into play here. If the length of swing becomes too long, it will be difficult, and ultimately impossible, to control. This causes off-center hits.

To achieve maximum controllable distance and power in your golf swing, it's important to reach what's known as the "maximum leverage point." That is, the position where the butt end of the club is as far as it can be from the ball *while still swinging in balance*. That italic phrase is crucial, because power without control does infinitely more harm than good in the golf swing. It's like owning a car that will go 100 mph but has a faulty steering system. The next accident may literally be just around the corner.

Ironically, most golfers routinely reach this point in their swing quite by accident. It generally occurs when they are trying to hit a lay-up shot. They swing more easily than they normally do—which certainly helps improve their chances of making solid contact—but since they are not striving for distance, they make a swing that, while long enough, isn't so long that they

Addressing the ball and starting the swing

can't control it, which is often the case when they have a driver, fairway wood or long iron in their hands.

Here are three points to keep in mind when trying to make a swing that takes full advantage of this maximum leverage point.

First, the forward spine angle you establish at address must be maintained throughout the swing. This provides a constant point to swing around.

Second, at the top of your backswing, your shoulders should be turned 90 degrees to the target line. This amount of shoulder turn provides the arms, and therefore the club, a direct path back to the ball. To test this, place a club parallel to the target line, near your toes. Hold a second club so it rests across your upper chest and your shoulders. Assume your address position—again, stressing that you bend from the waist and your spine angle remains constant—and turn your upper body to the right until the shafts are at a 90-degree angle. You may find that you need to either open or close your stance slightly to achieve this optimum 90-degree shoulder turn, which makes this an excellent drill to work on for practice at home.

Finally, the trail arm must retain its relationship to the trail shoulder as the arm folds on the backswing. To determine this position, hold both arms straight out in front of your sternum or breastbone. Then, without consciously turning your upper body, move the target arm back until you feel the muscles in your chest tighten to a locked position. This point will vary depending on an individual's flexibility. The point the target arm reaches, in relation to your shoulder, will be the optimum position for your arms in the backswing. Going past this point will cause you to alter your spine position or bend your lead elbow.

As a general rule, a swing that is too long will lead to inconsistency while one that is too short doesn't allow a player to effectively use the leverage of the arms and upper body. In brief, a backswing that is too short leads a player to *hit at* the ball rather than *swing through* the hitting area. However, PGA Professionals almost never see a backswing that is too short.

Putting It All Together

All golfers making a full swing at the ball should rotate their upper body 90 degrees from the target line in their backswing. In reality, most golfers can't achieve this degree of rotation because they either aren't flexible enough or they don't play and practice enough. However, they can achieve a fuller upper-body rotation with a correct address and a simple move at the start of the swing.

Full swing sequence with shaft shows weight shift.

The First Move

Begin your backswing, what I like to refer to as the swing away, by drawing your trail hip back so your lead shoulder turns down and your arms start back. At the completion of the backswing, your trail hip is over your trail heel. The trail hip doesn't slide away from the target, but neither does it turn. If a rod were standing vertically behind you in line with your trail shoulder, with the move, your trail hip would hit the rod in the backswing. The feeling is one of sitting down into your trail-hip socket. There is no weight shift or change of weight from one side to the other. There is only a difference in pressure, which is felt in the feet. The head stays centered over the ball.

In making this move, the club will travel straight back from the ball for the first 18 inches or so. Then, just as importantly, your upper trunk will begin to rotate around your spine and have space to rotate fully. This move not only eliminates the sway or slide to the rear of the body, but it also prevents a reverse pivot, which is far more common than the sway. A reverse pivot occurs when your weight is shifted to the target foot during the backswing. Then, in the forward swing, the weight is shifted to the trail side. At impact, you are leaning backward away from the target, which usually results in a very weak hit and poor direction.

To make the move fully effective, you must set up properly to the ball. A sound address position is vital. Most golfers take a closed position without realizing it. The shoulders and feet are aligned to the target itself, or in extreme cases even to the right of the target. As a result, the clubface is aimed to the right. If you swing the club on a natural plane, the ball is going to go far right of the target. Therefore, an adjustment in the forward swing is made, usually by throwing the trail shoulder out toward the ball in an effort to get the club moving down the line of flight to the real target. Invariably the club comes over the top and across the line of flight from outside to inside. This produces a pull or hook if the face is closed, or a pull slice if the face is open at impact.

Other address faults that restrict a full upper-body turn include playing the ball too far forward in the stance so the trail shoulder angles out toward the target line and ball. This restricts full upper-body rotation. A stance that is too narrow promotes an over-rotation of the lower body, which counters any effort to turn the upper body properly. The idea is to keep the lower body steady at this point so the upper body can have something to turn against and develop a powerful coil for the forward swing.

Too many golfers stand too straight at address when they should tilt their spine from 3 to 9 degrees to the trail side. This expedites the starting move and the 90-degree rotation of the upper trunk.

Two things derive from this tilt. It lowers your trail hand so you can easily grip the club without stretching your trail arm or shortening your target arm. Thus, you will not be inclined to get the trail shoulder pointing out toward the target. It also puts your torso in position to more readily begin the swing.

The position you want at address is the well-known railroad track in which the feet, hips and shoulders form a line parallel to the target line. That parallel line must be directed to the side of the actual target. Most golfers do not achieve this setup and otherwise get into poor address positions because they step into the ball with their eyes on their feet or on the ball and the club. They then step toward the target, which gets them closed at address. Tour professionals step in while looking at their target.

By keeping your eyes on your goal, you are sending target information to the brain and letting your body instinctively respond to that data. We all have athletic instincts, and one of them is to line ourselves up correctly to hit a ball toward a target, if our focus is on the target.

An optical illusion occurs the farther away the target is from you. It appears smaller and this can affect your setup. Imagine that when looking down the line of flight while getting into your address position, you key your vision on a large tree to the left of the target. An imaginary line from that tree back to your feet/hips/shoulders will be parallel to your target line. When hitting a short iron, align your feet/hips/shoulders directly to the tree. With middle irons, the alignment is a little to the side of the tree. With a driver, the alignment is farther to the side to allow for the optical illusion that makes it appear smaller. Here are five recommendations for setting up properly.

1. Widen your stance so that, with the driver, the width measured from the center of your feet is that of the outside of your shoulders. The width is proportionately less as the club gets shorter so the ankles are under the shoulder joints.

2. Close your stance a little, with your trail foot pulled back a little more from the target line than the target foot. This is important especially if you lack flexibility. You can do this with all clubs, even your wedge. It makes the rotation of the upper trunk to 90 degrees that much easier.

3. The base of your sternum (center of your chest) should be pointing directly at the ball so that the trail arm moves most effectively, staying below the target arm at the start of the swing away and until it folds.

4. Golf is a stability sport, so distribute your weight from the balls of your feet to your heels, not from the balls out to the toes.

5. Golfers tend to stand with knees that are too straight. Be sure there is some flex in your knees so you can use your joints properly. Kind of sit back with your hips out behind you in a skeletally balanced position.

You are now ready to complete the full swing.

The backswing begins with the move of the trail hip back over the trail heel. If you start the action with the hands, the club will move too much to the inside. By the same token, the arms will go where the shoulders take them, so the move in effect creates your swing plane.

At the top of the backswing, the butt of the grip should be as far from the ball as possible. Your trail arm is below the target arm when the club starts back, then it folds and the wrists hinge.

The Forward Swing

You start the club forward by tilting your torso to the target. The lead hip effectively is withdrawn just as the trail hip was in the backswing. There is only a transfer of pressure to the lead foot. In the earliest stage of the forward swing, the arms come down more than they move forward. Only the target hip is active at this point. The trail hip more or less stays back. It doesn't rotate yet, thereby storing power for the moment when it does rotate through impact. As a result, early in the forward swing there will be more tilt to the trail side than there was at address.

By swinging the arms down and holding back the trail hip rotation, you avoid hitting from the top. The trail arm continues to extend past impact and is extended fully only when past the ball.

Swing sequence shows full swing from swing away through finish.

Driver at impact

Think of the swing as a linear motion, not one of centrifugal force. If you rotate the trail hip too early, you create centrifugal force, which releases the club too soon. This is why golfers hit from the top or come over the top and cast the club. You want to store centrifugal force until it is needed. By keeping the trail hip back early in the forward swing, you get a natural "late hit." When it is released, you have a very strong motion through impact.

A Final Thought

Throughout this book, we've tried to give you useful information in an easy-to-understand form. Golf instruction can be complex and overwhelming, even for experienced players. Certainly, in this chapter, we've given you a lot to comprehend, although we hope we've done it successfully. That said, here's one last thought that should tie it all together, whether you're a beginner or a low-handicapper trying to shave just one more stroke from your score or answer one more question you may have about the swing. At the end of the day, a golf swing is a great golf swing for you if it does one thing and one thing only: helps you make solid, consistent contact.

"The measure of a golf swing isn't its aesthetic beauty, although we would all like to have a swing reminiscent of Sam Snead's," says the legendary British professional John Jacobs. "However, the only true purpose of the swing is to move the club through the ball squarely to the target at maximum speed. How this is precisely done is of little significance at all, so long as a player's method enables this to be done repetitively." This repetition depends on how well players have matched their swing to their athletic ability, physical conditioning and skill level.

Questions and Answers

Q: *I have a tendency to sway so badly on my backswing that my right foot actually rolls to the right. Is there anything I can do to help prevent this?*

A: Work on the starting move with the torso and only move the hip over the heel.

Q: *I tend to take the club back to the inside on my backswing. Are there any drills that will help prevent this?*

A: Try this: Address the ball with a 5-iron but place another ball directly behind the clubhead. As you begin your backswing, concentrate on rolling the second ball straight back along the target line. In the first move away from the ball keep the arms and the upper body connected.

Q: *I've heard that Byron Nelson had what he called his "Magic Move." What was it?*

A: Nelson would drop the club into the slot to begin his downswing by tucking his right elbow against his right hip. In fact, if he wore a contestant's badge on his belt near this spot, he found that by the end of the round he would often have a small scrape where his right elbow would repeatedly hit the badge. Byron is quick to point out, however, that it didn't take him long to figure out he should move the badge rather than change his swing.

Q: *I'm 6-feet-3 and am just taking up the game. Should I study the swings of other tall players?*

A: That's an excellent idea. When he was a youngster growing up on the island of Fiji, 1998 PGA Champion Vijay Singh, who is 6-2 carefully studied photos of Tom Weiskopf's (6-3) swing from a 1977 issue of *Golf Digest*. Since you are tall, it would also be very helpful to watch videotapes of a tall player swinging the club to see how well he coordinates the timing of his swing. Remember that height is not the only physical characteristic you should match up. You may need to look at the swings of several players.

7

The Keys to
Successful Putting

*"All there is to putting is keeping the head still and the face
of the putter moving squarely across the line to the hole. The
problem is there are at least 1,000 ways to do this."*

—Tommy Armour

The late Harvey Penick taught that "A good putter is a match for anyone but a poor putter isn't a match for anyone."

It's worth noting that Mr. Penick was a very good putter whose best-known pupils were Ben Crenshaw and Tom Kite, who were also very good on the greens.

Ben Hogan was also a very good putter until late in his career. It's worth noting that his favorite game in practice rounds was to award a point for hitting a fairway and one for hitting a green in regulation. At the end of the round, the player with the most points won, and that player was usually Ben Hogan. In his retirement, he often half-jokingly suggested that golf would be a better game if greens were shaped like funnels and putting was eliminated altogether.

One of the oldest sayings in golf is "You drive for show and putt for dough," and there's certainly an element of truth in this, although poor drivers find themselves scrambling all day and no one can hope to sustain that type of play with any success—at least not for very long.

A textbook case that proves the importance of putting is the 1938 PGA Championship at Shawnee Country Club, when the diminutive Paul Runyan demolished long-hitting Sam Snead, 8 and 7, in the 36-hole match-play finals.

"In all honesty and fairness, Sam wasn't yet the great player we think of today," said Runyan, a two-time PGA Champion. "But even then he was magnificent. He would routinely out-drive me by 40 or 50 yards, but I was playing extremely well and putting as well as I ever did (which, it's worth noting, is as well as anyone ever did). Sam became frustrated and began pressing, which of course you cannot do and hope to be successful. Good putting is not only a great equalizer, but it's also a great psychological weapon, especially in match-play situations."

The cold, hard reality is that the better you are, the more important putting becomes, because your number of putts per round represents a larger percentage of your total strokes per round. Consider this: Studies over the years have consistently shown that for a typical low-handicapper, putting can account for between 40 and 45 percent of his or her total strokes per round.

If you attend a professional tournament, the importance the players place upon putting becomes obvious when you see how much time they spend on the practice green, practicing and refining their technique.

But if you ask PGA Professionals what percentage of their lessons deal with putting, the answer will be shockingly low. Why is that?

One theory is that people consider putting an art that you're either blessed with or aren't. Therefore, there's no point in wasting valuable lesson time when you could be learning to smash out 300-yard drives.

A second theory is that people consider good putting to be a fleeting thing—a skill that varies from round to round and something that no amount of lessons or serious practice can affect in any consistent fashion.

Both are equally wrong.

In truth, there are people who do seem to have a special talent for accurately reading the line and speed of a putt, but this isn't to discount how much they practice to refine that talent. Take the case of Billy Casper, for example. Casper won two U.S. Opens and a Masters and more than 60 professional tournaments, in no small part because he was one of the game's finest putters. In fact, after Casper won the 1959 U.S. Open at Winged Foot, Ben Hogan quipped, "If he [Casper] couldn't putt he'd be selling hot dogs out here."

But was Casper's putting skill a gift he was given at birth? Hardly.

"When I was a youngster I would practice putting long after the other kids had gone home," Casper once explained. "I found that if I practiced putting in the dark, it greatly improved my sense of feel and touch. I'd practice for hours, alone in the dark."

Since everyone has a different physical and psychological makeup, there are no pure absolutes in putting. Just consider the differences among some of the players who are generally considered some of the greatest putters in history.

Walter Hagen, Arnold Palmer and Tom Watson were all very aggressive putters, in part because this reflected their personalities but also because in their prime they were supremely confident and didn't worry about leaving themselves a three- or four-foot putt coming back if they ran their first putt past the hole. Tiger Woods is also a very aggressive putter.

On the other hand, Bobby Jones, Jack Nicklaus and Ben Crenshaw were more conservative putters, preferring to have their putts die at the hole. Again, this reflected their personalities but in no way reflected a lack of confidence in making short putts.

Palmer, Casper and Gary Player had strokes that allowed them to "tap" the ball, with very little movement of the clubhead after impact, while Crenshaw, Seve Ballesteros and Brad Faxon have very long, flowing strokes.

Players like Jones, Bobby Locke and Ben Crenshaw all had strokes that were very much like a door opening and closing. Depending on the length of the putt, the clubface would open on the backswing, much as a door or gate swings open, and then close to a square position upon impact. Other players such as Tom Kite and Loren Roberts prefer to keep the clubface moving back and forth along the target line as much as possible, again given the length of the putt. Snead, for example, would practice his stroke for hours, simply putting along a yardstick on his hotel room floor.

Nicklaus, Hagen and Lee Trevino tended to crouch over the ball, while Jones, Crenshaw and Nancy Lopez stood fairly erect.

But that said, almost all these and other great putters did share a fair number of fundamentals or principles in their putting—guidelines that are worth incorporating in your game.

Understanding the Fundamentals of Good Putting

The following series of fundamentals may seem simple or obvious, but as with all fundamentals it is important that you take the time to make sure you incorporate them into your putting. The best way to do this is to have your PGA Professional give you a putting lesson to ensure that you are actually doing what you *think* you are doing. One of the subtle difficulties of this game is that our bodies often trick us. That's why a trained set of eyes is so valuable, no matter how skilled you may be.

An Overview

There are basically two main considerations or factors in putting. The first is distance control, which is determined by the amount of forward and backward

Putting position after impact

swing of the club. The second is direction, which is largely determined by ensuring that the clubface is pointing at a 90-degree angle to the target line at impact.

In the pages that follow, we will cover these areas in greater detail, but here is a brief synopsis of the key putting principles.

At address, you should stand with your ankle joints under your shoulders. Push your hips back and up and let your arms hang from your shoulders.

You should hold the club with a grip that feels comfortable but take care to grip the club lightly. A tight grip pressure creates tension in your hands, arms and shoulders.

Your eyes should be directly over the ball, since placement of the ball is crucial to helping ensure solid contact. Ideally, the ball should be positioned in the middle of your body. Positioning your eyes over the ball will help you align your body and the clubface to the target.

During the putting stroke, keep your head and body still. Putting should be the only motion in golf in which the body and head remain very still. Ideally, only your upper arms and shoulders should be moving. If your hands and wrists move independently of your arms and shoulders, it becomes more difficult to control the distance and direction. It is important to have an even stroke and pace. Moving the club head back and forward the same distance and pace will improve distance control.

Finally, there is no mystery to where the ball is going to go when you strike it. It's going to go wherever the clubface is pointing at impact.

Getting Started

In the preceding section, we gave you some basic principles of good putting. Now we'd like to give you the fundamental techniques that can help you become a good, consistent putter.

Pre-swing putting alignment

GRIP—Unlike the grip for the full swing, which has evolved to help players create speed and power in the swing, the putting grip exists to provide control and accuracy above all else.

Just as there are a variety of grip styles for the full swing, there is an even wider variety of grips for putting. Indeed, how you choose to grip the putter is among the most individual and idiosyncratic elements in the game. You can putt with all 10 fingers on the grip. You can interlock or overlap any variety of fingers. You can putt with either hand gripping the butt of the club. You can even putt with the hands split apart, which is a method advocated by two very, very good putters, Paul Runyan and Phil Rodgers. Whatever style you develop, the key is to establish a grip that is (1) comfortable and (2) allows the hands to complement each other. It is crucial in putting that the hands work as a unit, with no one hand dominant.

Here is a thought that has helped a great many players become and remain good putters: However you grip the putter, never allow your target or lead wrist to "break down" after impact (and certainly never before!). By maintaining the angle your target wrist had at address, you help ensure that the face of the putter will be square to the line at impact and that you'll neither add nor reduce the effective loft of the putter. In fact, one reason so

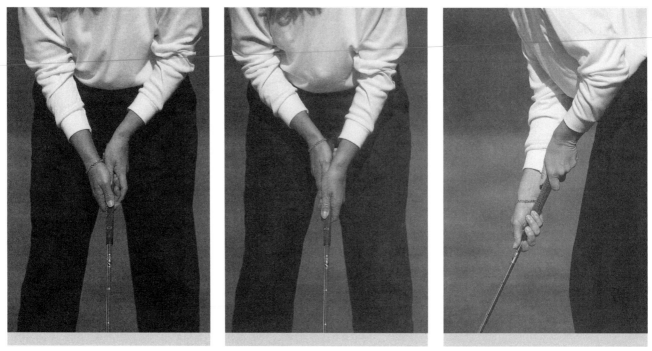

Conventional putting grip   Cross-handed putting grip   Split putting grip

many players elect a cross-handed method of putting is that it helps maintain this wrist angle.

If you have difficulty either comprehending this concept or making it work for you, here's something you might try: Wear a watch on your target wrist and slide an object such as a pencil, pen or, even better, a wooden tongue depressor under the watch so it rests across the top of your forearm and wrist. Now practice stroking some putts. The pencil will prevent your wrist from breaking down, and will also help you develop a stroke that keeps the putter traveling along the target line for an optimum amount of time.

Grip pressure is another area, like the grip itself, which is largely a matter of individual preference. Just as in the full swing, some players prefer a very light grip pressure while others instinctively grip the club more tightly. A good test, however, is to assume your normal grip and putting stance and then check for tightness in your forearms. If your forearms feel tight, you may want to loosen your grip pressure slightly. Tension in your forearms can very often lead to a jerky, inconsistent stroke.

STANCE—Again, as in so many areas in putting, how you stand to the ball is largely a matter of what feels most comfortable to you, as long as your stance allows you to position your eyes over the ball and that the ball is positioned at least in the middle of your stance as we discussed earlier.

The keys to a proper putting stance are similar to the full-swing position, with some minor alterations. First, stand so your ankle joints are positioned under your shoulders. Push your hips back and up and let your arms hang naturally from your shoulders.

Logic dictates that the ideal stance would be one in which the feet, hips and shoulders are parallel to your target line, since this should give you the best chance of delivering the putter squarely to the target line. However (and this is a big however), human nature often works against logic, and in this case, with good reason. A very large number of outstanding putters play from a *slightly* open stance, for two reasons: first, for many people, an open stance allows them to more easily see the proper line of the putt, and second, by opening their stance they feel they can keep the putter moving along the target line for a longer period of time.

It's worth noting that some outstanding putters such as Bobby Locke, Nick Faldo and Billy Casper putted from a closed stance, but they really are in the vast minority. Still, if you are having problems with your putting, *slightly* closing your stance may be an option worth discussing with your PGA Professional.

BALL POSITION—Just as in the full swing, ball position is an often-overlooked fundamental, but in the case of putting, it becomes increasingly important. Why? Because if the ball is positioned incorrectly in your stance, it can cause you to either hit your putts off line or, more likely, cause you to intuitively adjust your stroke to compensate for this fundamental error, which will invariably lead to inconsistency.

Path of a curving putt

Putting practice drill

Putter face tape shows you where on the putter you're striking the ball.

The proper ball position is one that will allow you to position your eyes over the ball *and* deliver the putter squarely to the ball. If the ball is too far back in your stance, the tendency will be for the clubface to be marginally open at impact. Conversely, if the ball is too far forward, the face of the putter will already be closing down slightly. Notice we used the words "marginally" and "slightly." That's important, because when you're aiming at a 4 1/4-inch target, you don't have much margin for error.

AIMING PROPERLY—It is impossible to overstate how important it is that you learn how to properly aim and align yourself to the target. As many as 70 percent of missed putts are the result of faulty aim, not a flawed stroke. If you aren't capable of aiming the putter toward your target, then even the most technically perfect stroke in the world isn't going to get the job done on any consistent basis. Just consider this: If you have a perfectly level, 10-foot putt but aim just 2 degrees to the right or left of the target (or mis-align your putter to the same degree) your odds of making the putt decline dramatically—and continue to decline the farther you are from the hole.

A full putting stroke

One way to dramatically improve your ability to aim the ball properly is to align the clubface to an intermediate target. After you've studied your putt and determined the proper target line, take one more look at the putt from behind the ball and pick out something distinctive on your intended line that is a foot or two ahead of the ball. It can be an old pitch mark or an off-

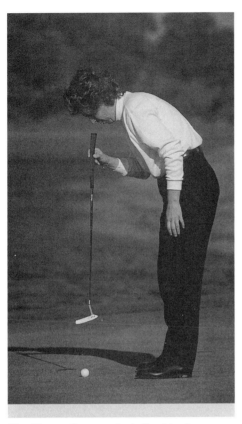

Checking eyeline over the ball—side view

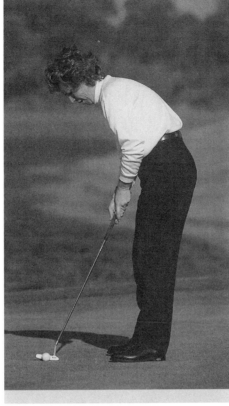

Putting stroke at impact

Checking eyeline over the ball—front view

Putting position at address—front view

Putting from off the green

colored blade of grass. Once you've picked this intermediate target, address the ball and align the blade and the ball to *this* target, not your ultimate target.

Here are three thoughts that might help you improve your aiming: First, after you've carefully marked your ball, replace it so that one of the logos is aimed at the intermediate target you've selected. Tiger Woods always does this. This will help you aim the clubface squarely to the ball, since the logo and the top edge of the putter blade should sit at right angles to each other. Next, experiment and try this step that two-time PGA Champion Nick Price makes in his pre-shot routine. Like a great many players from earlier generations, Price addresses the ball, then lifts his putter and carefully places it ahead of the ball. He finds this helps him ensure that the putter is aimed squarely at his intermediate target—and it gives him just one additional boost of confidence. Finally, as you prepare to putt and are taking one last look at the target, make sure you look at your *intermediate* target and not the hole itself. Eyeing one target and aiming at another can only create confusion for you and could add a last-minute element of doubt.

READING GREENS—Here is one area where some players simply seem to have an uncanny edge. It's as though they have a gift for reading how putts are going to break given the contours of the green and the playing conditions, and have a remarkable ability to detect subtleties that may escape others. That said, reading greens isn't something you can either do well or not at all. Understanding some basics can dramatically help you improve your ability to judge the break and speed of your putts.

First, being able to gauge the speed of a putt is crucial to figuring out how much a putt is going to break. It stands to reason that a putt hit on a wet or even damp green will be slower than one hit on a dry, firm surface.

Next, be aware which direction the grass is growing. This is particularly true of Bermuda-grass greens. If the grain is growing toward you, the putt will be slower than if it is running away from you. A good way to test this is to check the color of the grass. If the grain is growing toward you, the grass will appear darker and duller, while grass growing away from you will appear shiny. Another check is to study the top edge of the cup. If the grass is growing away from you, the surface on the far edge of the cup will be shorter and darker than the grass on the near side of the hole, because it has been cut nearer the roots. And don't forget the grain will have more effect on the ball later in the day when the grass has grown a bit. This is especially important with Bermuda grass. Keep in mind that in the late afternoon, the grain of the grass will cause the ball to break toward the setting sun. Three other thoughts: Putts will tend to break toward bodies of water and will generally break away from mountains, and wind will definitely affect a putt, depending on how strongly it is blowing and how sheltered the green is by trees.

While correctly reading a green is obviously important, here's a good piece of advice: don't over-read your putts. In order of importance, you should (1) study the putt from behind the hole; (2) take a look from the low side of the putt (the side the ball is going to break toward); and (3) look from behind the hole, although a large number of Professionals guard against this because it can provide confusing information. Finally, take one last look from behind the ball and then pull the trigger. In the vast majority of cases, your first instinct is going to be the right instinct so you should trust it. Develop a routine and stick to it.

CONTROLLING DISTANCE—In the previous section we discussed the importance of direction control in putting, but here is something to consider: When you hit a poor approach putt, do you generally err on the distance you hit the putt or the direction? If you think back over your rounds, the chances are you'll discover that your mistake was one of distance and not direction. You either hit the ball too firmly or not firmly enough, and you're not alone in making this mistake. People invariably focus so intently upon direction—finding the right line—that they give short shrift to distance.

To help improve your sense of distance control, it's a good idea to become less "hole-bound." In other words, find some practice drills that will allow you to concentrate on developing a feel for distance control rather than being consumed with the effort to hole putts. One such drill is to take a few balls and practice putting to the fringe of the green, varying each putt's length so that you hit a longish putt to the far fringe with one ball and then a shorter putt to the near fringe with the next. Your only focus should be letting the ball roll softly against the fringe.

A technical tip that may help you better control the speed and distance of your putts is to vary the length of your stroke as the putts vary in length. The longer the putt, the longer the stroke away from the ball and through the ball and, conversely, the shorter the putt the shorter the stroke back and through the ball. Just as you don't want to decelerate on the forward stroke, neither do you want to think "hit" on longer or slower putts. Instead, try to establish a comfortable "one-two, forward-back" rhythm to your stroke.

Another consideration concerning distance is the individual's personality. Some people are naturally aggressive and feel comfortable taking a strong run at putts. Their philosophy is summed up by 1985 PGA Champion Hubert Green, who once explained that he liked to charge his putts because "99 percent of the putts I leave short don't go it."

A second school of thought is that it's better to hit putts just hard enough so that the ball either dies at the hole or just inches past. The beauty of this thinking is that a ball rolling slowly has a much better chance of falling in the side of the cup than a ball moving more quickly. That, and of course, you seldom leave yourself a nerve-testing putt coming back. The downside is that the slower a ball is rolling, the more it is affected by spike marks, old pitch marks, etc.

Here's one final thought on distance control: be realistic. Certainly, you'd like to make every putt, but depending on the distance and difficulty of a putt, it's important to be realistic and decide what putts you can honestly expect to hole and when you should try to simply leave the ball within easy makable range.

FINDING THE RIGHT PUTTER—Putters come in every conceivable style and design, from the classic to those bordering on the bizarre. Designing putters, it seems, is often an exercise in the search for the perfect mousetrap.

The foremost consideration when selecting a putter is that it looks and feels good to you. If a putter doesn't inspire confidence when you set it down behind the ball, then it's not likely to produce satisfactory results over the long haul.

Go through a putter fitting and find the type of head design and shaft offset that fits your alignment and setup.

Next, you should honestly assess your skill. If you have a precise stroke that allows you to consistently strike the ball with the putter's sweet spot, you can use a more forgiving putter that offers a more delicate feel. If, however, you're not that precise or don't play and practice as often as you'd like, a more forgiving putter with heel-and-toe balanced weighting might help you become more consistent.

Another consideration is the type of greens you most frequently putt on. If the greens are rather slow and bumpy, you need a putter with at least six degrees of loft, since this will allow you to get the ball rolling smoothly. If you putt on fast, smooth greens, you can get away with less loft, although it's worth noting that most players would benefit from a putter with at least four degrees of loft. Also, bear in mind that the effective loft of a putter is determined in large part by where your hands are relative to the clubface at contact. If your hands are ahead of the putter, you'll reduce effective loft; if your hands trail the clubhead, you'll add loft—yet another reason to develop a consistent stroke.

SOME ALTERNATE PUTTING METHODS—In recent years, two alternatives to the traditional method of putting have emerged and become popular—the long-handled putter and the cross-handed grip (left-hand-low grip for right-handed golfers).

The long-handled putter is an excellent option for people who have had problems making short putts. Since it provides a fixed center of gravity, it helps ensure a consistent length of stroke and there is much less possibility of manipulating the stroke with the hands and wrists. This is an excellent method for people who like to stand taller at address, and also for those who have experienced problems controlling their small muscles. If you have had severe putting problems, experimenting with a long putter can help develop a new set of neuro-pathways. Think of this as traveling down a highway that's been very bumpy for you lately. By switching putting styles, you're traveling a different route to the same destination.

While this method can be very effective for short putts, players like Rocco Mediate have been very successful with it on longer putts as well. If you watch him hit an approach putt, you'll notice that his method is very similar to sweeping with a broom, in that he controls the stroke with the large muscles of his shoulders.

Left-hand-low or cross-handed putting is particularly useful for players who are left-eye dominant, since it allows them to look at the ball from a different angle than the traditional putting method. It also helps ensure that the shoulders are level to the ground. The other advantage this method offers is that it helps prevent the lead wrist from cupping on the forward stroke, which helps the grip end of the club move forward for a longer period of time. The end result of this type of stroke is that the shoulders, not the wrists, control the putting motion. Karrie Webb is an excellent example of a player who successfully putts with this method.

Questions and Answers

Q: *Can the "Yips" be cured?*

A: The Yips or "Twitchies" as the British call them, are something of a mystery. While many players are never afflicted with the Yips, they tend to strike players at different stages of their career, and can afflict both good putters and bad. Toward the end of his competitive career, Ben Hogan was so plagued by the Yips that he very often couldn't bring himself to take the putter back from the ball. Master champion Bernhard Langer has had recurring battles with the Yips throughout his career, and has tried all sorts of putting styles in order to deal with the affliction. Can the Yips be cured? Not according to the prevailing wisdom which is summed up in the British saying "Once you've had 'em, you've got 'em." Incidentally, while the Yips generally afflict a player's putting, they can also have the same effect on driving and chipping the ball.

Q: *When the ball comes to rest in the first cut of rough near the green, can I putt the ball?*

A: It's a risky shot, but yes, you can putt it from the rough. The key is to position the ball well back in your stance, almost off your right or rear foot. Set your hands well ahead of the ball at address, and lift the club up sharply on the backswing. On the downswing, hit down sharply on the ball. This will cause the ball to pop into the air and land with topspin. The ball will settle quickly once it reaches the green, and will run smoothly toward the hole. This shot is risky, because there are no guarantees how the ball will react after impact. It requires a lot of practice, but it can be effective. Here's a variation of this shot that's worth trying: If you are facing a difficult lie in the greenside rough, play the ball back in your stance with your hands ahead of the ball. Turn the putter so that you are addressing the ball off the toe of the club, take the club away from the ball with a quick cocking of the wrist, and then hit down on the ball. By hitting the ball with the toe of the putter, you prevent the clubhead from getting caught up in the grass and turning over. The ball will pop into the air and land smoothly on the green.

Q: *Are there any rules of thumb when putting on wet greens?*

A: Any time you are putting on wet greens, the first thing to keep in mind is that the putt will be slower than it would be if the greens were dry. Most people instinctively know this, but often overlook the fact that the moisture reduces the amount that the ball will break.

Q: *I've noticed that an increasing number of players, especially LPGA Professionals, have switched to cross-handed putting. What is the advantage to this stroke?*

A: Many people believe this type of stroke helps ensure that your wrists don't break down or collapse at impact. They also believe that putting cross-handed helps keep the putter moving along the target line for a longer period of time than traditional methods. While this is a very effective method on short and medium length putts, many people find it awkward on longer putts, causing some players to alternate between the two types of strokes.

Q: *What are the advantages and disadvantages of using a long putter?*

A: If you have the "Yips," this can help you make more consistent contact, since a long putter uses the large muscles rather than the small muscles in your hands, which can become twitchy under pressure. Because the putterhead travels along the target line for a longer period of time than it often does with a normal putter, it is very effective on putts of 10 feet or less. The downside is that many people find that it is not an effective method for long or approach putts.

Q: *Is there any way of judging where I'm hitting my putts on the putterface?*

A: One very good way is to invest in some putterface tape. You simply apply it to the face of your putter, and when you strike a ball, it leaves an impression, telling you exactly where you struck the ball.

Q: *My home course has very fast greens, but I often play with friends on courses with slower greens. Should I switch to a heavier putter on slower greens?*

A: There are two schools of thought on this matter. One argues that by switching to a heavier putter you don't have to adjust your stroke. The other insists that by switching putters, you create an element of doubt, which can lead to a small lack of confidence and, therefore, inconsistent putting. The best advice is to work with your PGA Professional and decide which approach works best for you.

Q: *I'm a beginning golfer, and I've noticed that some players leave their golf glove on when putting while others remove it. Is there an advantage either way?*

A: People who take their glove off believe it gives them a better sense of feel. Those who leave it on—Jack Nicklaus and Lee Trevino, just to name two—believe that since they play all their other shots with a glove on, it provides a consistent feel. There's no one right answer, except for the one that works best for you.

Q: *If my putter breaks during a round, can I replace it?*

A: It depends. According to Rule 4-3 of the Rules of Golf, if a club is damaged in the normal course of play in a *stipulated round*, you may: continue to use the damaged club; repair or have it repaired if this does not unduly delay play; or replace the club with another club if it does not unduly delay play. That club, however, cannot be one in use by any other player on the course. If, however, a club is damaged other than in the normal course of play (e.g., in a fit of temper) and rendered nonconforming, it cannot be used or replaced. Most players, when they find themselves in this situation, try one of three alternatives. First, they putt with the longest iron in their bag, usually a 1- or 2-iron, striking the ball as low on the clubface as possible to reduce the loft. Second, they putt with a fairway wood, making sure to grip down on the shaft as far as is comfortable. The third alternative is to putt with your sand wedge, aligning the leading edge of the wedge with the equator or center of the ball. Of the three, this is the preferred approach, since the added weight of the wedge provides the truest roll, while the length of the club is closest to that of a putter. This alternative is also a good shot to have in your bag when your ball comes to rest on the apron of the green, up against the first cut of rough.

Q: *The greens on my home course were recently rebuilt and they are still on the bumpy side after a rough winter. I've always been a pretty good putter, but now I'm really struggling. Do you have any advice?*

A: First, keep reminding yourself that your fellow players are all in the same boat and are equally frustrated. Anything you can do to remain patient will give you a small edge. The other suggestion is to experiment with a putter that has a little more loft, since this may help you roll the ball slightly more smoothly. Another approach is to play the ball slightly forward in your stance, since this will also help you hit putts that hold their line a bit better.

Q: *What does "de-lofting" a putter mean?*

A: It has nothing to do with the design of a putter or anything you do to alter it. It has everything to do with what you do to the club during your stroke. Make a slight forward press (moving your hands slightly toward the target) as a way of beginning your putting stroke. This helps relieve tension and is a way of ensuring a smoother stroke. What happens, however, is that some people strike the ball with their hands leading the head of the putter. This results in the effective loft of the putter being reduced slightly. This de-lofting can be a problem since most putters have so little loft to begin with, and if you reduce it even further, the ball tends to skid along the ground for a longer-than-normal amount of time.

8

Improving Your Chipping and Pitching

In a perfect world, there would be no need to know how to chip and pitch the ball. After all, in a perfect world, you'd never miss a green.

Now ask yourself this question: How close to perfect is my game?

There are two key statistics you should keep track of when you try to assess the importance of improving your chipping and pitching.

The first is how many greens you miss in regulation. Two or three? That's very good. Five or six? Welcome to the PGA Tour, because that's about average for the best players in the world. So now we're getting closer to the real number, say seven, eight, nine or maybe more per round.

Now, how many times do you get up and down in one chip and one putt from off the green? Even if you reached the point where you got up and down just half the time, think of how many strokes you'd save per round. And this doesn't begin to factor in how many times a poor chip or pitch has left you taking three shots or more to finish a hole from just off the green.

Unless you're already a very good player—or at least a very good chipper and pitcher of the ball—it should be obvious why this is such an important chapter.

First, let's define our terms. Broadly speaking, a chip is a shot that spends more time running along the ground than it does in the air. A pitch is just the opposite.

Before getting into the fundamentals of hitting these shots, let's begin with a simple observation: The first rule of thumb is that safer is better. The idea is to play the shot that involves the smallest amount of risk while offering the largest possible margin for error.

To do this, you need to look at the variables affecting the shot. The first is the speed and slope of the green. The next is the height and firmness with which you play the shot. The third is the amount of spin you put on the ball, which is a function of the club's loft and the way you elect to play the particular shot.

Of the three, the first is a given. It's up to the individual golfer to accurately judge these conditions but he or she has no control over them. The second factor is also relatively straightforward, assuming you have the necessary fundamentals and execute the shot properly. It's the final factor—spin—that is difficult to control, since it is the final result of the first two factors, coupled with the ball and club being used.

With that in mind, the first rule should be that, except for specific shots, which we'll discuss later, your best choice should be the safest shot—and the safest shot is the shot with the least amount of air time.

This point is so crucial that it's worth highlighting:

Your best shot is the safest shot—and the safest shot is the one with the least amount of air time.

Having made the point about air time, we should take it even one step further and say that another good rule of thumb is for you to hit the shot that keeps the ball as close to the ground for as long as possible, because the higher you hit the ball, the more it will bounce when it lands on the green, and every time the ball bounces, the margin for error increases.

With that in mind, unless you are a skilled chipper and pitcher, whenever possible, putt the ball from off the green. There's an old saying, "A poor putt will usually get closer than a good chip," and like most old sayings, it contains an element of truth. Your next option would be to chip the ball with the least-lofted club possible. Your final option, then, would be to pitch the ball into the air with a lofted club.

First, Some History

Before getting into the basics of how to play these shots, it might be helpful to understand how they fit into the evolution of the game. In golf's early days, the ability to chip and pitch the ball was even more important than it is today. There were a variety of reasons for this.

First, until the development of the gutta-percha ball, golf balls flew relatively low and had trajectories that were wildly inconsistent, so playing the ball low and letting it run along the ground—the bump-and-run shot—was a safer play.

Next, greens were generally open in front, unguarded by bunkers, which made it easier to run the ball into the greens. And until the advent of widespread watering, greens were extremely firm and shots lofted into the greens would frequently take a bounce and run into the rough behind the putting surface.

Finally, strong winds were generally a factor on the courses in Scotland and throughout the British Isles and the East Coast, where the game first took root in the United States.

As the game has evolved over the years, it has become far more of a target game, since changes in equipment, course design and maintenance have led to a style of play that is more "through the air" than "along the ground." That said, however, when you watch players who learned the game by playing in Europe, you generally see very skilled chippers and pitchers of the ball, since the conditions on the Continent today place an even greater emphasis on those skills. That's certainly one reason European players did so well in the 2000 U.S. Open at Pebble Beach. Because the greens were so small, the Open placed an emphasis on chipping and pitching. And, of course, it's no coincidence that Tiger Woods won by such a huge margin. In 2000, he had as fine a short game as anyone in the world.

The Basics of Good Chipping
An Overview

In the pages that follow, we will go into greater detail concerning the skills needed for proper pitching and chipping, but in this section we will give you an overview of the necessary fundamentals.

Pre-swing Fundamentals

As we have said in the "Overview" section of other chapters, to grip the club properly stand with your ankle joints under your shoulders and, gripping the club's shaft with your trail hand (right hand for right-handed golfers), shake hands with the grip with your target (left) hand, placing the grip diagonally across the base of your fingers. Next, simply slide your trail hand down the shaft until the target thumb fits into the lifeline of the trail hand and the thumb pad of the trail hand covers the thumb of the target hand. Finally, if you favor an overlapping or Vardon grip, place the pinky finger of your right hand on top of the first two fingers of the target hand.

The stance and posture for a chip is somewhat different from those for a full swing. Begin by standing with your ankle joints under your shoulders, then push your hips back and up and let your arms hang down from your shoulders. Next, whatever club you've selected for this chip, set the angle of the shaft so it is more vertical than the lie of the club dictates. In other words, the shaft angle should closely resemble the more upright angle of your putter. This means that when you address the ball, the club will rest more on the toe of the club than it would for a full shot. The grip end of the club should be pointing toward the middle of your body, and your weight should be evenly distributed between the balls of your feet and the heels.

Chipping, from address through finish

Chipping with an alignment aid

To ensure proper alignment, stand behind the ball and visualize a line running from the target to the ball. This is your target line. Next, pick a spot on that line about six to 12 inches in front of the ball. This is your intermediate target. Once you've established your intermediate target, keep your eye on it as you walk up to your set-up position and place the clubhead behind the ball so it is aimed down your target line. Keep your eye on the target as you assume your address position.

The pre-swing fundamentals for a pitch shot are identical to those of a chip. The difference is that since you want the shot to have more air time than time running along the green, you play a pitch shot with a higher-lofted club.

The key to a pitch shot is making sure the golf club moves the same distance backward and forward and at the same pace. It is important to keep the upper trail arm (right arm for right-handed players) moving throughout the swing. If it stops on the forward swing, it will cause the wrist or elbow to bend and the club will strike the ball with an ascending blow. Ideally, the clubhead will be traveling on a level path at impact.

The most important consideration in good chipping is distance control. As in approach putting, most poor chips result from either leaving the ball well short of the hole or too far past it. With that in mind, you should develop a technique that will

Chipping with a fairway wood

allow you to make consistent, solid contact with each shot. These fundamentals will allow you to do just that.

GRIP—Very good chippers of the ball, such as Paul Runyan, employ their putting grip following the logic that a chip is more like a putt than a full swing. Since the fundamentals we suggest call for the club's shaft to be set in a very upright position at address, your putting grip might work well for you. Like so much in golf, it's a good idea to consult with your PGA Professional and find what works best for you.

Whichever grip you choose, bear in mind that a chip is very much a "one-lever" stroke, which means there is very little, if any, cocking of the wrists. In fact, 1964 U.S. Open Champion Ken Venturi, who had one of the best short games in history, likes to tell people to imagine their hands are molded together in a cast when chipping. It's a great image to keep in mind.

Certainly, there have been some players who were very wristy chippers (and usually wristy putters as well) and had phenomenal touch. The 1959 PGA Champion, Bob Rosburg, was one. But this type of stroke takes considerable talent and practice to perfect, so we'd like to suggest staying with a safer, more consistent method.

Chipping to a target

Another consideration is where you should place your hands on the club. Some people like to grip down toward the end of the grip, because they feel this gives them more control. Others prefer to grip the club with just an inch or so of the grip above their top hand. In truth, it's a matter of feel and preference. Again, you should experiment and find what works best for you.

Here are two final thoughts that may help you improve your chipping: Almost everyone agrees that you want to grip the club lightly, since this helps promote better feel. When chipping, always try to keep the back of your left or top hand moving on a line parallel to the target line. This will help keep the clubface square to the target.

One Club or Several?

One of the many reasons golf is so challenging and often confusing is that very often there is no one right method of playing any given shot, and that's certainly the case when it comes to deciding whether you should hit the majority of your chips with one club—your favorite, if you will—or use a variety of clubs.

Most PGA Professionals strongly recommend using a variety of clubs, because by doing so you don't have to alter your chipping stroke. For example, if you have a long chip you might use a 6-iron or even a 5-iron, but as the distance becomes shorter, go to a more lofted 8- or 9-iron. The stroke remains the same, but you vary your distance control by selecting the club with the appropriate loft. A word of caution here, however: Keep in mind that since you are striking the ball with your hands ahead of the club, you are decreasing the effective loft of the club. In other words, you are taking a 6-iron and giving it the loft of a 5-iron, and you want to guard against trying to play these shots with insufficient effective loft.

All that said, however, there have been some marvelous chippers who hit the majority of chips with one club, usually an 8-iron. Raymond Floyd, a two-time PGA Champion, is probably the best example. He is able to move the shaft forward and backward to change the loft of his club.

To be an effective chipper using just one club takes tremendous talent and touch to be consistent, but those who favor this method argue that using a favorite club provides an important element of confidence.

Whether you chip with one club or several, one thing that all good chippers and pitchers of the ball share in common is a pre-shot routine that is very similar to their putting routine. They study the shot they're facing, and determine the speed and contours of the green in order to judge the proper line.

Once they've done this, they pick not only an intermediate target to aim at, but also a circle about a foot or so in diameter into which they want to land the ball. Naturally, this spot will vary in distance according to the loft of the club they select, but bear in mind that you want to play the shot that provides maximum ground time and minimum air time.

The Basics of Good Pitching

Pitching is somewhat more complicated than chipping because you're adding height and, in some respects, spin to the equation, and you are making a swing that is longer and generally involves the hinging and unhinging of the wrists. Still, with practice and good fundamentals, you can become proficient in a relatively short period of time.

Pitch shot, from address through finish

FUNDAMENTALS—Many of the basics of good pitching mirror those of consistent chipping. Employ your full-swing grip with a light grip pressure. This is even more important when pitching the ball than when chipping, since a grip pressure that is too tight will hinder the proper hinging and unhinging of the wrists. You want to play from a slightly open stance, since this will allow you to see the proper line more easily than you could from a closed stance. And a slightly open stance pre-clears your hips and helps you deliver the club directly along the target line.

What varies when hitting a pitch shot is the ball position, both in your stance and relative to the position of your hands at address and impact. To a large degree, these are determined by the lie and the shot you want to play.

As a general rule, if you have a tight lie (playing off very close-cropped grass) or a poor lie in the rough, you need to play the shot with your hands slightly ahead of the ball, with the ball positioned back slightly in your stance, just as you would when hitting lower, running chip shots. This will cause the ball to fly on a lower trajectory and run farther, but it will allow you to make cleaner, more consistent contact.

As the lie improves, however, you can position the ball more toward

Pitching over a hazard

Pitch shot, half-swing

Pitch shot, downswing through finish

Add loft to your pitch shot at setup by moving the shaft back and the ball forward.

the middle of your stance, with your hands either even with the ball or fractionally behind. This will allow you to employ the full loft of the club, whether it is a pitching wedge or sand wedge. Bear in mind, that given a consistent ball position, the more you position your hands behind the ball, the more effective loft you add to the club, the higher the ball will fly and the softer it will land.

Some Special Shots

Once you've mastered the basics of chipping and pitching the ball, the fun can really begin. By working with your PGA Professional, experimenting, and practicing, you can learn all sorts of imaginative shots that can save you strokes around the greens. Here are a few shots worth trying to add to your arsenal.

THE 3-WOOD CHIP—This is a shot popularized by Tiger Woods. When your ball comes to rest in the rough just off the green, forget using a wedge and try a 3-wood, choking down on the grip, but playing it just as you would a chip with an iron. The club has just enough loft to get the ball up and running smoothly, but the rounded sole and leading edge will help prevent the club from getting caught up in the grass.

THE CUT SHOT—If you watch tournament golf on television, you'll notice that the players are able to hit high, soft shots with seemingly little effort. Here's one way they do it—they play this shot like a shot from the sand bunkers. The key is leaning the shaft back *before* they actually grip the club. This adds a tremendous amount of effective loft to the club. Then they place their hands on the club, with the ball played slightly forward of center in their stance. The next step is crucial: They address the ball by aiming the *clubface* at the target, and then assume a fairly open stance. The key is that you aim the clubface, and not your body, at the target. Then you swing the club back along a line that parallels a line drawn along your toes, knees and hips. This line will be outside the target line, and will allow you to cut across the target line on your downswing. The combination of this swing path and the open clubface will add tremendous effective loft to the club, and allow you to hit high, soft shots without any flicking of the wrists in the hitting area.

One word of warning: Although this shot can generally be played from most lies, if you choose to play it with the ball sitting up in the rough, make sure you align the leading edge of the club with the bottom of the ball. The mistake golfers often make is setting the club well below the ball at address, which causes them to cut under the ball and usually leave it in the rough.

THE BUMP-AND-RUN—This is a valuable shot to learn if you play a course with greens that are either elevated or guarded by mounds. Very often you won't have enough room between the mounds or banks and the hole to safely loft a shot that ends close to the hole. If that's the case, a different but far riskier shot is to pitch the ball into the bank and let it bounce toward the hole. The key is to pick a spot where you want the ball to land, then pitch the ball into the spot, figuring that it will hit the slope, bounce into the air, and roll slowly toward the hole. The variables to consider are many: the height and thickness of the grass on the slope; how hard you hit the ball; which club you should use; and how far the ball has to carry once it hits the slope. Again, this is a very risky shot and one that, in truth, often costs more strokes than it saves. But in the closing holes of a match, it's one worth trying if you're willing to invest the time to practice it properly.

THE "TEXAS WEDGE"—If the bump-and-run shot is one of the riskier shots in the short game, the Texas Wedge is one of the safest. Simply put, when you find yourself off the green—even by several yards—and in a situation where the pressure is high, the lie is marginal, and your nerves are more than a little shaky, this is a shot you should consider. What you are doing is basically putting the ball from off the green. Spin isn't a factor. Neither is trajectory. You've reduced the shot to two considerations: the line and how firmly you have to hit the ball to get it to—not into—the hole. If it happens to go in, so much the better, but golf has a way of punishing the greedy. The only suggestion is that, depending on the length of the shot, you might consider widening your stance for stability and moving the ball slightly forward in your stance, so that you strike the ball with the clubhead moving along the flattest part of the stroke. Again, bear in mind that you are trying to get the ball near the hole, so focus your attention on the line and the speed of the putt.

Questions and Answers

Q: *Recently I've seen a lot of advertising for chipping clubs. Are these worthwhile?*

A: If you have trouble chipping the ball, they are certainly something you might consider. The rounded soles and low center of gravity make them more forgiving than traditional irons. Why not talk it over with your PGA Professional and see if there are demo clubs available in the golf shop that you could try?

Q: *I practice a lot, but I never get the same results on the course as on the practice area. I think I'm making the same shots, but I'm not getting the same results. Any ideas why?*

A: Here are two thoughts: First, you're probably using practice—or range—balls to practice. These are designed to stand up to constant pounding, and are much harder than the balls you probably use in competition. As a result, they perform differently and probably pitch lower and run farther. Next, practice greens are rarely cut as short as the greens on the course, which is something you should keep in mind for your putting as well.

Q: *Should I take the pin out or leave it in when chipping or pitching?*

A: It's largely a matter of personal preference, although if you're facing a fast, downhill shot, the pin could act as a backstop.

9

Taking the Fear Out of Bunker Play

One of the biggest differences between good players and higher-handicappers is their attitude toward bunker play. For the good player, facing a shot from the sand is an opportunity. For weekend golfers, it's often their worst nightmare come true.

Here is a classic case in point:

Playing the 72nd hole of the 1988 U.S. Open at The Country Club in Brookline, Mass., Curtis Strange hit his approach to the small green into one of the front bunkers. The huge gallery reacted with horror. But in truth Strange, one of the best course managers of his generation, knew exactly what he was doing.

"When I looked at the shot, I knew that the front bunker was the only place I could miss the green and still have a really good chance of making a par," said the captain of the 2001 United States Ryder Cup team. "The rough was brutal around the green, so I couldn't miss it either long or wide. The sand was perfect at Brookline, so I knew the odds were pretty good that the ball wouldn't plug."

The ball came to rest on an upslope, Strange played it to within a couple feet of the hole, made par to tie England's Nick Faldo, and then won the 18-hole playoff the following day.

When the legendary Bobby Jones was collaborating with golf course architect Robert Trent Jones on the design of the Peachtree Golf Club in Atlanta, he neatly summed up a good player's thinking about bunkers as compared to other hazards.

"Trent," he said. "The difference between a sand bunker and water is the difference between a car accident and a plane crash because you can usually walk away from a car crash and you can often save par from a bunker. Plane wrecks and water are a totally different story."

In truth, if you have a proper sand wedge and a sound understanding of the mechanics of playing a bunker shot, playing from sand is one of the easiest shots in the game. Why? Because you never have to strike the ball, which means that you have a relatively large margin for error. You can actually misplay the shot and still get your ball onto the green.

How Bunkers Evolved

It's entirely possible that, if golf hadn't had its roots in Scotland, sand bunkers as we know them might not play such a prominent part of the game.

Many of the earliest courses—The Old Course at St. Andrews being the most obvious example—evolved from linksland. This was sandy soil exposed when the sea receded centuries ago and shaped, in no small part, by the strong winds of the ocean that swept across it, creating all sorts of swales and mounds and baffling contours.

Linksland, by its sandy nature, was particularly susceptible to the winds at St. Andrews, where The Old Course lies was "Common Ground," set aside for the community's use. Golf was only one of the uses. It was also used for grazing sheep, and the animals would often burrow into the turf seeking shelter from the cold, harsh winds. The winds would eat away at the exposed soil, creating natural bunkers, some of which were quite large, deep and fearsome.

Prestwick, the site of the first 12 British Opens, has several such bunkers, and other famous—or infamous, depending on your point of view—bunkers include the Hell Bunker at St. Andrews, The Graves at Musselburgh and The Crater at Portrush in Northern Ireland.

Bunkering on modern courses is a far more benign matter, but the real reason bunkers are no longer the menace they once were can be credited to Gene Sarazen's invention of the sand wedge in 1931.

Sarazen, who won all four professional major championships and seven majors in all, was tormented by his sand play. In that respect, he was like every other player of his generation. Bunkers were generally unkempt—today, for example, there are no rakes at No. 1 rated Pine Valley in New Jersey—and players had to use niblicks, which had 9-iron loft and were unsuited for the job. The club would dig into the sand on impact, forcing players to try and pick the ball cleanly, which was a risky play at best.

In 1931, Sarazen was taking flying lessons from Howard Hughes and he noticed that when the plane's rudder was turned down, the plane went up and vice versa. Sarazen wondered if the same theory might apply to a golf club that would help players control shots from the sand.

"The more I thought about it the more it seemed to make sense," Sarazen recalled years later. "I called Wilson [Sporting Goods] and had them send me a box of niblicks. Then I went and bought all the solder I could find and began experimenting with it, putting it on the soles of the irons. I'd add some here and file some there, and then I'd go over to the beach and hit shots out of that real powdery sand. Finally, I got it just right and I couldn't wait until I got over to the British Open at Prince's in England.

"On the trip over, I started worrying that the R&A might ban the club, so during practice rounds I'd keep it head-down in my bag and then bring it back to my hotel at night," Sarazen continued. "Once I brought it out for the first round, it was too late for them to do anything about it. The club worked like a charm and I won by five strokes over MacDonald Smith, and I won our Open that year, too. Oh, all the fellows couldn't wait to get their hands on one of their own."

Once they did, the game of golf was changed forever. Sand bunkers were now hazards in name only, at least for skilled players. It's safe to say that in the modern era, the huge majority of professionals and low-handicap amateurs are at least competent bunker players and some, like Sam Snead, Gary Player, Seve Ballesteros, Amy Alcott and Tiger Woods, are geniuses with sand wedges in their hands.

The concept behind a sand wedge is simple. Unlike other irons that have a leading edge that is lower than the trailing edge, on a sand wedge the angle is reversed. In addition, the sole or flange is cambered, or rounded slightly, and is wider than on a pitching wedge. The combination of these three factors produced a design that allows the clubhead to glide through the sand rather than digging into it.

Because of the sand wedge's design, players could now hit a shot that allowed the clubhead to slide under the ball, causing the sand it displaced to throw the ball into the air. That's a crucial point to remember: **In a basic sand shot, the sand forces the ball into the air. The clubhead should never contact the ball.**

Sand wedges come in a wide variety of designs and you should decide which is right for you based on personal preference, your skill level, the playing conditions and how you intend to use the club. This is another case when working with your PGA Professional can pay huge dividends.

For example, if you play most of your golf on courses that have fine, powdery sand in the bunkers, you need a club with more bounce (the combination of the width of the flange and the angle between the leading and trailing edges of the sole), since this will allow the club to glide through the sand more easily. It might also be helpful to experiment with a wedge that is slightly heavier than normal. If, on the other hand, you play courses where the sand is firmer and more densely packed (as is the case in most courses in the northern United States and Canada), you'll benefit from a wedge with less bounce.

A second important consideration is whether or not you intend to use this wedge as a pitching club from the fairway as well. If you do, you need to find a club designed in such a way to slightly reduce the bounce. Otherwise, the clubhead will skid and bounce when it hits the turf, resulting in thin shots.

Spine tilt to match slope of the bunker

Playing from Bunkers
Overview

In the pages that follow, we will cover the specifics of bunker play in detail, but in this section we want to provide you with an overview of the pre-swing and in-swing fundamentals.

Many golfers consider the greenside bunker shot one of the easiest in the game because you never actually contact the ball. They understand that when played properly, all they have to do is remove the sand from under the ball and the sand will move the ball out of the bunker. The same fundamentals that we discussed in the full-swing chapter apply to playing a bunker shot.

Pre-swing Fundamentals

When gripping the club, stand with your ankle joints under your shoulders and hold the club in front of you at a 45-degree angle, with your trail (right hand for right-handed players) holding the shaft. With your target (left hand for right-handed players), shake hands with the grip by simply placing the club's grip diagonally across the base of the fingers. Next, slide your trail hand down the shaft until the thumb of the target hand fits into the lifeline of the trail hand. At this stage, the target-hand thumb is covered by the thumb pad of the trail hand. If you choose a Vardon or overlapping grip, slide your right pinky finger so it rests on top of the pointer and index fingers of the left or target hand.

To assume a proper stance, stand with your ankle joints under your shoulders. Push your hips back and up and let your arms hang naturally from your shoulders. Your weight should be evenly distributed between the heels and balls of your feet and your sternum should be aligned with the ball. Finally, simply tilt your shoulders so your trail shoulder (right for right-handed players) is lower than your target shoulder.

To align yourself properly, stand behind the ball and draw an imaginary line from the target to the ball. This is your target line. Next, pick a spot on the target line about six to 12 inches in front of the ball. This is your intermediate target. Keeping your focus on the intermediate target, walk into your set-up position and place the clubface behind the ball (taking care not to let the club touch the sand) so it is looking down the target line. Continue looking down the target line as you set your ankles under your shoulders, and then assume your proper address position, and address a spot that is the desired distance behind the ball.

In-swing Fundamentals

To better understand the fundamentals of a bunker shot, draw a six-inch circle around the ball, and then pick the ball out of the sand and set it aside. Next, assume your address position and practice swinging your sand wedge and removing sand from the circle. Once you are successful, place a tee in the circle and hit the tee out of the circle and onto the nearby green. When you are able to remove the tee consistently, replace the ball and repeat the swing that was successful in removing the tee.

Bunker shot with an uphill lie

Downswing through finish from a greenside bunker

Just as in putting, individual styles of bunker play vary from one player to the next, but there are certain fundamentals that remain fairly constant for all good bunker players. In this section, we'd like to give you a basic framework to build your bunker game around. We believe this method is the safest and most consistent method for playing from the sand. If you watch good players, you'll notice that almost all of them will have a set routine.

STUDY THE SHOT—Just as you would for any shot, from a drive to a short putt, take the time to carefully examine the shot you face. Your first consideration must be your lie, since this will determine what type of shot you are able to play. For example, if the ball is buried (sitting down in the sand) but you are very close to the pin, the chances are you will have to hit a very risky shot that will keep the ball near the hole. Once you've examined your lie, figure out where you need to land the ball to get it close to the hole. Finally, visualize the type of shot you need to play. Is it a high, soft shot? If the lie allows you to spin the ball, is it worth the risk? Or do you need to play a shot that will allow the ball to release on landing and run to the hole?

ADDRESSING THE BALL—Once you've decided on the shot you want to play, pick an intermediate target a foot or so from the ball and aim the clubface toward that target. Now for a crucial point to keep in mind: The higher and softer you want to hit the ball, the more you need to tilt the shaft backward at address to add loft. Only after you've aimed and set the clubface should

Using a putter from a greenside bunker

you place your hands on the grip. One of the most common mistakes poor bunker players make is gripping the club and *then* rotating the shaft to open the clubface. Once you've aimed the clubface and gripped the club, assume your stance. Almost to a person, all good bunker players employ an open stance, since this preclears their hips and makes it easier to slide the club under the ball. It also restricts the length of your backswing while making it easier to make an upright swing. If you have a good lie, the ball should be

Downswing through impact and finish from a fairway bunker

Clubface position for a slightly buried lie

Clubface position for an extremely buried lie

positioned forward of center in your stance, with your hands even with the ball or fractionally behind. Here's a good thought to keep in mind: If your hands are ahead of the ball at address and impact, the effective loft of the club will decrease and the ball will fly on a lower trajectory. If the hands are behind the ball, you will be adding loft. This is good to remember when learning to hit specialty shots.

Next, carefully work your feet a couple of inches into the sand. This does two important things: First, the Rules of Golf prohibit players from "testing" the sand to gauge its firmness. The Rules do, however, allow you to set your feet in the sand, which will give you some idea of its consistency. Coarse, wet or densely packed sand will accentuate the "bounce" of the club, increasing its effective loft. Dry, sugary-type sand will allow the club to slice through the sand more easily, and so it requires more effective bounce. Next, by working your feet into the sand, you automatically lower your swing center, which will help you slide the club under the ball without making a conscious effort.

Finally, keep in mind that you cannot sole your club in a hazard. This means that if your club touches the sand or any other part of a hazard prior to your downswing, you incur a one-stroke penalty.

Full swing bunker shot from an extremely buried lie

PLAYING THE SHOT—Over the years, people have advised golfers to "hit a couple of inches" behind the ball, which is fine advice but it doesn't take into account variations in the type of density of the sand. The image of taking a slice of sand the size of a dollar bill seems to work better for the vast majority of golfers.

Next, try and match your backswing to your follow-through. In other words, if you have a long shot, make a long swing.

Another useful swing thought is not to allow the toe of the club to pass the heel. This will help ensure the clubface stays open throughout the shot.

CONTROLLING THE DISTANCE OF YOUR SHOTS—There are four basic factors that can be used to control the height and distance of your shots.

Full swing at the top and finish from a greenside bunker

CLUBFACE POSITION—The more loft you add to the clubface by moving the shaft back at address, the higher and shorter the ball will carry and run. Two considerations that factor into this are ball position (forward for higher, softer shots and back for lower shots) and hand position (even with or behind the ball for higher short shots and ahead of the ball for lower shots).

SWING SHAPE—The steeper the angle of approach into the ball, the higher and shorter the shot will fly. A good way to visualize this is to imagine the ball will come out of the sand on the same trajectory that the club enters it. This isn't strictly true, but it is an effective image.

LENGTH AND PACE OF SWING—All things being equal, the more clubhead speed a swing generates, the farther the ball will carry and run. Most players find it easier to vary the length of their swing to control distance. Since the follow-through usually mirrors the backswing, many players control the length of their shots by varying the length of their follow-through.

THE AMOUNT OF SAND DISPLACED—Again, this will vary given the texture and density of the sand, but as a rule, the more sand you cut out from under the ball, the shorter the shot. However—and this is important to note, particularly in firm sand—the closer you come to the ball, the more spin you'll impart on your shot and the quicker it will check up on the green.

111

Top of the swing through impact and finish

Learning Some Specialty Shots

As you become more proficient from the sand, there are a variety of shots you can develop that can help you save strokes from difficult situations. Here are a few.

Setup in a waste bunker

BURIED LIES—Even the best players in the world get a sinking feeling when they approach a greenside bunker and see their ball sitting down in its own pitch mark. If they've short-sided the hole and the hole is cut nearby, they feel even worse, knowing that they have probably made a two-shot mistake. When this happens, you have to take your medicine and do your best. The shot can be played, but it's very difficult to get it to stop very quickly.

The first rule is to address the ball with a square or even slightly closed clubface, since this will help the club dig into the sand behind the ball. Position the ball back in your stance, at least in the middle, and it often helps to play from a square or just slightly open stance, with your weight on your target side. You want to hit this shot with a sharply descending blow.

Entry and setup in a greenside bunker

Greenside bunker shot showing top of backswing through impact and finish

Drive the club into the sand behind the ball and don't worry about making a follow-through, because there won't be much of one, if any. You may want to experiment and try this shot with a pitching wedge or even a 9-iron, since these clubs will dig into the sand more easily than a sand wedge. Finally, accept that the ball will come out without much spin and will run once it hits the green. Allow for it—and vow never to leave yourself on the short side of another green.

UPHILL LIE—When the ball comes to rest on an upslope, it leaves you with a relatively easy shot, especially if the hole is cut close to the bunker. First, remember that the slope adds effective loft to the club, so it will help the ball come up on a high trajectory. When you address the ball, really dig your back foot into the sand for stability and then align your shoulders so they parallel the slope of the bunker. For most shots from this lie, you want to have a square clubface. You don't need a long swing for this shot, since it could cause you to lose your balance. Just swing along the slope and accelerate the clubface into the sand close to the ball—and don't even think about a follow-through. The ball should pop out nicely, even if it is slightly plugged. It won't have much spin, but the high trajectory will help it stop fairly quickly.

DOWNHILL LIE—Now this can be a tough shot. First, make sure to dig in your front foot for stability. Play the ball back in your stance slightly, and tilt the shaft to compensate for the loss of effective loft caused by the lie. Align your shoulders to the slope and concentrate on sliding the clubhead under the ball with a lot of acceleration. Finally, this is a shot where you want to concentrate on maintaining your knee flex throughout the shot, because there is a tendency to rise up out of the shot, resulting in a skulled shot that either flies over the green or, worse, plugs in the face of the bunker.

HITTING A "SPINNER"—If you face a shot that you need to stop quickly and have become fairly confident in your bunker play, here's a shot that can help you put plenty of spin on the ball. First, you must have a very good lie. If the ball is sitting down, this shot is too risky. Address the ball with an open stance and an open clubface, with the shaft tilted back at address, and have your weight balanced equally on both feet or even favoring the right side marginally. Position the ball well forward in your stance and set your hands and eyes behind the ball. This combination sets you up to apply tremendous amounts of spin to the ball, as well as lots of height. The difference—and what makes this so risky—is that you swing with great speed and loft, clipping the sand just under the ball, and then finishing with a high follow-through. This is a dangerous shot, but it can be a very dramatic and effective one to have in your arsenal.

PUTTING FROM THE BUNKER—If, after all this, you're still uncomfortable playing from the sand, here's a shot that can be a lifesaver. The problem is you need to have the right conditions. You can putt from the bunker if you have a very good lie; if the bunker doesn't have a lip or a long, steep face; and you aren't trying to get close to a hole cut near the bunker. If all these conditions are met, here's how you play the shot:

Play the ball forward in your stance. You can use your regular putting stance, but a square stance is ideal. You want the ball forward in your stance—say off the target foot—because you want to sweep the ball off the sand. Don't try to tap down or trap the ball. You'll just drive it into the sand. You might be better off using your full-swing grip, since you'll probably need to hinge and unhinge your wrists to generate enough speed to get the ball out of the bunker. Your main consideration is to sweep the ball first, before hitting the sand.

This is a very safe shot if the conditions are right. Learn it—but also invest in some bunker-play lessons from your PGA Professional, because these perfect conditions only come along every so often.

PLAYING FROM FAIRWAY BUNKERS—There are two important considerations before you even think about the distance you need to hit this shot. The first is your lie, because the lie dictates what kind of shot you'll be able to play. But the next is equally important, and that's the height of the bunker's face. **Your first job is to get the ball out of the bunker. Don't get greedy and don't try to be a hero. Take a club with enough loft to get out of the bunker.**

With this shot, it's vitally important that you strike the ball before you hit the sand. This is a shot you want to pick off the sand with a sweeping type of swing. To help you do that, work the inside of your feet into the sand so you have a solid base to swing from. This is especially important with the trail foot. You do not want to sway off the ball with this shot. **Remember, if you dig your feet an inch into the sand, choke down an inch on your grip.** This will help you guard against hitting the sand first. Play the ball toward the middle of your stance, since this will help you hit the ball first. If the bunker has a very low face, it's worth taking one more club than you need for the distance, since this will allow you to make a more controlled swing and will help guard against swaying or excessive motion. Play for either the front or fattest part of the green, since it's often hard to judge how the ball will react when it lands, so you need to give yourself the largest possible margin for error.

One final thought: Depending on the distance you need to reach the green, it's a good idea to choose a fairway wood over a long iron. The increased weight of the wood's sole will help get the ball into the air more easily, and the design of the club will help it glide through the sand should you hit behind the ball.

THE LONG BUNKER SHOT—If you hit your approach into a bunker that is well short—50 or so yards—of the green, you're facing a very difficult shot, especially if you elect to try to play some sort of explosion shot with a sand wedge. Here's a safer approach: Pitch it with a short iron, with a 7-, 8- or 9-iron or a pitching wedge, just as you'd pitch the ball from off the green. The fundamentals are almost identical. First, judge how much loft you need to clear the face of the bunker. Select your club and address the ball with a slightly open stance. Your hands and eyes should be ahead of the ball and your weight should favor your left side. Take the club straight back from the ball, and strike down on it with a descending blow, making sure you strike the ball before you hit the sand. **Do not try to scoop or flick the ball out of the sand.** Strike down on the ball and trust the loft of the club to get the job done. This is a very safe and effective shot for players of every skill level.

PLAYING FROM GRASS BUNKERS—Many courses, especially those built in the last 25 years, have deep grass bunkers guarding the greens. These can leave players facing very challenging and even frightening shots, but in truth, playing from these bunkers is very much like playing from sand bunkers.

The first consideration is the lie. If the ball is sitting down in the deep grass, you're in the same position you'd be if the ball were buried in the sand. It will be impossible to spin the ball and it's anyone's guess how it will come out and what the ball will do once it hits the green.

If you face this shot, you need to get as much of the club on the ball as possible. To do this, position the ball back toward the middle of your stance and set your hands and eyes over the ball. Flex your knees and maintain that flex throughout the shot. Grip the club firmly, don't squeeze it to death, but you must have a strong grip on it—and take the club back with a sharp hinging of the wrists. On the downswing, you want to hit down smartly on the ball with a descending blow and accelerate the club through the grass. **Do not quit on this shot.**

If you get lucky and the ball is sitting up in the grass, you've got a much easier shot. The danger is addressing the ball with the leading edge of the club well under the ball. If you do this, you run a very good risk of sliding the club right under the ball at impact, leaving it in the bunker. The key is aligning the leading edge of the club with the bottom of the ball.

Questions and Answers

Q: *I bought an old sand wedge at a yard sale. I like the looks of the club but the face is pitted with rust. Can this be repaired?*

A: It can, but here's a tip. Don't bother. The pitting actually can help add spin to your shots because it increases the friction between the club and the ball. And yes, it's perfectly legal.

Q: *What's a Dual Wedge?*

A: Years ago, equipment manufacturers designed clubs that you could use from the sand and as a pitching club. The problem is they didn't perform either task very well. Our suggestion is to work with your PGA Professional to get fitted for the combination of wedges that is best suited to your game.

Q: *My regular playing partners suggested I buy a 60-degree wedge. But we're only allowed 14 clubs and I already have two wedges. Any suggestions?*

A: Look at your long irons. If you're like most players, they look like they just came out of the box because they're so difficult for most players to use successfully. Why not replace your 2-iron or 3-iron with a 60-degree wedge. After all, most players take more than half their strokes within 100 yards of the hole.

Q: *Can you suggest a foolproof drill that will help me become a better bunker player?*

A: Foolproof? No. Good? Yes. The next time you are practicing your bunker shots, place a tee in the sand so that the top of the tee is level with the top of the sand. Place a ball on the tee and then focus solely on making a swing that will sweep both the ball and the tee out of the sand. If you do this drill, you'll develop a swing that cuts through the sand at just the proper level and path. When you're playing and find yourself in the sand, make your last thought before you play your shot "Clip the tee out of the sand." You'll be surprised how well it works.

10
Shotmaking

Once you've developed an understanding of the pre-swing and full-swing fundamentals and have incorporated them into your game, it's time to move onto what many people feel is the essence of golf: shotmaking.

Being able to shape shots from side to side, control their trajectory and play from a wide variety of lies and in any conditions is one of the hallmarks of an accomplished golfer. Once you are able to "control your ball," you are ready to elevate your game to a new level of skill, subtlety, challenge and enjoyment.

Once you understand the fundamentals, the key to becoming a proficient shotmaker is practicing these shots so that you can hit them under the pressure of competition. Simply being able to hit a fade or draw on the practice range isn't enough. The key is being able to hit these shots when you need to get the ball into the fairway or near the pin at a tight spot in a match. With that understood, let's review the fundamentals that are the keys to successful shotmaking.

We believe the best way to develop a good grip is to stand erect with your ankle joints under the shoulders, holding the club at a 45-degree angle in front of you with your trail hand (right hand for right-handed golfers). Place the club diagonally across the base of the fingers of your target hand (left hand for right-handed golfers), then simply slide your trail hand down the shaft until the thumb of the target hand fits into the lifeline of the trail hand. The thumb of the target hand is covered by the thumb pad of the trail hand and the little finger of the trail hand rests on top of the first two fingers of the target hand.

To establish a stance that will help you create and maintain balance in your golf swing, stand with your ankle joints under your shoulders and your weight evenly distributed between the balls and heels of your feet and evenly balanced between your right and left foot. Once you have done this, push your hips back and tilt forward from the bottom of your hips until your sternum is pointed at the ball. Finally, tilt your shoulders until the trail (right) shoulder is lower than the target (left) shoulder.

To align yourself properly, stand behind the ball and visualize a line running from your target to the ball. This is your target line. Then pick a spot on that line some six to 12 inches from the ball. This is your intermediate target. Once you have established your intermediate target, walk into position and place the club-head behind the ball, aimed at your intermediate target. Make sure you keep your eyes on that intermediate target as you get into position and assume your stance.

Curving the Ball from Side to Side

If you go to a tournament and study good golfers, you'll find that they tend to prefer either a slight left-to-right (fade) or right-to-left (draw) ball flight. But when they need to, they have the ability to hit shots that either fade or draw or, if necessary, hook or slice dramatically. This is one part skill and one part understanding how to hit these shots.

In the earlier section on fundamentals, we urged playing from a square or neutral address position. One reason for this is that it gives the majority of players the best chance of delivering the club squarely to the ball at impact. Everything else being equal, this will help produce a straight ball flight.

To deliberately curve the ball, however, you need to make some adjustments, primarily in your address position.

HITTING A DRAW—To draw the ball from right to left, you want the clubhead entering the hitting area from inside the target line. To do this, the simplest approach is to close your address position—in other words, pull your trail side back from the target line. This sets your feet, knees, hips and shoulders in position to make an inside-to-down-the-line-to-inside swing, which will put a counterclockwise spin on the ball, causing it to curve to the left. You need to aim the clubface where you want the ball to start. This swing shape will allow your club to rotate faster than your body through the hitting area, while this swing thought will help ensure you swing along a proper path to produce a draw.

Three further thoughts: The best club to practice a draw or a fade with is a 5-iron, since it has enough loft to easily get the ball airborne while still putting enough sidespin on the ball. The more loft a club has, the more difficult it is to curve the ball. Also, bear in mind when playing this shot that the ball will tend to have lower flight and run farther than it would if played with a standard shot, because when hitting this shot you are actually taking "effective" loft off the club. In other words, a 5-iron will really have the loft of a 4-iron at impact. For that reason, make sure you take a club with enough loft to play this shot. It is very difficult to hit a hook with a long iron because the shape of your swing causes the clubface to close down, reducing the true loft of the club and causing most players to have too little effective loft if they try to play this with a long iron.

HITTING A FADE—When hitting a fade, you need to address the ball with a slightly open stance—that is with your target or forward foot pulled back away from the target line. This promotes taking the club away from the ball outside the target line, and also ensures returning to the ball from outside the target line as well. This swing path allows the clubface to cut across the ball at impact, producing a clockwise spin that curves the ball from left to right.

Because the swing you make with a fade has the body ahead of the club, a fade will fly higher than normal and will tend to stop the ball more quickly when it hits the ground. For this reason, many people believe it is a safer, more easily controlled shot than a draw. But keep in mind that because the shape of a fade swing actually increases the effective loft of a club, the ball will fly higher than a normal shot, but it won't carry as far. In effect, for example, when playing this shot with an 8-iron, you will actually produce a shot that has the trajectory and distance of an 8 1/2-iron.

Two Other Approaches

While we believe the method explained in the previous section is the preferable way to learn to curve the ball, there are two other schools of thought.

The first calls for altering your grip, making it stronger (turning your hands to the trail side) to hit a draw, or making it weaker (turning your hands to the target side) to hit a fade. We discourage this approach, since if you have a good, neutral grip you should be able to work the ball from side to side by following the fundamentals described earlier in this chapter. Changing your grip from shot to shot is a recipe for inconsistency.

The second approach calls for altering the clubface angle at address. To do this, you align your body to the spot you want the ball to start, but aim the clubface at the place you want the ball to finish.

The problem with this approach is that your body instinctively reacts to what your eyes see, which makes this approach inconsistent. In other words, if you shut a clubface at address, the tendency is not to fully release the club at impact. Another problem is that it's very difficult to use this approach with a wood or fairway metal club.

Hitting the Ball High or Low

Being able to control and alter the height or trajectory of your shots can be invaluable when playing in windy conditions or when attempting to fashion a shot that can help you get out of trouble. The good news is that learning to play these shots is relatively easy and requires only some simple adjustments in your address position and the shape of your swing.

HITTING THE BALL HIGH—To hit the ball higher than normal, you need to add effective loft to your club. Here's how you accomplish this. First, play the ball slightly forward in your stance, which should be slightly open. Next, make sure your hands are slightly behind the ball at address which sets the shaft tilted slightly back, and make your normal golf swing. Keep in mind that this shot will not fly as far as it would with your normal swing, and it should fade slightly and stop quickly when it lands. Take these factors into account when planning your shot.

HITTING THE BALL LOWER—This is an excellent shot to have when playing in strong winds or when trying to play out from under trees. Again, just as when you're trying to hit a higher-than-normal shot, the first step is a slight change in your address position. You want to play the ball marginally back of center in your stance, with your hands positioned ahead of the ball. Many players also find it helpful to close their stance slightly while gripping down somewhat on the club. The shaft is now tilted forward and you simply make your normal swing.

When hitting this type of knock-down shot, you are actually reducing the effective loft of the club, turning a 7-iron into a 6-iron or less, so plan accordingly. Also, this shot will tend to draw slightly and run when it hits the ground. Finally, you want to resist the temptation to hit the ball hard, since the harder you hit the ball, the more it tends to "balloon" into the air, which defeats the purpose of the shot. Your key thoughts are to keep your hands traveling ahead of the ball at impact and concentrate on making crisp, solid contact.

Playing from Uneven Lies

One of the elements that complicate (or make more intriguing and challenging, depending on your point of view) shotmaking is that the game is not played on a level surface. Just think back on your last few rounds and count up how many times you were required to play a shot from an uneven lie—either uphill, down-hill or sidehill. Each type of lie produces a different ball flight and, therefore, requires alterations to your address position and swing.

UPHILL LIES—Of all the uneven lies you might face, this is the easiest to deal with because it actually helps get the ball into the air. In fact, when faced with a player who has difficulty understanding the concept of hitting the ball with a properly descending blow, many PGA Professionals will have them hit shots from a slight uphill lie.

At address, your two main concerns are to build a stance that will prevent swaying and to determine the bottom of your swing. You want to stay centered over the ball as much as possible. At address, you want the angle of your shoulders to mirror the angle of the slope. You may also find it useful to grip down on the club.

When playing from an uphill lie, your key thought should be to swing along the angle of the slope. Bear in mind that the lie will add effective loft to the club, making the ball fly higher—but shorter—than it would from a level lie. You should allow for these considerations when making your club selection and addressing the ball.

DOWNHILL LIES—This is a far more difficult and complicated shot than playing from an uphill lie. This is because it lessens the loft of the club. Still, if you understand the fundamentals it's a shot you can learn to master with practice. Basically, it mirrors what you do to play from an uphill lie.

At address, your shoulders should mirror the angle of the slope.

The key to playing this shot is to swing along the angle of the slope for as long as possible, since the tendency is to hit a thin shot from this sort of lie. Keep in mind that playing from a downhill lie actually removes effective loft from a club, producing a lower-than-normal trajectory.

BALL BELOW YOUR FEET—Like a downhill lie, this is a difficult shot, in large part because it is so difficult to maintain your posture and balance throughout your swing. At address, your first concern is to tilt your spine forward so your arms hang freely and you are the correct distance from the ball. Your weight will be centered over your ankles and your knees flexed comfortably. It is vital that you maintain that flex throughout your swing, since the understandable tendency is to hit a thin shot. You want to take full advantage of the length of the club, so grip it at the very end of the shaft. Finally, the ball will tend to fly to the right from this sort of lie because of the change in shaft angle, so you must allow for this when aiming the club.

Setup for a sidehill lie, ball below feet

BALL ABOVE YOUR FEET—This shot is not nearly as difficult as one played when the ball is below your feet, but it still presents a challenge unless you understand the fundamentals. At address, you need to grip down on the club, since the ball is actually closer to your body than it is from a level lie. Your weight should be over your ankles and your spine tilt will be more upright. This is really more of an arm swing, with minimal body motion. The more the ball is above your feet, the greater the tendency for the ball to fly to the left of your target because the clubshaft is at a flatter angle.

Grassy or Bare Lies

When you hit the ball into the deep rough off the tee, your first job is to get the ball back into play. The biggest mistake is to try and get greedy and hit a shot that the lie won't allow you to get back into a position to save par. If you leave it in the rough, you've turned a one-shot mistake into a two-shot error or worse. If the ball is in rough so deep and/or wet that you can't advance the ball more than a few yards, you simply have to accept your punishment, take a sand wedge, and pitch the ball back into the fairway. However, if the lie is decent, you can play a shot that will allow you to either reach the green or come close enough to save par.

Setup for a sidehill lie, ball above feet

Your first decision has to do with club selection. You want to select the club with the maximum amount of loft, even if this means that you may only be able to come up short of the green. Your odds of getting up and down from in front of the green are probably better than from a bunker or, worse, the rough around the green. Remember, golf is a game of percentages, and the most successful players are those who keep the odds in their favor.

Once you've made your club selection, you need to make a swing that is steeper than your normal swing. To do this, loosen your grip pressure. The steeper angle of approach keeps as much grass as possible from coming between the clubface and the ball. To that end, if you have a choice between playing a long iron or a fairway wood from the rough, always go with the fairway wood.

The design of the club reduces the chances of it catching in the thick grass, while the lower center of gravity and the added loft helps get the ball into the air.

To make this steeper swing, address the ball with a slightly open stance and aim left of your ultimate goal. Loosen your grip pressure and play the ball slightly forward of center in your stance and set your hands even with or just behind the ball. Take the club away, allowing your wrists to hinge fully, and then hit down on the ball, making a high finish.

Here's another thought to keep in mind: If the ball comes to rest in a lie that is so bad that you honestly believe you might not be able to make even decent contact and advance the ball any appreciable distance, you always have the option of declaring an unplayable lie, taking a one-stroke penalty, and dropping the ball (a) within two club lengths of the point where the ball lay but not closer to the hole, or (b) behind the point where the ball lay, keeping that point between yourself and the hole, with no limit to how far back from that point you can go.

Around the Greens

If you find yourself in the rough around the green, the lie becomes even more important. If the ball is sitting up slightly, you can play a shot that allows you to slide the clubhead under the ball. The key to this shot is to align the leading edge of your wedge with the bottom of the ball and not the base of the grass. Otherwise you run the risk of cutting too far under the ball and leaving it in the rough. If the ball is sitting down in the grass, play the shot the same way you'd play a bunker shot.

One final thought about greenside rough. While you never want to "short side" yourself by missing the green on the side closest to the hole, you also want to avoid hitting the ball where players walk from the green to the next tee. The grass in this area will be trampled and could leave you a shot that is far more difficult than it would be otherwise.

Catching a "Flyer"

When your drive lands in the first cut of rough, the grass is still short enough for you to get plenty of club on the ball. The problem is that the grass is just long enough to come between the ball and the clubface. This causes the ball to come off the clubface with much less spin than it normally would, which results in a lower trajectory. The ball will end up running farther than it would from the fairway, so you need to make an adjustment, either in your club selection or in how hard you hit the shot. The same holds true when playing in wet conditions, since the moisture that comes between the clubface and the ball has the same effect on your shot.

Playing from Hardpan

When your ball comes to rest on very hard, bare ground, you've found yourself in another "good news, bad news" situation. The good news is that if you play the shot properly, you can put tremendous spin on the ball. The bad news is that you must be very precise in order to play this shot properly.

If you are near the green, the safest shot is to simply putt the ball, since that provides the best chance of making solid, predictable contact. However, if you need to play a pitch, chip or full shot, you need to reduce the amount the club skids on impact, because if you hit the ground before you hit the ball, the club will bounce off the hard ground and you will hit a thin shot. To reduce skid, avoid a sand wedge if at all possible. Play the ball back in your stance with your hands ahead of the ball at address. Make full wrist hinge and hit down on the ball, trapping it against the hard ground. The key thought is to strike the ball before you hit the ground.

Playing in the Wind

There's an old Scottish saying, "If there's nae wind, it's nae golf" and, indeed, wind presents one of the central challenges in the game, particularly on the links courses where the game was, if not born, certainly nurtured. Being able to judge the strength and direction of the wind and knowing how to play in it are vital elements in becoming a complete golfer. When the winds blow, golf requires patience, concentration and an added attention to detail in order to be successful.

Before getting into the mechanics of playing shots in the wind, here's a thought to keep in mind: If you are playing near a large body of water or in a humid climate where the air tends to be heavy, the wind will have a greater influence on the ball than it will in the thinner air of the mountains or desert. Also, the stronger the wind blows, the more effect it will have on every shot, including pitches, chips and even putts. For this reason, if you regularly play on a windy course, you might consult with your Professional to find a ball that flies at a lower trajectory, since this will help minimize the influence of the wind.

PLAYING AGAINST THE WIND—The key to playing this shot is to resist the temptation to hit the ball hard, for this will only increase the effect of backspin, causing the ball to balloon into the air and come up well short of your intended target. The best advice when hitting a shot into a strong wind is to knock the ball down by hitting a low-trajectory shot as described earlier in this chapter. Another option is to simply take more club than the shot would normally require and make an easy swing, focusing on making solid contact. It's also worth experimenting with choking down on the grip, since every inch you grip down on the club equates to one less club in distance. When playing a driver, there are two schools of thought: The first calls for teeing the ball lower than normal and slightly back in your stance, since this will allow you to strike the ball with less loft on the clubface. The other school of thought argues that by teeing the ball lower you tend to hit it with a descending blow, causing it to balloon up into the wind. The best advice is to work with your PGA Professional and see which approach works best for you.

The good news about playing shots into the wind is that it can be a tremendous advantage on approach shots and shots around the green. The same effect that reduces distance off the tee—an increase in backspin—helps stop the ball on the green.

PLAYING DOWNWIND—Again, this is a good news, bad news situation. The good news is that it will help you gain distance off the tee (but good news only if you hit it straight, otherwise it only helps get you further into trouble) but bad news because it also makes it difficult to stop the ball on the green, since the wind reduces backspin.

CROSSING WINDS—There are two approaches to dealing with side winds. One school of thought from most highly skilled players recommends curving the ball into the wind. For example, if the wind is blowing from left to right, hit a draw and hold it against the wind. The problem with this approach is even the most skilled player will sometimes look on in horror as that gentle fade turns into a hook as there's a lull in the wind after impact. Most PGA Professionals believe a safer approach is to favor the side of the hole that the wind is blowing from and simply let the wind carry the ball back to your target. This approach takes the spin off the ball and it will run in the direction the wind carried it.

Playing in Bad Weather

The first rule when playing in wet or cold weather is to constantly remind yourself that your fellow competitors are in the same weather and all you can do is make the best of a bad situation. The second rule is to simplify your game as much as possible. Avoid risky or marginal shots. Play for the center of the fairways and greens and, above all else, play it safe.

When it is raining, you must concentrate on keeping your hands and grips dry. Make sure you have a towel to dry your grips and a second towel, draped inside your umbrella, to dry your hands. It's also a good idea to have a golf bag with a cover. This will help keep your grips dry. The longer you can keep your clubs dry and yourself comfortable, the better off you'll be.

In cold weather, your focus must be on staying warm as long as possible. Dress in layers of clothing rather than heavy, bulky clothes. Many people find it useful to soak their hands in very warm water just prior to the round and at the turn. Wearing gloves or mittens between shots is a good idea and so is carrying a hand warmer. It's also important to wear a hat to help your body retain heat. However, if you wear a stocking cap, make sure you can still hear the sound of the club hitting the ball, since this is an important element of your feel. Also, keep in mind that in cold weather, the amount of clothing you wear will shorten your swing, and golf balls do not carry as far, so take this into account when planning your shot.

Playing in Heat and Humidity

First, while slow play should be avoided at all costs, when it is very hot and humid you should pace yourself. Be ready to play when it is your turn, but don't race between shots. Dehydration begins the minute you step outside in hot weather. You should drink water or an electrolyte-balanced sports drink on every hole, rather than waiting until you feel thirsty. By that time, you are already becoming dehydrated and drinking a lot of liquid can lead to cramping. Wear light-colored clothing, since dark clothing tends to attract heat, and also wear a hat to keep the sun off your head. It's also important to put sunscreen on exposed skin. Bear in mind that perspiring is one way your body cools itself, but even if you don't perspire very much, you must still take care to drink plenty of liquid. Finally, drinking alcoholic beverages is never a very good idea when trying to play your best golf, but it's particularly bad when playing in heat and humidity.

Questions and Answers

Q: *I play several rounds a year in cold weather and always use a hand warmer. I know that balls fly farther in warm weather than in cold. Can I use a hand warmer to keep balls warm?*

A: Afraid not. It's a violation of the Rules of Golf.

Q: *What is the key to hitting shots that spin back on the green?*

A: Hall of Famer Sam Snead is fond of telling the story about the high-handicapper who asked Sam how to get the ball to spin back on the greens.

"How far do you hit a 5-iron?" Sam asked.

"About 100 yards," the man said.

"Why in the world would you want it to back up?" Sam asked.

The key is to make crisp, solid contact with the ball. Anytime turf comes between the ball and the clubface, it takes spin off the ball. At address, set your hands slightly ahead of the ball and try to replicate that position at impact. This will help you strike the ball with a crisp, descending blow.

Q: *When your drive ends up in a divot hole, what's the best way to play the shot?*

A: The first thing you should do is accept the fact that golf can sometimes be an unfair game, and when you hit a good drive that ends up in a divot hole, it's a perfect example of just how unfair it can sometimes be. You must remain calm. The key is to make solid contact, striking the ball with a descending blow. At address, set the ball back in your stance, with your hands ahead of the ball. Focus on making a well-timed swing, do not rush the downswing.

Q: *In the fall, when I hit shots off line, they often come to rest on top of leaves or pine needles. How do I play this shot?*

A: The first thing to keep in mind is that you should not ground your club, since this could cause the ball to move, resulting in a one-stroke penalty. The key is to address the ball with the club slightly above the leaves. Take it away slowly on the backswing and concentrate on repeating your normal swing. You want to make the cleanest, most-solid contact possible. Also, bear in mind that when you are playing from trouble, the first thing you want to do is escape the trouble; the next consideration is to make sure you don't hit the ball into even more trouble.

Q: *Is there anything that top players practice that average players neglect?*

A: Several things, but learning how far you carry each club can really help when you are trying to hit shots close. Top players know just how far they can carry each club. In part, it's because they practice and hit these shots, but it's also because they hit the ball so squarely time after time. There's no telling how many strokes per round the average player could save if he or she could begin to control the trajectory and know the true distance of the shots made with every club.

11

The Importance of Proper Equipment

Not so long ago, in the years leading up to the most recent revolution in golf equipment, Lee Trevino was asked about a new club that had just been introduced to the market.

Trevino dismissed the claim saying, in effect, that it's the carpenter not the tools that matter.

But not long afterward, Trevino surveyed the changes in clubhead design, shaft construction and the myriad new golf balls and admitted he'd been wrong. More than ever before, finding the proper equipment is crucial not only to improving, but also, for the best players in the game, to remaining competitive.

It only stands to reason that there is no "one-size-fits-all" rule when it comes to equipment. Everyone is different, both physically and in the way he or she swings a golf club. And yet, all too often people will base their club-buying decision on any number of ill-conceived reasons such as: (1) what the hottest player in the game is endorsing; (2) what's on sale; (3) which advertising claim is the most seductive; and so on and so on.

In truth, properly fitting equipment to a golfer is incredibly complicated and requires experience and knowledge of both a golfer's needs and the available equipment options. In all honesty, unless you have that experience and knowledge, trying to make this decision by yourself puts you very much in the same boat with the lawyer who has himself for a client.

Our very first suggestion, therefore, is to work closely with your PGA Professional when making decisions concerning equipment. Professionals are schooled in this area as part of their training and education, and must be able to demonstrate their knowledge and expertise before being qualified as PGA Professionals. Just as important, however, is the fact that your PGA Professional is familiar with your game, and therefore your equipment needs.

That said, in this chapter we'll provide you with the information that can help you make some intelligent decisions on equipment.

The single most important consideration should be finding clubs and balls that fit *your* game as opposed to something that works well for Tiger Woods or Karrie Webb. Self-delusion is a terrible—and often expensive—thing when it comes to buying equipment.

Fortunately, just as equipment technology has dramatically increased in recent years, so has the technology that allows golfers to fit every aspect of their equipment to their games.

Today, people marvel at how far the top players drive the ball and how precisely they hit their approach shots. Certainly, part of this can be explained by excellent instruction and superb conditioning—of both the players and the courses they play. But a great deal of the credit must be given to improved equipment and the technology that allows players to find the equipment that is perfectly suited to their needs.

Perhaps the biggest advance has been in the development of clubfitting stations, where advanced equipment measures such factors as the exact launch angle of a shot, swing speed, swingpath angle, spin rate, the energy transfer to the ball and the distance the ball will carry. By incorporating all this information into a swing model, a PGA Professional can determine the optimum equipment specifications for you.

While not every PGA Professional has such sophisticated equipment, an increasing number of equipment manufacturers have demo-testing days at clubs and courses where you can be tested to determine what equipment specifications are best suited to you.

YOUR CLUBFITTING OPTIONS—The first decision you have to make is where and how you're going to get your clubs. The first option is to simply buy them right off the rack, much as you would a new suit. If you're lucky, these stock clubs will fit you adequately, or may just require a little fine-tuning by a PGA Professional. The next option would be to have your PGA Professional send your specifications to a manufacturer, who will custom-build a club or a set for you.

Once you've decided where and how you're going to purchase your equipment, there are several factors we think you should consider:

APPEARANCE—The simple fact is that if you don't find a club appealing to your eye, you'll never really feel fully confident with it in your hands. There's an old saying that "a club has to fit your eye before it fits your game," and there's a lot of truth in that. For many years, when so-called game-improvement clubs were introduced, players who had learned to play with classic blades never really felt comfortable with the newer designs. By the same token, many younger players who learned to play with these designs look at the classic blades and find them too unforgiving.

Here's something to keep in mind when it comes to equipment, especially putters, drivers and wedges: If you have a club that you like but it isn't working for you just now, set it aside but don't sell it, trade it or throw it away. If a club looks good to you at one point, it will inevitably look good to you again—and when it does it will work well for you, too.

WORKMANSHIP—A set of golf clubs, or even an individual club such as a driver, is a significant investment. The good news is that if you purchase clubs from a reputable manufacturer and are fitted properly, they are something that you can use for a very long time. We strongly suggest that if it comes down to a question of quality versus price, you go with the quality.

PROPER FIT—We discussed this earlier in this chapter, but it bears repeating. **The best and most expensive clubs in the world are worthless unless they fit you and your game properly.** We will go into each of the following elements in more detail later in this chapter, but for now let's simply review the different variables you need to consider when being properly fitted for a club.

SHAFTS—Many people believe that the shaft is the most important element in clubfitting. The considerations include the shaft's flex, weight, material, step pattern and kick point. Today, shafts come in five basic materials. The choice you make may well come down to personal preference—how the club feels when you hit a shot—but certain types of shafts are generally better suited to different types of players.

Standard steel shafts come in a variety of step patterns and flexes and can accommodate the needs of a wide variety of golfers. They tend to be the heaviest of all the shafts.

Lightweight steel shafts, as the name suggests, have the advantage of being lighter than traditional steel shafts, which is an advantage for women, seniors and some junior golfers.

"No-step" steel shafts offer greater flexibility and tighter tolerances than traditional or lightweight steel shafts in being matched to a player's swing.

Graphite shafts are lighter than steel shafts and they also allow manufacturers to control the amount of torque or twisting the shaft experiences during the swing.

Graphite composite shafts, like regular graphite shafts, are lighter than steel shafts but the addition of other substances in their manufacture can make them easier to fit to a player's specific needs.

Steel and graphite blends are a new development. They promise the lightness of graphite with the feel of steel shafts.

Weight is a crucial element in determining the proper shaft, as well as a player's swing speed, which is why careful measurements and fitting—as well as feel—are the keys to selecting the right shaft material and stiffness for you.

CLUBHEAD DESIGN—The clubhead should be visually appealing, but also should be designed in a way that accentuates the positives in your swing while reducing the negatives. For example, if you generally slice the ball, you want to make sure the clubface is square or even slightly closed. Also, a larger clubhead and face is generally more forgiving than a standard club design. The size, composition and design of a clubhead and where you contact the ball are determining equipment factors in the launch angle and the spin rate of a shot.

LIE—The club should rest squarely on the ground when you address the ball with the toe slightly elevated. The crucial factor, however, is not the lie of the club at rest but at impact. This can be tested by your PGA Professional using a lie board.

LOFT—The club's loft should be complementary to your swing and game. This is particularly true with the driver.

BULGE AND ROLL—The vertical and horizontal curvature of the clubface of a wood should also complement your game and swing shape. This factor could be altered with wooden clubs but is predetermined in today's metal woods, as are considerations such as the squareness of the clubface and the amount of offset, which is the amount the shaft is set ahead of the leading edge of the club. Increased offset can help a player square up the club at impact. This is a particular benefit for players who tend to slice the ball.

SWINGWEIGHT AND OVERALL WEIGHT—Again, these two variables should be matched to you and your swing.

GRIP—Since this element provides your only contact with the club during the swing, it's vital that the shape, size and material be suitable for your needs.

SET COMPOSITION—This final factor should take into consideration not only your game but also the type of courses you play.

Some Further Explanations

Now that you have a broad overview of equipment and clubfitting, we're able to go into more detail about the various elements that need to be considered when you are fitted for one club or an entire set of clubs.

SHAFTS—As we mentioned before, many people believe the shaft is the most important consideration when it comes to proper clubfitting. It's also the least understood.

Many people believe that the shaft produces power, when in truth, what it does is harness it. That's one reason it's so crucial that the shaft be constructed in a way that will allow it to deliver the power generated by your swing at the optimum moment of impact. If the shaft releases power fractionally too soon or too late, it can cost you distance and can also lead to inaccurate or inconsistent ball-striking.

Until the 1930s, the vast majority of shafts were made of hickory, although the first steel shaft appeared as early as 1891. In fact, the USGA didn't legalize steel shafts until 1924. The R&A followed suit seven years later. Hickory presented any number of complications for players. First, the shafts would warp and swell when exposed to moisture. Next, practice as we know it today wasn't possible because the shafts couldn't tolerate the stress of hitting one ball after another. It was only with the development of the steel shaft that hour-long practice sessions became possible. Finally, hickory shafts would torque or twist from side to side during the swing. This required very precise timing and also meant that players of the time developed very "handsy" swings.

Even the rudimentary steel shafts were a vast improvement over hickory, but by today's standards they were quite crude. In fact, it wasn't until the introduction of frequency matching in the 1980s that shafts could be tested throughout a set to ensure consistency.

"I basically played with the same set of irons throughout my career," recalls 1973 British Open Champion Tom Weiskopf. "When frequency matching came along, I had my irons tested and found that the shafts in two of the irons were slightly different from the shafts in the other irons. It was interesting because I always had to hit shots slightly differently with those two clubs."

Now not everyone has the feel or talent of Tom Weiskopf, but that anecdote reveals just how precise shaft construction and testing has become, and also offers further evidence that great care should be taken in obtaining shafts that properly fit your needs.

Beyond shaft length (which should be based upon the length of your body segments and not your height as is commonly believed), the three fundamental considerations are the shaft flex, design and materials.

A steel shaft's flex is determined in large part by the thickness of the shaft's wall. The thicker the shaft, the stiffer and heavier it will be. It will also require more strength and/or swing speed to produce the optimum results. Typically, shafts are labeled R (Regular), S (Stiff) and X (Extra Stiff) and generally have gradations within those groups. For example, an S-300 shaft will be marginally stiffer than an S-100. Many manufacturers even have an L (Ladies) flex with different swingweights, as well as an "A" flex for senior golfers.

The next consideration in a steel shaft is the step pattern. A shaft's narrowing from top to bottom is usually accomplished by a series of steps. The width and location of the steps, along with the stiffness of the shaft, result in a "kick point," which is the point of maximum flex. The location of the kick point can determine the trajectory of the shot. As a general rule, the lower the kick point the higher the trajectory. This makes a lower kick point preferable for golfers who lack the strength to launch the ball high into the air. On the other hand, many top golfers prefer a higher kick point, since they believe this gives them greater control and they don't need help getting the ball airborne.

The final consideration is the shaft's material. Graphite and other synthetic materials are a popular alternative to steel. They are generally lighter, for one thing, which allows people with less strength or slower swing speeds to produce more clubhead speed and, therefore, more distance. Recent advancements have also made it possible to control the shaft's torque or twisting, which had been a problem in early graphite shafts. Graphite also offers greater shock absorption, which is an enormous benefit for people who suffer from arthritis. It's worth noting that there is a wide variety in the composition and quality of graphite and other composite shafts, and this is generally reflected in the cost of the shafts.

CLUBHEAD DESIGN—This is an area where there has been a tremendous evolution in recent years. The use of lightweight metals has made it possible to design clubheads that are much larger and more forgiving than what we have come to think of as traditional clubs. The larger the clubface, the larger and more forgiving the "sweet spot," or optimum hitting area. The benefits of this design for the average and high-handicap golfer are enormous, since this type of club minimizes their mis-hits. More accomplished players, however, find it difficult to work the ball with these clubs, since they tend to negate the amount of spin—especially fade or draw spin—you can put on the ball. Players also complain that they don't get quite the same amount of feel or feedback from their shots.

There are two other considerations when it comes to the design and composition of your irons. The first is whether they are forged or cast. Traditionally, irons have been forged from relatively soft steel, and then ground and filed to exact specifications. Cast clubs are typically made of harder metal than forged clubs and are generally more forgiving but offer less feel or feedback to the player. The other consideration is the amount of offset, which is the distance between the leading edge of the hosel and the leading edge of the blade. Players who tend to slice the ball benefit from clubs that are slightly offset.

The question of clubhead size and design is an excellent topic to discuss with your PGA Professional, since he or she can carefully analyze your swing and equipment needs.

LIE—A club's lie determines how it relates to the ground both at address and, more importantly, at impact. Players who carry their hands low at address and/or have flatter swing planes need clubs with flatter lies. Conversely, players with upright swings need clubs with more upright lies. If a club's lie doesn't fit your swing, it can result in errant shots. For example, if you have an upright swing but play with irons that have lies that are too flat for your swing plane, you run the risk of catching the toe of the club in the turf at impact, resulting in shots that fly to the right of your target. The opposite is true if you have a flat swing plane and clubs that are too upright.

Your PGA Professional can check your club's lies with a lie board. In fact, it's a good idea to have your clubs checked annually to ensure that the lies are correct.

LOFT—The amount of loft obviously varies throughout the set and manufacturers generally adhere to a fairly standard pattern of lofts. It's important to note that some manufacturers intentionally make their clubs "weaker" by adding more loft per club than is standard, especially in the longer irons. As a result, shots get into the air more easily but don't carry as far. Why? Because it helps the vast majority of golfers get the ball into the air more easily. Just as is the case with your clubs' lies, it's a good idea to have the lofts and launch angles checked by machine every year as well.

LENGTH—If you stand next to a person of average height and your hands are positioned virtually the same distance from the ground, why would you need longer clubs? Having said that, some people prefer longer clubs since, everything else being equal, a longer club produces a longer radius and greater clubhead speed. This is one reason many players on the Senior PGA Tour and the LPGA experiment with longer than standard shafts in their drivers. The downside is that a longer shaft (and therefore a longer swing arc) can be difficult to control, so what you gain in distance you may lose in direction—and centered contact. That said, in recent years, the standard length of a driver has gone from an average of 43 1/2 inches to as much as 45 inches. The crucial consideration in shaft length is where you contact the ball on the clubface. If a shaft is too long or too short, it can cause you to mis-hit the ball.

FACE ANGLE—Woods—which can be made out of any material—are designed with both horizontal and vertical curvature. This is what's known as "bulge and roll." Of the two, bulge is by far the most important. Bulge helps counteract the effect of off-center hits. For example, if you hit the ball toward the toe of the club it will put a counterclockwise spin on the ball, helping to curve it back to the left and vice versa. Roll can affect the trajectory of your shots. For example, a ball hit high on the clubface will tend to have a higher flight than a ball hit low on the club. As mentioned earlier, while traditional wooden woods could be altered to change bulge and roll, with metal or composite clubheads the bulge and roll is established during the manufacturing process and cannot be altered.

SWINGWEIGHT AND TOTAL WEIGHT—Total weight (or dead weight) is fairly obvious. It is simply the weight of the component parts of the club taken as a whole. Depending on the weight of the shaft, grip and head, it can vary from 12 ounces to 13 1/2 ounces. Swingweight is a method of standardizing the functional weight of a club. A club is placed on a swingweight machine similar to a scale, with most clubs falling within the "C" or "D" range. It's worth noting that if you place a club on a swingweight machine and then drape a dollar bill over the hosel, it will add one point to the measurement. For most golfers, an ideal swingweight will lie in the D-1 to D-3 range. Most ladies, juniors and seniors will benefit from a swingweight in the high "C" range, while stronger players using longer clubs favor a higher swingweight, even into the "E" range. Dead weight varies from club to club, with the driver often being the lightest club in the bag.

GRIP—The size, shape and composition of a grip are important because your grip is crucial to your ability to control the club. The size of a grip is often overlooked by beginning golfers, but it can dramatically affect your ball-striking. For the vast majority of players, a grip is the proper size if, when you hold it in your target hand, your middle two fingers barely touch the pad at the base of your thumb. If a grip is too small, it can lead you to overwork your hands, producing a hook. If it is too big, it hinders your hand action and can lead to slicing. For these reasons, some players prefer thicker or thinner grips.

For much of golf's history, grips were made of strips of leather wrapped around the shaft. That has completely changed with the development of rubber composition grips that slide over the butt end of the club. These grips are available in a wide variety of styles. One of the most popular among people who play regularly in high heat and humidity is a grip that contains cord. The rougher surface provides added control, however it can be somewhat painful for sensitive hands.

One final thought: Some players prefer grips that have a small ridge running vertically along the underside of the trip. These "reminders" help ensure they place their hands on the club the same way every time.

SET COMPOSITION—The Rules of Golf allow you to carry 14 clubs, but beyond that, you're on your own when deciding what clubs should make up your set, as this story about Ben Hogan illustrates.

One of the most famous photos in golf history is Hy Peskin's classic shot of Ben Hogan watching his 1-iron approach fly toward the 18th green in the final round of the 1950 U.S. Open at Merion. Years later Hogan discussed that shot with a writer.

"It was a difficult shot because I had to decide whether to hit the 1-iron or a 4-wood," Hogan said. "I finally went with the 1-iron because it gave me a better chance of running the ball back to the hole."

The writer was puzzled because usually players will carry either a 1-iron or a 4-wood, but not both since they hit the ball approximately the same distance.

"Excuse me, Mr. Hogan, if you carried both a 1-iron and a 4-wood, what club did you leave out of your bag?" the writer asked.

"A 7-iron," Hogan said, "because there are no 7-iron shots at Merion."

Few players are capable of that sort of analysis, but if you take a good look at your game and the course you're playing, you can make some sound decisions about what clubs you should include—and exclude—from your set.

First of all, can you consistently hit your long irons well? The majority of golfers cannot, so why not replace them with a 4- or 5-wood, 7-wood, 9-wood or a trouble wood with a lot of loft and a lot of weight on the sole. This club is great for hitting high, soft approaches or for playing from the rough. Also, if you miss a lot of greens or play a course with heavily bunkered or elevated greens, why not invest in a 60-degree wedge? Finally, if you have trouble hitting a driver consistently because you can't generate enough clubhead speed to match the launch angle, why not look at a driver with additional loft, up to 14 degrees? These help you get the ball airborne and are more forgiving of mis-hits. The truth of the matter is that if you cannot generate more than 70 mph of clubhead speed, you can't reasonably expect to be successful with any iron with less loft than a 5-iron.

Golf Balls

Nowhere are the advances and improvements in equipment more obvious or dramatic than they are in the golf balls that are available today. It isn't so much that the balls go farther than those of just a generation ago, but they are far more consistent than they were 25 years ago. In addition, the wide variety of golf balls available today allow players to work with their PGA Professional to find the ball that is best suited to their game. The key is experimenting with every variety of ball to find which type best suits your swing and game.

The dimple design and symmetry, the material that makes up both the cover and the core, and the ball's weight and size determine the flight characteristics of a golf ball. In order for a ball to be considered "conforming" or acceptable for use in USGA and R&A competitions, it must pass tests for size, weight, dimple design and symmetry, initial velocity and overall distance.

The shape and symmetry of the dimples is central to a ball's flight characteristics. Early feathery balls were smooth and did not become truly playable until they had been nicked by use. Eventually ballmakers began marking their balls with random markings before settling on varying dimple patterns in 1908.

Over the years the number and patterns of dimples that manufacturers have experimented with have resulted in combinations that allow a ball to fly higher or lower than a standard ball.

Golf ball construction varies from the traditional three-piece ball, which has a core wrapped with elastic windings covered with material that varies from balata (rarely used any longer in favor of synthetic and less-expensive materials), to two-piece balls which are basically a large core and cover. There are also manufacturers producing four-piece balls featuring a core, windings and two covers.

Traditionally, wound balata-covered balls have been favored by better players because balata is a softer material than synthetics such as Surlyn and produces higher spin rates. That said, balata cuts and bruises far more easily than synthetics and therefore is less durable. Very little pure balata is used anymore, as manufacturers have developed synthetic blends that produce a soft feel but are more durable.

Wound balls with composition covers offer a slightly lower spin rate than balata-covered balls, but are far more durable.

Increasingly, manufacturers are turning to blended center/composite cover balls because they can produce a greater variety of balls that produce a greater variety of spin rates. The harder the cover and center, the lower the spin rate, producing a ball that goes farther but is more difficult to manipulate around the greens.

Spin rate is a matter of personal preference. A player like Spain's Sergio Garcia likes to shape shots from side to side, so he would prefer a ball with a higher spin rate. At the same time, a player such as Mark Calcavecchia, who relies on basically just one shot pattern, prefers a ball with a lower spin rate.

So-called "Ladies'" feature spin rates suitable for slower swing speeds.

Compression is one of the least understood characteristics of golf ball design. Explained simply, compression measures a ball's amount of deflection when a standard, measurable force is applied. This is measured on a scale of 0–200, with 200 reflecting a ball so hard that it does not compress at all when the force is applied. For every 1,000th of an inch of deflection, the rating is reduced by a point. A ball that compresses 100/1,000ths of an inch is a 100-compression ball. Most balls range from 80 to 100 compression.

Compression has a marginal effect on a ball's performance. It is more important as a matter of feel. Some players want the hardest possible ball they can find while others prefer a softer feel.

A Final Thought

While it's true that you can't "buy a golf game," the recent advances in equipment design, manufacture and fitting can certainly help you shave precious strokes from your scores. Advances in technology will always change the performance characteristics of golf equipment. The key is determining what equipment is right for you—and the best person to help you with these decisions is your PGA Professional.

Questions and Answers

Q: *I tend to hit Surlyn-covered, two-piece balls farther than wound balata balls, but I have more control around the greens with the balata balls. Can I play a Surlyn ball from the tee and then switch to a balata ball around the greens?*

A: Sorry, that's against the Rules of Golf (Appendix 1-b, One Ball Condition), which state that once you begin a stipulated round with one brand and type of ball, you must finish with the same brand and type of ball. The only element that can vary is the number on the ball.

Q: *Can I use different-type grips on my irons and woods?*

A: As long as the grips conform to the Rules of Golf (Rule 2-2), you can use any type of grip on any of your clubs. Note, however, that grips with a flat side can only be used on putters.

Q: *I've heard that golfers who played in the hickory-shaft era could drive the ball as long as today's players. Is that possible?*

A: Yes and no. Many players of that era were prodigiously long. Bob Jones was very long, as was the young Sam Snead. One player, Jesse Guilford, was nick-named "Siege Gun" because of his length. The difference is that the golf balls are light-years better today, as is the course conditioning.

Q: *If the swingweights of my clubs vary, is there anything I can do other than send them back to the manufacturer?*

A: Absolutely. Ask your PGA Professional to apply some lead tape to the back of the clubs. This should be done by a trained PGA Professional, since the placement of the tape can affect the trajectory of your shots. For example, if the tape is placed near the bottom of the club, the ball will tend to have a higher trajectory than it would if the tape were to be placed along the top edge of the club.

Q: *Is it legal to have a graphite shaft in my driver but steel shafts in every other club?*

A: Totally, 100 percent legal. In fact, if you look in the bags of the world's best players, you'll notice that a large number will do exactly what you do. Many players believe they simply get more feel with steel shafts in their irons.

Q: *At a recent tournament, I noticed that several of the professionals on the practice tee were trying out as many as eight or 10 wedges. Why so many?*

A: Unlike a few years ago when players had to customize their wedges, today manufacturers produce clubs in a staggering variety of configurations. Players can order clubs with the loft, lie, shaft, flange, bounce and scoring lines to fit their game and the courses they play. The good news is, so can you. The days of the hot rods are over. Today you can buy what you want right off the rack.

Q: *I've read that many good players have stiffer shafts in their drivers than in their other clubs? Is this true, and if it is, why do they do this?*

A: Today, players of all skill levels should take advantage of testing to determine what factors will produce the ultimate launch angle. This may not result in a stiffer or weaker shaft in their driver, but it will almost certainly result in some changes in their equipment selections.

Q: *I hit the ball fairly straight with my irons but tend to slice the ball with my driver. Any thoughts?*

A: First, the driver is the longest club in your set (unless you have a super-long putter). For that reason, you have to make a swing that is rhythmic enough to allow you to deliver the club squarely to the ball at impact. Remember that the more loft on the clubface, the more vertical spin, while less loft will produce more horizontal spin. For that reason, it's important to have the face angle of your clubs checked as part of a fitting program.

Q: *Why does loft matter when choosing a putter?*

A: If you look at slow-motion footage of a ball struck with a putter, you'll notice that it skids along the grass momentarily before it begins rolling toward the hole. You need a putter with enough loft to get the ball up and running as soon as possible. The faster the greens, the less loft you need on your putter. Also, bent-grass greens require less-lofted putters than Bermuda greens.

Q: *I recently started playing with a 60-degree wedge. I like the club but very often I come up short of the green, because the ball flies so high. Could the problem be that there's more than 60 degrees of loft to the club?*

A: It's possible, and you could have your PGA Professional check the club by putting it on a lie/loft machine. A more likely source of your problem, how-ever, is that you are swinging too hard, trying to get too much out of the club. With a 60-degree wedge, the harder you hit the ball the higher it tends to fly, and therefore, the shorter it will carry. Experiment with making easier, softer, swings and see if the results aren't a little more like what you have in mind.

Q: *When I'm on the practice tee I very rarely hit big slices or hooks, but when I'm on the course the ball curves more than when I'm practicing. Could this have something to do with the range balls?*

A: It could. Range balls are two-piece balls designed to absorb enormous amounts of pounding, day after day. If you play with wound, balata balls, you may notice a difference, since these are designed to spin more than range balls, accentuating hook or slice spins. You'll also find that wound balls will fly higher than practice balls, as well. This is one reason that at the PGA Learning Center, we offer four different types of practice balls, so every visit is like a ball-testing program. Also keep in mind that most people will swing harder on the golf course than on the practice range. That could be another reason.

Q: *I play most of my golf in very hot, humid conditions. My hands perspire quite a bit, which makes it difficult to grip the club, even when I wear a glove. Are there any types of grips that can help me?*

A: You might experiment with some of the new gloves on the market that are designed to help fight this problem. The most important part of keeping the grip tacky in those conditions is to wipe the grip clean before use.

12

What You Need in Your Bag

Deciding what to carry in your golf bag is largely determined by the size of your bag and the weather conditions you'll be facing. Still, if you follow these common sense suggestions you should have any contingency covered.

Strictly in terms of golf equipment, you should carry at least two sleeves (six) balls as a minimum, and depending on your handicap and the difficulty of the course you're playing, you might well need more. If you wear a glove, you should have at least two and probably three if you are playing in hot, humid or rainy conditions. You'll also need tees and ball markers, but not nearly as many as you'll discover you've accumulated over the years.

You should also carry a current edition of the Rules of Golf as well as a small notebook where you've jotted down any recurring swing or short-game problems and the solutions your PGA Professional has suggested to get you back on track.

There's no need to turn your bag into a medicine cabinet, but there are some medications and ointments you should carry. For example, no matter where you play, you should carry sunscreen and lip protection with a minimum SPF (Sun Protection Formula) of 15 and probably higher, especially if you have fair skin and burn easily. The dangers of skin cancer are not to be taken lightly. It's also vital to carry the appropriate medications if you are allergic to bee stings or insect bites, and to let your playing companions know what to do if you are stricken. It's also a good idea to carry some aspirin or other pain relievers such as Advil. While all the over-the-counter pain relievers are good for the aches and pains that come with the game, recent medical studies indicate that aspirin can be a potential lifesaver—literally—in the case of heart attacks. It's also wise to carry some adhesive bandages in assorted sizes, as well as a small container of an antiseptic to prevent a cut or blister from becoming infected. Finally, don't forget to include an insect repellent that won't leave a sticky or greasy film on your skin, particularly on your hands.

You shouldn't overlook energy and nutrition when preparing your bag for a round of golf. Put a piece of fruit or a high-energy snack bar in your bag (although if you don't eat the fruit, remember to remove it following your round or you may be in for a nasty surprise the next time you play). Also, if there isn't plenty of water on the course, you might pack a bottle of water as well.

Preparing for Wet Weather

If rain threatens, it's important to carry whatever you need to help keep you as dry and comfortable as possible. It's particularly important that you find a way to keep your hands and grips dry, since wet hands and grips virtually ensure you won't be able to control either your shotmaking or your score.

The first item you should pack is a good, lightweight rainsuit or, at the very least, a waterproof or water-resistant wind shirt—and the newer the better, since there have been tremendous advances in material and design that make this clothing more efficient, water-resistant and comfortable. You might also pack an additional hat in case yours becomes drenched.

You should carry at least one additional large towel as well as a smaller hand towel, and here's a tip: drape one towel across the top of your clubs to help keep them dry, and hang another towel under your umbrella—which should have a spread of at least 58 inches and be of sturdy construction so it will hold up under strong winds and driving rain.

Just as staying dry is paramount in wet weather, when the temperatures drop you want to do whatever you can to keep warm. It's especially important to keep your hands warm so you can maintain feel for as long as possible.

For cold weather it's a good idea to pack an extra sweater and, if it's raining, a second woolen cap to prevent the heat from escaping. A hand warmer is also a good investment if you play a fair amount of golf in chilly temperatures.

13

How to Think Your Way to Lower Scores

Y ou can have the most technically perfect swing in the world and still post high scores round after round.

You can also have a beautiful putting stroke and a sound short game and still be a high-handicapper. Why?

Because if you don't know how to control your emotions and think your way around a golf course, the chances are you'll never get to the level you deserve for all the hard work that you've done to improve your skills.

Ben Crenshaw, the captain of the 1999 United States Ryder Cup Team, was once mired in a frustrating slump. He was swinging well and, of course, his putting was always a saving grace in his game. A writer asked Ben what was keeping him from winning again.

Ben Crenshaw once said that the most important distance in golf is the area between the ears—where you do your thinking.

"I'm this close," he said, holding his hands about six inches apart and then moving them to either side of his head. "Unfortunately, this is the most crucial distance in golf."

Another testimonial to the importance of mental strength in the golf game came in 1971, when Bobby Jones died following a long, degenerative battle with syringomyelia, a disease that slowly wasted his body. Upon learning of his death, Ben Hogan said: "Bob Jones was sick for so long, and in fighting so hard to live, he finally revealed his greatest strength to us. It was his strength of mind."

Now clearly, few of us will ever approach the sort of mental toughness possessed by the likes of a Bobby Jones, Ben Hogan or Jack Nicklaus, just to name three players who excelled in this crucial part of the game. But there are disciplines we can all develop to help us manage both our emotions and our golf games. That will be the goal of this chapter.

HOW'S YOUR SELF-IMAGE?—One reason for Tiger Woods's phenomenal success is that, even from an early age, he came to believe that he was a very special golfer, destined for greatness. Part of this was certainly instilled by his parents, particularly his father. Once he began experiencing success, it only fueled his confidence. He won the U.S. Junior Amateur three times, then went on to win the U.S. Amateur three times before becoming a professional. To no one's surprise, that pattern of success has continued on a pace that will rank him as one of the game's greatest players, since he is already the only player to ever hold all four major professional titles at the same time.

Former PGA Champion Lanny Wadkins, who won 21 tournaments on the PGA Tour, was once asked if he was surprised that he enjoyed so much success as a professional.

"Not at all," Wadkins said. "Because I had won at every level as a junior and as an amateur."

No one ever claimed that Lanny Wadkins lacked for a positive self-image, and the same is undoubtedly true for virtually every other successful golfer.

But while an overall positive self-image is important, it can also go a long way toward improving specific areas of weakness in your golf game. Take the case of Sam Snead.

By any standard, Snead was one of the greatest players in the game's history, yet curiously enough, he never won the U.S. Open. There may be any number of reasons for this, but the one that he gives the most credence is his *belief* that he couldn't putt the lightning-fast greens at the Open.

"I'd get on those greens and I'd be squeezing the rubber right out of the grip," he said once in a discussion with Dr. Cary Middlecoff and some other golfers. "I was all right on the long putts, but no one ever missed more short putts than I did."

Even from an early age, Tiger Woods believed he was destined for greatness as a golfer.

"Sam," Doc replied, logically enough. "No one ever had more short putts than you did."

The point is that in his own mind, Sam didn't believe he could handle the greens, and therefore lacked the confidence to be effective. His was a self-fulfilling prophecy.

The lesson in all this is fairly straightforward: If you have a weakness in your game, you must identify it and work with your PGA Professional to correct it. Once you have, however, the next step is to test yourself and prove that you are proficient in that element of your game.

Talk yourself into success—If there is one key quality that all champions have in common, it is fundamental optimism. They simply believe in themselves and their ability to perform. They are like Larry Bird, who always wanted to take the last shot in the closing seconds of a tight basketball game, or a pitcher like Roger Clemens who wants to start in the final game of the World Series.

Can you imagine players like Jack Nicklaus or Tom Watson berating themselves over a poor shot or even thinking for a nanosecond that they couldn't pull off a shot, no matter how difficult? Of course not.

Many sport psychologists argue that you can actually use the strength of your mind to improve weak areas in your game. For starters, you can eliminate negative thoughts by reviving positive memories.

Let's say you're playing a match in the club championship and on one of the closing holes you hit your approach shot into a greenside bunker. Instead of berating yourself for hitting a poor approach or bemoaning the fact that you're not a good bunker player, try this: As you approach the green, try to recall instances when you hit good bunker shots. Visualize how you played the shot, and actually try to get a mental image of yourself playing the shot. This may give you the confidence you need to play the shot successfully.

A classic case reflecting the power of positive thinking was Tom Watson's memorable pitch shot on the 71st hole of the 1982 U.S. Open at Pebble Beach. His tee shot on the par 3 carried into the deep, thick rough behind the green. As they studied the shot his caddie, Bruce Edwards, said, "Get it close."

"Get it close?" Watson said. "We're going to make it."

And he did.

Of course, there's no real substitute for experience. Any good player will tell you that the more often you play a shot under pressure, the more comfortable you become and, therefore, the better your chances of success.

A textbook example of this was Ben Hogan's dramatic 1-iron approach to the 18th green in the final round of the 1950 U.S. Open at Merion. Hogan needed to make a par 4 to get into a playoff with Lloyd Mangrum and George Fazio. Under tremendous pressure, he striped a 1-iron onto the green and two-putted, going on to win the following day.

After his round, a writer asked Hogan how he was able to play the shot as calmly as he did.

"Because I've been playing it every day in practice," Hogan said.

LEARN HOW TO CONCENTRATE—Concentration means different things to different people, but for the past several decades Ben Hogan's ability to totally focus on the job at hand has stood as the ideal they have tried to emulate—probably to their great detriment.

It was said that Hogan had the ability to focus his concentration with laserlike precision. In truth, while he possessed considerable discipline and powers of concentration, his real gift was in knowing how to shut himself off from any distractions. A good example is this advice he gave to 1948 Masters Champion Claude Harmon.

Harmon was the longtime PGA Professional at Winged Foot Golf Club, the site of the 1959 U.S. Open. On the eve of that Open, Hogan gave Harmon, a close friend, some advice.

"Claude, your problem is that you play 'happy' golf," Hogan said. "You can't do that if you want to have any chance at Winged Foot. Everyone is going to want to shake your hand and wish you good luck. What you've got to do is just keep your head down and don't make eye contact with anyone. Just concentrate on your game."

Harmon was an affable man by nature, and the thought of ignoring his friends and other members was difficult for him. Still, he gave it his best shot.

"It almost killed old Claude," Sam Snead recalled. "At Winged Foot, there's a long walk between the ninth and the 10th tee, and it goes right by the clubhouse. Those members would be out there calling to him: "Hey, Claude," "Good luck, pro." Claude would just walk along, looking at the ground. Finally, after about three rounds he couldn't take it anymore." He finished tied for third with Mike Souchak, behind the winner, Billy Casper, and Bob Rosburg.

The real secret to concentration doesn't lie in trying to isolate yourself from the world for the length of the round. No one—no, not even Ben Hogan—could really do that. The best thing you can do is learn how to vary your focus, as well as carve the round up into periods of narrowed concentration.

On the face of things, Lee Trevino would appear to be the polar opposite of Ben Hogan when it comes to methods of concentration, but in truth, Trevino's approach makes the most sense for the majority of golfers.

By his own admission, Trevino's chattering and wisecracking helped him relax, particularly when the pressure increased. One year he was paired with the late Davis Love Jr. in the final round of a tournament. As they left the first tee Love, who was a quiet man, said to Trevino, "Lee, I'm just as nervous as I can be. If it's all the same to you, I won't be doing much talking today."

"That's okay, Davis," Trevino said. "I'll do enough talking for both of us."

While Trevino might talk and joke on his way to the ball, once he reached it he became deadly serious. The joking stopped. He carefully studied his shot and his options. He studied the lie and the wind and factored in all the other considerations. Once he decided what type of shot he was going to play, his focus sharpened even further and shifted to actually playing the shot. At that point, his concentration was absolute.

By copying Trevino's approach, you achieve the maximum concentration at the *appropriate* time. That is the key.

One of the late Harvey Penick's favorite and most quoted pieces of advice to his pupils was "Take dead aim." In a very real sense, what he was talking about was focusing your concentration.

It might be useful to approach concentration as a three-stage process, much as Trevino does.

In the first stage, there really is no need to concentrate on the game. Instead, use the time when you are between shots to relax and enjoy yourself. Talk with your friends or caddie. Take time to appreciate the beauty of the course. This is a time when you can refresh yourself and recharge your powers of concentration.

As you approach your ball, you move to the second stage of concentration. Your focus shifts to the shot you're facing. How is your life? What is the wind doing? Where is the trouble that you must avoid? What sort of shot do you feel comfortable playing? Once you've absorbed all the relevant information, you move to the third stage, and your focus becomes total.

In the 30 seconds or so that you are in stage-three concentration, you've selected the club you plan to hit, visualized the shot and even visualized your swing or an element of your swing by concentrating on one (or at the most two) swing thoughts. Do not let any negative thoughts linger in your mind. Be positive at all times.

If, for any reason, your concentration lapses or doubts enter your mind, don't be afraid to step away from the ball. If you lose confidence or your concentration is broken, your chances of hitting the shot properly are greatly reduced.

Billy Casper, a former Masters and U.S. Open Champion, was almost fanatical about this. If he was distracted when preparing to play his shot, he'd step away from the ball, put the club back in the bag, and begin his pre-shot routine again.

You might think that's excessive, but Doug Sanders would probably disagree.

In the 1970 British Open at St. Andrews, Sanders faced a putt of some two feet that would give him a one-stroke victory over Jack Nicklaus. Sanders addressed his putt and then, at the last moment, bent down to remove something from the line of the putt. Without repeating his pre-shot routine, he settled back over the ball and stroked his putt. It missed, and the next day Nicklaus beat him in an 18-hole playoff.

LEARNING TO RELAX—This may be difficult to believe, but learning to relax in the course of a round—especially as the pressure builds—is a crucial element of concentration. There are certain things that everyone can do that will help them relax.

The first thing is remember to breathe. When 1993 PGA Champion Paul Azinger was learning to play, his friend, who was a former boxer, repeatedly stressed this to him. Tom Watson got the same advice from Byron Nelson.

"Byron noticed that I tend to do things pretty quickly by nature,"

Watson has explained. "I tend to walk quickly, not linger over shots, and the pace of my swing is fairly quick. All that was fine with Byron, as long as I remembered to really breathe. If you don't get enough oxygen, you can't think clearly."

This is particularly true when you are facing a very difficult shot under pressure. As you stand behind the ball visualizing your shot, take a deep breath and slowly exhale. Most people will find this helps settle their nerves.

A great many players find music helps them relax between shots. Former British Open Champion Peter Thomson thinks of his favorite classical music. Sam Snead and Jack Nicklaus favor waltzes. Fuzzy Zoeller whistles softly. Pick a favorite, rhythmic piece and try humming it as you walk between shots—this also helps you slow the pace of your walking, which will help you relax as well.

The great Walter Hagen often advised people to "stop and smell the roses along the way," and that is excellent advice for golfers in the course of their rounds. How often have you seen photos of players at Pebble Beach gazing out over Carmel Bay? Tom Watson and Jack Nicklaus come to mind, and no one is more intense than they are on the course.

Golf courses are among the most beautiful places on earth. Take advantage of the opportunity you have to share in that beauty.

"Don't forget to breathe" was advice a former boxer gave to Paul Azinger when he was just starting to compete in tournaments. It is a key to playing well under pressure.

BE KIND TO YOURSELF—Golf is challenging enough without beating yourself up over a missed putt or a poor shot. With that in mind, here are some suggestions that can help you stay on an even keel. After all, when you get frustrated and/or angry, it's almost impossible to think clearly and rationally.

1. **Play one shot at a time.** Don't worry about the shot you just played or others you will be facing. "It isn't very original to say that golf is played one shot at a time," Bobby Jones once said. "But it did take me many years to realize this was true."

2. **Accept poor shots.** "I always figured I was going to hit six or seven poor shots in a round, so when I did hit one it didn't bother me," Walter Hagen explained. Tommy Armour took Hagen one step further. "The low-handicap player only hits between five and 10 truly good shots in a round. The rest are just good misses."

3. **Don't compare yourself to others.** Set realistic goals for your game and your round, and only judge yourself against those goals. Also, keep in mind that everyone has bad days when things don't go their way.

4. **Never complain, never explain.** One of the truest statements in golf is that "every shot makes someone happy." If it's a good shot you've played, you're pleased. If it's a poor shot, your opponents are relieved.

5. **Be realistic.** Don't hold yourself to arbitrary or unreasonable standards. If you used to play to a low handicap but don't have the time to practice, it's unreasonable to expect to play as well as you once did. You only get out of your game what you put into it.

6. **Keep the game in perspective.** Win or lose, score well or poorly, in the end, golf is still a game. After Jack Nicklaus lost to Tom Watson in their dramatic duel in the 1977 British Open at Turnberry, his friend Ken Bowden met him and said he'd understand if Nicklaus didn't want company for dinner. "Heavens, Ken, it's just a game. Of course we'll have dinner." If Jack Nicklaus can have that attitude after losing the British Open, none of us should be too hard on ourselves.

7. **Be patient.** Golf is a game of ebb and flow, good breaks and bad breaks. The most successful players are those who minimize their mistakes and wait for their opportunities.

8. **Have a game plan.** Know what holes you can reasonably expect to score well on and which require you to play defensively. When Raymond Floyd won the 1986 U.S. Open at Shinnecock Hills, he said simply, "I had a game plan and I didn't deviate from it once in the entire tournament."

9. **Trust your strengths.** Harvey Penick used to tell his students that "plain vanilla isn't too bad." In other words, if you have a bread-and-butter shot, stick with it. Don't try a shot you're uncomfortable with unless it's absolutely necessary—and never try a shot you haven't worked on in practice.

10. **Remember that everyone else is in the same boat.** If you're feeling the pressure in a tournament, try to keep in mind that everyone else is feeling it as well. This is particularly important if you are playing in difficult weather conditions. If you are playing in wind, cold or rain, shut your game down and try to play as conservatively as possible. Remember that par is a number that is relative to the conditions.

Last but certainly not least, it's vitally important to set realistic goals based upon your skill level. If you are a legitimate 14-handicapper, it's not realistic to think you're going to break par. If you delude yourself into thinking you will, you will reach your frustration level very early in the round.

Two-time U.S. Open Champion and Captain of the 2001 United States Ryder Cup Team Curtis Strange was once asked what his greatest strength was.

"I don't kid myself," he said.

Neither should you.

14

Making the Most of Your Practice Time

Gary Player, one of just five players—along with Gene Sarazen, Ben Hogan, Jack Nicklaus and Tiger Woods—to win the career professional Grand Slam, is fond of saying that the harder he works, the luckier he gets—and he must be a very lucky player because he's a very hard worker.

Now it's not realistic to expect to be able to practice as much as a Gary Player or any other professional, but you can learn to make the most productive use of your practice time.

One of the first keys to improving is practicing properly, as veteran PGA Professional Bob Toski is constantly reminding people.

"Practice doesn't make perfect," he has often said. "Perfect practice makes perfect."

But if you do it incorrectly, practice also makes permanent.

That's one very good reason for you to work closely with your PGA Professional to determine what elements of your game need the most work and what specific drills, exercises and corrections will help you correct your flaws and lower your scores. No matter how talented a player you are, trying to diagnose and correct the problems in your game without a coach is an invitation for trouble. It's like trying to diagnose what ails you and then prescribing the proper medication—or worse, performing surgery on yourself.

One of the biggest drawbacks to improvement is human nature itself. Even though almost all of us realize that we should concentrate our practice time on those areas of our game that are the weakest, invariably we

It's a good idea to take notes and review your instructor's corrections.

wind up spending our time doing what we do best. The best examples of this are players who are talented shotmakers but average putters. What do you suppose they wind up practicing when they go to the course? More often than not, shaping one beautiful shot after another. Putting is an afterthought—if that.

Here's a simple approach to determining what percentage of your practice time should be devoted to the different elements of your game: Keep a chart of your game. In other words, after every round write down in a notebook how many times you hit your driver, fairway woods, long, middle and short irons and wedges, and how accurate you were with each club. Also keep track of the number of times you chipped or pitched the ball, hit bunker shots (both long and short), and the number of putts you took. Pay particular attention to the number of times you three-putted greens, noting whether this was caused by a poor approach putt or by missing a short second putt.

Do this for several rounds and you will see a distinct pattern emerge. You'll not only see clearly what your strengths and weaknesses really are, but also where you take the most strokes—and if you are like the majority of golfers, you'll discover that area is in the short game, which also happens to be the area that most people neglect when practicing. As a general rule, at least half of everyone's practice time should be devoted to the short game, whether they are a scratch golfer or a high-handicapper.

Develop a Plan for Practice

Here's where working with your PGA Professional can really pay off in lower scores. Once you've completed accurately charting your game, sit down with your PGA Professional and interpret the results. Your instructor may see trends in the results that aren't immediately apparent to you and this will help you focus your practice on the areas of your game that *really* need work.

Your next step will be to establish a practice routine that realistically fits your schedule and your true desire to improve. This routine will include focusing on your long and short games, specific areas that need attention (such as playing from bunkers), physical conditioning, course management (playing lessons are a valuable learning device that your coach may use) and the mental side of the game.

When developing a practice schedule, keep in mind that practice is far more effective when done over relatively short periods of time as opposed to long, grueling hours spent simply pounding ball after ball on the practice tee.

A good time to practice is immediately following a lesson, since the instruction you received from your PGA Professional is fresh in your mind. You not only *know* what you were taught, but can *feel* it as well. Another good time to practice is immediately following a round since this is a time when you've just identified a current problem in your game. Once you (and your PGA Professional) have fixed the problem to your satisfaction, call it a day.

Just as there are good times to practice, there are certainly times when practice becomes counterproductive.

For example, when you become physically tired, it's time to put the clubs away. Why? Because practice when you are tired can cause you to ingrain errors in your swing or putting stroke, creating poor shots and a lack of confidence. Whenever possible, you want to end your practice sessions on a positive note.

And just as you can become physically tired, if you are truly concentrating on the job at hand, you can become mentally exhausted as well. Generally, you can tell this is occurring when you lose interest or your mind wanders. Keep in mind that during a practice session, just as when you're on the golf course, you should focus intently on every shot or putt. Have a plan for every shot and visualize it from beginning to end. If you have trouble staying focused, write down all of your interfering thoughts, then see how they can be eliminated (e.g., hunger, etc).

"I never hit a shot, whether in practice or during a round, that I don't have a very clear, focused picture of it in my head," Jack Nicklaus has said on many occasions.

Neither should you.

There are two schools of thought concerning practicing in poor weather. The first argues that you should avoid it, since it can lead to poor concentration and mechanical errors that you will need to correct. The second school argues that since you are inevitably going to play in difficult conditions, you need to practice in order to prepare for them. The logical, compromise approach seems to be to practice sparingly in poor conditions.

Finally, there are days when you will be frustrated by your lack of progress. This happens to all players. Take the long-term view that by getting better in small steps, your overall game improves.

Keeping Practice Interesting

One way to keep practice interesting is to challenge yourself with inner-directed competitions. For example, here are some games you can play that will help you maintain your focus throughout your practice sessions.

SET GOALS—No matter what part of your game you are working on, you will realize greater success if you set specific numerical goals for yourself. For example, rather than simply hitting putt after putt on the practice green, say

PGA Professionals can often identify problems that can be traced to faulty or ill-fitting equipment.

to yourself, "I'm not going to leave until I make five three-footers in a row from all sides of the cup." Then vary the number and distance. Or if you struggle with right-to-left breaking putts, do the same thing with them. The same holds true with bunker shots: Keep practicing until you can successfully execute a specific number of shots from the sand. And you can do this with every club in the bag. Is driving the ball into play a problem? Then pick an area 35–45 yards wide and set a goal that you will drive five balls in a row into that driving area. The width of the landing area and number of balls you hit into it will vary according to your skill level, but the idea remains the same.

Here's one other thought to keep in mind: When hitting balls on the practice range, set the balls far enough away so that you must take at least a few moments between shots. This will give you time to think between shots rather than simply pounding one ball after another into the distance. Try to make your practice like playing a round, by changing clubs and targets with each shot.

PLAY A ROUND ON THE PRACTICE RANGE—The danger of hitting balls on the practice range is that it doesn't mirror the realities of a round of golf. To solve this, work your way through your bag, just as you would during a round. In other words, if during a round of golf at your usual course you hit a driver and a 6-iron on the first hole, then do the same thing on the practice tee. If the next hole is a long par 5, hit your driver, a fairway wood and a short iron, and so on. And you should be realistic, so every now and again, hit a lob shot, just as you would if you missed a green. If you are an accomplished player, you should also try to shape shots, since this will give you the confidence to either fade or draw the ball into the fairway or the green. The point of this exercise is not only to help you hit the necessary shots on the course, but also to keep you mentally sharp during your practice session.

While you're at it, try as much as possible to key your practice to your playing experience. For example, Gardner Dickinson once noticed that Ben Hogan would frequently end his practice sessions by hitting 3- or 4-woods and asked Hogan why. Hogan told Gardner that when he grew tired toward the end of a round, he hit poor (by his considerable standards) shots with his fairway woods. He felt that the best way to fix this was to hit those clubs at the end of his practice sessions when he was tiring.

Here's one other suggestion: When you are warming up prior to your round, just before you leave the practice tee, hit three or four shots with the club you plan to use on the first tee—and whenever possible, make the last shot you hit a good one, since this will give you a little added confidence to help settle those first-tee nerves.

PLAY "CALL SHOTS"—This is a game you can play with a friend, and it will help both of you improve. If you played basketball as a kid, you probably played a game called "Horse." The game went something like this: The player who has the honor picks his or her shot, let's say a jump shot from 15 feet. If that player makes the basket, the other players have to follow. If they miss, they get a letter, beginning with "H." The last player to spell horse wins. In "Call Shots," the player with the honor calls the shot, say a fade with a 5-iron to a target 170 yards down the practice range. The player who comes closest to the target, while hitting the correctly shaped shot, wins a point. This game will not only help you keep mentally focused during your practice time, but will also help correct any weaknesses in your shotmaking, because your opponent will almost certainly call shots that play to your weaknesses.

PLAY YOUR "WORST-BALL"—This is a great way to practice if you can find a time when the course isn't crowded, perhaps in the early evening. Play two balls, but always play your next shot from the worst position of the two. For example, if one drive lands in the fairway but the other stops behind a stand of trees, play the ball that's in trouble. This will be a challenging form of practice and will help you develop confidence in your ability to scramble when in trouble.

Drills and Practice Devices

Perhaps no other sport lends itself to the use of drills and practice devices to the extent that golf does. This is true, in no small part, because PGA Professionals and their pupils focus so intently upon improvement. Drills and practice devices offer positive reinforcement for the points made on the lesson tee and practice green.

Before trying any drill, it's important to consult your PGA Professional to make sure that the specific drill is designed to help solve your particular problem. If it isn't, you may wind up with a cure that's worse than the problem. Once you do agree on a drill or series of drills, this can be enormously beneficial for a number of reasons.

First, a good drill properly executed will quickly help replace a bad habit with a good one, often by instilling the feeling of a proper address or in-swing position or motion or sensation (feel). More precisely, it allows you and your PGA Professional to focus on the specific part of your body or swing that needs attention. Finally, to focus on the positive side of your game (which is often overlooked) allows you to reinforce elements that you are doing correctly.

Another value of drills goes back to a point we made earlier. Golfers, like all human beings, are creatures of habit. Under the stress of competition or when we tire late in a round, we naturally fall back on our bad habits or

Starting pace drill

swing faults. When this happens, it is very helpful to have a drill you can fall back on to get you on an even keel. For that reason, we strongly suggest that you carry a notebook that contains both your tendencies and the drill or drills that can help you correct the problem quickly, often in mid-round.

While the value of a drill targeted specifically to your needs by a PGA Professional is indisputable, the value of learning aids is a dicier matter. Without question, there is no other sport that inspires such a collection of gadgets that promise to "(1) add 50 yards to your drives; (2) correct your slice; (3) make you the second coming of Ben Crenshaw on the greens; (4) all of the above and so much more, all for three easy payments of $19.95. Send your check or money order today." If you doubt this for a second, just turn on your television early on any Sunday morning, when the advertisements and infomercials for practice aids are rivaled only by weight-reduction miracles and machines designed to give you abs of steel.

Before spending a dime on any of these would-be cure-alls, we can't stress enough the importance of consulting with your PGA Professional to judge whether what the aid promises to fix is something that you actually need to cure; whether it lives up to its claims; it is reliable and properly manufactured; it is easy to use and cost-effective. If you can't answer yes to most or all of these questions, the only thing your purchase may improve is someone else's profit-and-loss statement.

Off-Course Practice

Ben Hogan may not have invented practicing but he certainly deserves credit for helping make it as popular as it is today. Hogan once famously said that there weren't enough hours in the day for him to devote to practice, and that's certainly true for the majority of golfers who have to schedule their practice time around work, school or other important responsibilities.

But just because you can't get to the course doesn't mean you can't arrange to squeeze in some quality practice time. Here are some suggestions:

AT HOME—Your home is a wonderful place to work on your game. For starters, if you have a large enough yard, you can hit balls into a net. Even if that's isn't possible, just making practice swings is a good idea. Work on your swing mechanics at a slow speed. This will build strength in your golf muscles, and help build a repeating swing. Even with limited space, you can probably find a place to practice chipping and pitching, and if you have a carpet that's fairly close-cropped, you can also practice your putting stroke. Another good idea is to have your PGA Professional cut down a club so that you can refine your grip while watching television. There are also practice devices with grips that are molded to help you fit your hands in a standard position. Again, you should check with your PGA Professional to make sure that these hand positions reflect the proper grip for you. When it comes to gripping the golf club, one style certainly does not fit all.

Another wonderful means of practice is the use of video. Not only is the equipment more affordable and easy to use, but it is becoming increasingly sophisticated in terms of features such as computer-generated models and motion analysis. There is a wide variety of commercial videos dealing with every facet of the game, and PGA Professionals have welcomed this technology as a way of enhancing their instruction. By reviewing videos of their lessons, pupils can accurately focus on those specific areas where they need to improve.

While video instruction tends to get the most attention, don't overlook audio-tapes, particularly those that focus on the psychological elements of the game. With so many golfers commuting by car to work or on errands, audio instruction can be a tremendously valuable tool in your attempts to improve. Also, don't be shy about asking your PGA Professional to record the key instruction points of your lessons on video or audio so that you can review them at your leisure.

AT THE FITNESS CENTER—Now we get to the heart of the matter: Just how serious are you about improving? Of the thousands of golfers who are willing to work long and hard on the practice tee and putting green, only a slender percentage are willing to commit to a regimen of health and fitness, even today, when those are increasingly important concerns for people of every age group. Today's professional golfers and top amateurs are diligent about staying in shape, because they know it is a vital element in their quest for lower and more consistent scoring. Some fitness facilities, such as HealthSouth, which operates a facility at the PGA Learning Center, can test you for golf-specific fitness and then recommend a conditioning program.

If you are committed to improving your golf (and your quality of life) you would be well-advised to seek out a sports-medicine physician and a fitness trainer and have them design a program of exercise and diet that will not only increase your golf strength but also your endurance. This is especially important if you find that you lose energy (and therefore, concentration) late in your rounds, causing your scores to rise over the closing holes.

THE MIND GAME—Former Ryder Cup Captain Ben Crenshaw once joked that he was "this close to playing well." As he said this, he held his hands about six inches apart and placed them on either side of his head. "Unfortunately, these are the most crucial inches in golf." There's no question that one element that makes golf so challenging is that it is as much a mental challenge as it is a physical test. Witness this story told by former British Open Champion Tom Weiskopf.

"I was playing a practice round at Colonial one year with Ben Hogan and another player from Ben's era," Weiskopf recalled. "I won't use the guy's name but he was a strong player, maybe one of the best shotmakers who ever lived. Anyway, we're watching him hit one beautiful shot after another and finally Ben turns to me and says, 'If we could screw another head onto [his] body, he'd be the greatest golfer who ever lived.'"

There are many stories dating back to World War II that testify to the role that imagination can play in maintaining a solid golf game—and emotional well-being—even under the most desperate circumstances. The most dramatic examples are those of British and American prisoners of war. Several of these prisoners were fine and avid golfers prior to the war and occupied their time in prison by mentally playing rounds of golf over their favorite courses. Others would use imagination to design courses. What made these stories so extraordinary was that almost immediately upon their return home, they resumed playing with no appreciable loss in skill.

A similar, if less dramatic, testimonial to the power of mental imaging is told by Hall of Famer Sam Snead.

"Even from the beginning, when I was just hitting balls with an old swamp maple limb, I'd get a picture of each shot in my mind before I hit it," Sam recalls. "Then I started thinking that I might be able to imagine an entire round. I used to do this at Augusta, because I knew the old girl so well. The night before a round at the Masters, I'd lie in bed, close my eyes, and imagine every single shot and putt in a perfect round. It didn't work every time, but I do think it helped more often than not."

Working on the psychological parts of your game, like concentrating on the health and fitness elements, may not be as exciting as fine-tuning your full swing, but the results can be every bit as dramatic when you tally your score at the end of a round.

Conclusion

There's no question that the cornerstone of any improvement you hope to make must be an intelligent practice regime that includes both the full swing and the various elements of the short game, health and fitness, and a determined focus on the mental side of the game.

Furthermore, it is vitally important that your odds of improvement are greatly increased if you work with a PGA Professional who knows both your strengths and weaknesses, and also which approach to learning is best for you. In addition, your PGA Professional will also recognize how large a commitment to practice your schedule will realistically allow and, therefore, determine what is a realistic program for you, given your ability, desire and availability.

For these reasons, we also strongly suggest that once you find a PGA Professional you are comfortable with and have confidence in, you stick with that person and resist the temptation to listen to the advice of others, no matter how well intentioned or well qualified. Building a swing or short game—or correcting a problem—is often a process that evolves over time and requires making a series of small changes that build upon each other. For example, you may have a problem slicing the ball because your swing shape is such that the clubhead strikes the ball from outside the target line with an open clubface. A friend may give you advice to get you to change your swing path, without noticing that the root cause of the problem is a faulty grip that must be corrected before any other changes can be made.

A classic case in point is Ben Crenshaw, who came out on Tour as one of the game's brightest new stars and then went into a mysterious and confusing slump. Since everyone loved Ben, everyone was eager to give him advice, and he was so nice he listened to them and only grew more baffled.

Finally, he returned home to Austin, Texas, and sought out Harvey Penick, the legendary teacher who had taught Ben to play as a child and had nurtured his game throughout his amateur career. The two went to the practice tee at Austin Country Club and Mr. Penick watched Ben hit a few balls and then told him to stop.

"Don't ever wait this long to come see me," the gentle Mr. Penick said sternly.

With that, he made a couple minor changes and Ben Crenshaw was back on form and on his way to winning his first of two Masters.

One final thought on the importance of practice: In golf, you only get out of the game what you put into it. Period.

Of all the millions of words ever spoken about the game, no truer words than those were ever spoken.

Questions and Answers

Q: *I was watching a golf telecast and one of the commentators said that good players never practice into a left-to-right wind. Is that true, and if it is, why?*

A: By and large, it's true that they try and avoid this if possible. The reason is that the wind blows your weight toward your toes, and in fighting to stay balanced, you may develop bad habits.

Q: *I'd like to bring one club to my office, because sometimes I can go out to a nearby practice facility and hit balls during my lunch hour. Which club should I take?*

A: We're tempted to say your putter, since putting accounts for such a large percentage of the strokes you take per round. But if we had to pick a club for hitting full shots, we'd suggest this: Why not take a 5-iron, because it's a club that is relatively easy to fade or draw the ball with, as well as hit it on a high or low trajectory. Having said that, we suggest that you alternate hitting the 5-iron for a few days and then switch to a pitching wedge or sand wedge to work on your short game.

Q: *I love to practice, but as I've gotten into my 50s, I've noticed that after hitting balls for any period of time, I develop unbelievable pain in my elbows. How can I prevent this?*

A: First, you should check with your doctor, but it sounds like tendinitis or "Golfer's Elbow." This is caused by repetitive stress. Many people who do the same thing over and over, such as typists, develop this. It can be treated with medication, but the simple solution may be to scale back on practicing your full swings and work a bit more on your putting, chipping and pitching, since these are less stressful. There are also bands that you can place around your forearms to help reduce the stress on your elbows, but again, our first suggestion is to check with your doctor.

Q: *I try to focus very intently whenever I play or practice. I try to block everything out, even to the point of isolating myself at the far end of the practice range or going to the course late in the day when there are fewer people around. The problem is that I simply cannot focus that intensely for a long period of time, and I become frustrated. Any suggestions?*

A: The history of golf is filled with stories about players who had the remarkable ability to totally shut themselves off from the outside world during a round. One such story concerned Ben Hogan and Claude Harmon in the final round of the 1948 Masters. Harmon made a hole-in-one on the treacherous par-3 12th hole. As they were walking off the green Hogan, who was keeping score for Harmon, asked his friend what he made on the hole.

"Why, Ben, I made an ace," an astonished Harmon said.

"Oh," said Hogan, marking it down on the scorecard.

Another story involved Joyce Wethered, who was playing in the 1920 English Women's Championship. As she prepared to hit the putt that would give her the victory, a freight train roared past on the adjacent rail line. Wethered was unfazed and calmly ran in the putt. Later, her opponent, Cecil Leitch, asked her if the train hadn't bothered her.

"What train?" she asked.

The truth is, total concentration of this type is extremely rare and almost impossible to sustain. A much better approach is to divide the round into 30-second moments of concentration for each shot. Prepare your shot as you approach the ball and judge what type of shot the conditions require you to play. Once you've made the decision, then go into your cocoon of concentration as you address the ball and play the shot. This approach allows you to concentrate when you need to, while keeping you from becoming mentally exhausted.

Q: *I'm a low-handicap golfer and strike the ball fairly consistently, but I seem to have a problem determining just how far I hit each club. I hit to target greens on our practice range but then when I get to the course, I've noticed that the ball doesn't carry the same distance it did on the range.*

A: The answer may be that the practice balls you hit on the range are designed for durability and probably have a thicker cover than the balls you play with during a round of golf and, therefore, will fly at different distances and trajectories. To better gauge how far you hit each club, take a dozen balls that you usually play with and number them from one to 12. If you can find an isolated spot on the course, hit the balls, noting which you hit solidly and which you hit either thin or fat. Then go out and pace off the distance to the majority of balls, discounting those that were mis-hit. This will give you a far more accurate idea of just how far you hit each club than hitting balls on the range. Also, when doing this, bear in mind the wind (try to do this when the winds are calm), the humidity (the ball will carry slightly farther in dry conditions) and the dampness of the ground (ideally, you want to do this when the ground is soft, so that the ball won't run very far and you'll be able to determine how far you carry the ball with each club, which is the important distance you need to know). Knowing your average carry distance for each club will help you with your course management.

15

How to Get the Most Out of Lessons with Your Professional

The best way for any golfer to make sustained improvement is to develop a relationship with a qualified PGA Professional. This is true whether you are one of the world's best players or just beginning to play. But like anything else, there's a right way and a wrong way to take lessons and knowing the difference can make improvement a lot easier and more rewarding. Here are some guidelines that will help you get the most from your lessons.

1. **Set realistic goals**. So you want to be a scratch golfer? Who doesn't? But is that a realistic goal? Probably not right away, so the first thing the two of you need to do is set a realistic goal for your improvement. The first question you need to ask yourself is whether you're willing to commit the time and energy it takes to make a major improvement, or are you willing to settle for less improvement? Real improvement takes time, as this story from 1964 U.S. Open Champion Ken Venturi reveals.

   "I was an amateur living in San Francisco and working for a man named Eddie Lowrey, who had caddied for Francis Ouimet when he won the 1913 U.S. Open," Venturi recalled. "Eddie was a good friend of Byron Nelson and he arranged for Byron and me to play. I shot a 66 and was feeling pretty good about myself. After the round, I kept waiting for Byron to say something but he never did. Finally, I asked him what he thought of my game. He told me there were

Finding a teacher whose approach to instruction matches your approach to learning is a key to success.

three or four things we needed to work on. He asked me if I thought I would be able to change my grip. I said I thought I could and asked him how long the change would take. He told me it would take about six months before I was truly comfortable with the change and able to trust it under pressure."

If it takes a player of Ken Venturi's caliber this long to make a change—albeit a grip change which is one of the most difficult changes to make—it should give you some idea of the commitment real improvement can require.

2. **Seek out the proper instructor**. It's important to understand that people learn in three fundamental ways: auditory (through hearing), visually (through sight), and kinesthetically (through feel). Teachers will use your preferences in the way they teach. The first rule is to find a professional whom you respect and with whom you are comfortable. It is a testimonial to the late Harvey Penick that he could help forge two champions—Tom Kite and Ben Crenshaw—who have totally different approaches to learning. Kite is an analytical

person by nature who enjoys tinkering with his game and loves nothing more than spending hours on the practice tee or putting green. Crenshaw, on the other hand, is a totally feel player, who relies on his instincts and would much prefer playing to practicing.

3. **Get into golf shape**. Again, this gets back to the question of commitment, but the reality is the best instruction in the world won't do much good if your body isn't in good enough condition to execute a proper swing or make the delicate shots around the greens. This is especially true if it is early in the season and you've spent the winter months without touching a golf club.

    In different chapters of this book, we deal with specific exercise, strength training and stretching programs that can help get you into the proper condition to play your best golf, but the point we want to make here is that it is absolutely crucial that you get into reasonable condition if you hope to take full advantage of the hours you'll be spending on the lesson tee and practice ground.

    One final thought: Just as you shouldn't begin a round of golf without warming up your muscles properly, you shouldn't begin a lesson without having at least done some stretching exercises and having hit a few balls. This will help loosen your muscles and help focus your attention on the job at hand.

People learn in many different ways. Visual, auditory and kinesthetic methods are predominantly used in golf lessons. It's important you find a PGA Professional you feel comfortable with and whose teaching methods complement the way you learn.

4. **Have your equipment checked**. Very often a player's problems can be traced at least in part to either faulty equipment or clubs that are not properly fitted to a player. For example, a professional might be able to trace the cause of inconsistency to a shaft that is too stiff or a club that doesn't sit properly on the ground at address. The problem may even be something as simple as grips that are slick and worn, forcing you to hold the club too tightly. If your clubs don't fit you properly, your PGA Professional will work with you to find a set

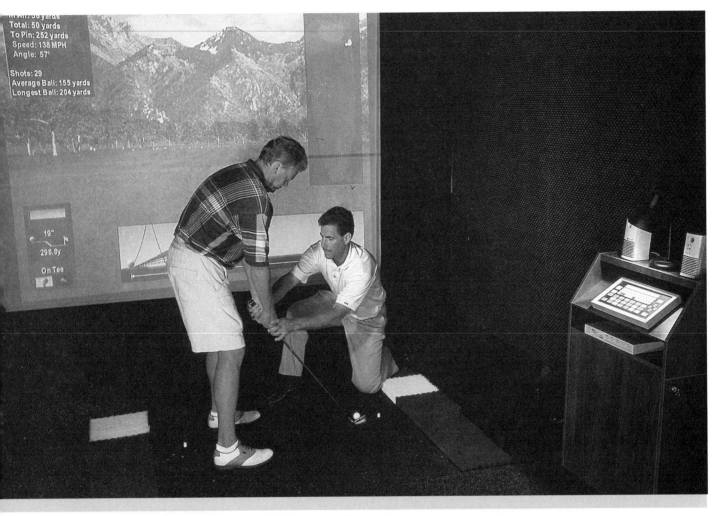

Total: 50 yards
To Pin: 252 yards
Speed: 138 MPH
Angle: 57°

Shots: 29
Average Ball: 155 yards
Longest Ball: 204 yards

19"

298.8y

On Tee

State-of-the-art technology can help your PGA Professional fit you with the proper equipment.

that meets your needs. Sometimes your Professional can make minor adjustments to your clubs to make them fit you properly. Remember, your grips should be cleaned after every few rounds with cleanser and hot water and replaced when showing wear. It's also a good idea to have the lies and lofts of your irons checked at least once a year, and more often if you are an avid golfer who plays and practices frequently.

5. **Stay patient and open to suggestions**. Very often the instruction you receive will be different from other ideas you may have heard or read before. That's why it's very important that you trust your instructor and go into the lesson with realistic goals. The truth is, it may take several lessons before you can see a noticeable improvement. If you try to make changes too fast, you might get worse before you begin to get better. More instruction and less change is the ideal situation.

6. **Know your weaknesses**. It's important to understand that people have a tendency to fall back into their old habits under pressure. This is just a simple fact of human nature. For example, if you tend to swing

too fast and get out of rhythm when you face a big shot or tough situation, you and your coach should recognize this tendency and work on ways to manage this weakness, especially under pressure. For example, one very good way of dealing with pressure is to have a simple, repeatable pre-shot routine that you can follow, since this will help eliminate doubt and help establish a rhythm that will carry into your actual swing. Former U.S. Open and Masters Champion Billy Casper is an excellent example of this. If he changed his mind about club

Identifying the weaknesses in your game and getting instruction to help correct the problems will usually result in lower scores.

selection or was distracted, he would go so far as to put his club back in the bag and begin his pre-shot routine all over again.

7. **Take notes**. No one's memory is infallible, so it's a good idea to take notes immediately after each lesson. You and your teacher should go over what you worked on, as well as your most common mistakes and what your teacher suggested to correct them. This will be more effective if you take advantage of videotape technology. Have your lessons videotaped to retain as a record of your progress—and to remind you of the areas you and your PGA Professional are working on. It's also a good idea to chart your rounds. Note how many fairways and greens you hit and how many putts you needed for your round. Also record how often you got up and down from greenside bunkers or when and where you missed the greens. Go over this information with your teacher before each les-

Keep in mind that there's a big difference between simply practicing and practicing intelligently. Your PGA Professional can help you learn the difference.

son. Look for your patterns. This will help him or her keep track of your progress as well as get an idea about which part of your game needs improvement.

8. **Practice intelligently**. Practice shouldn't be an endurance test. Simply beating balls for hours on end is not an effective way to practice. If you are making swing changes, take your time and concentrate on what you've been working on with your teacher. It's important to give yourself enough time to think between swings. Also, here's a plan that will help you get your new and improved game from the practice tee to the golf course, once you've made the necessary changes and are beginning to see positive results. Play a round on the practice tee. Begin by playing the first hole—actually visualize the hole and the ideal shot you want to play from the tee. Then move to the second shot and so on. This will sharpen your concentration and you'll be surprised how much it helps once you actually have to record a score.

9. **Don't overdo it**. The late Harvey Penick had a wonderful saying when it came to instruction: "An aspirin will probably cure what ails you but taking a whole bottle will kill you." His point was that you should avoid the temptation to exaggerate the changes your teacher suggests. For example, if your professional suggests you strengthen your grip and you begin hitting the ball more solidly, don't try to pick up an extra 10 yards by making your grip even stronger. Golf doesn't work that way.

10. **Have some fun**. Last but certainly not least, keep in mind that golf is a game and the point is to have fun. Keep in mind that improvement very rarely runs along a straight line. There will be ups and downs, good days and bad days, and frustration is a very big part of improving. Try to emulate Ben Hogan's attitude: "I used to love waking up in the morning because I looked forward to heading to the golf course to practice and play. I just loved trying to improve a little every day. That gave me the greatest pleasure of all."

16

10 Secrets to Match-Play Success

While the professional tours play stroke- or medal-play competitions week in and week out, for most amateur golfers, when they play with their friends on the weekend, they wind up playing some sort of friendly match, usually a nassau (see page 185) or individual match.

Indeed, if you look at the phenomenal popularity of the Ryder Cup Matches, you can make the case that it's based on people's desire to see the best players in the world going head-to-head in a match-play format.

Medal play is essentially conservative in nature because par is always a safe score, while soaring to a large number with a double bogey or worse can effectively shoot a good player out of an 18-hole tournament. It's just too difficult to recover from. But match play allows players to take far more risks because if a gamble fails, all you've lost is one hole—a temporary setback but one you usually can recover from.

Players are split over preference between match and medal play. Many prefer medal, arguing that the fairest way to determine the best player in any given tournament is 72 holes of medal play. Still others, like Sam Snead, far prefer match play because they relish the opportunity to face down an opponent. They just enjoy that added element of competition. That said, however, the best players—Bobby Jones comes immediately to mind—prefer 36-hole matches to 18-hole matches because they realize that over just 18 holes, a lesser player might get lucky—or elevate his or her game to a higher level—and beat a superior opponent.

While you still have to play good, solid golf to win in match play, here are some strategies that can help improve your chances.

1. **Play the course, not your opponent**. While you certainly want to be aware of how your opponent is playing and how the match stands, it's important to avoid the trap of getting swept up in the emotion of the match. And while you might want to beat your opponent into the ground and win by the largest possible margin, it's a waste of energy and focus to personalize the competition.

2. **Always play first**. Whenever possible, play first because if you hit a good shot, it will increase the pressure on your opponent and possibly force him or her to hit a poor shot. Walter Hagen, who won five PGA Championships at match play, would often start a game by hitting a 3-wood from the tee because while he might leave himself a slightly longer approach shot, by playing first he might get an edge over his opponent.

3. **Get the ball into the hole first**. Again, this is a way of increasing the pressure on your opponent. This also gives you the advantage of not having to worry about the putt you have left. You shouldn't rush your putt by any means, but do putt out if possible.

4. **Always assume the worst**. This might be the most important rule of match play. There's nothing that sets you back quicker than assuming you have a hole won, only to see your opponent pull off a miracle shot or sink an impossible putt. It's like a two-stroke swing in medal play: It gives your opponent a boost and sets you back. This doesn't mean you shouldn't be optimistic. Far from it. But you should always temper your optimism with a healthy dose of reality.

5. **Take it one shot at a time**. Just as in medal play, you have to try very hard to play one shot at a time. Don't dwell on the past, since you can't do anything about what has already happened. Don't start rehearsing your victory speech, either. When the time comes to play, concentrate on the shot at hand and only the shot at hand.

6. **Play to your par**. There's an old saying in match play: "Par is always a good score." The thinking is that over an 18-hole match in, say, a U.S. Amateur Championship, par will win more holes for you than it will lose. Now, depending on your handicap, par is the score you figure you need to shoot in order to win a hole. For higher-handicappers, "par" might be a bogey or even a double bogey. You may get to a point late in the match when you have to gamble, but establishing your par and sticking to the game plan that will allow you to match that number will win you more than your share of holes— and matches.

7. **Watch your opponent**. People are creatures of habit. But under pressure, they tend to get out of their routine. They walk faster. Or slower. They become indecisive over what shot to play or which club to use. The top professionals, on the other hand, always stay with their routine. For example, Tiger Woods will never hit a putt until he has sighted a tunnel for the line of his putt. That's why he so often

will study a putt with his hands cupping the bill of his cap. When you notice that your opponent is struggling or has gotten out of his or her routine, it's a golden opportunity to stay relaxed and try to increase the pressure even more.

8. **Don't look ahead**. There's a temptation when you are in front in a match to look ahead to the next round of the draw. This is especially true in the early rounds of a championship if you are favored to beat a less-accomplished player. The danger is that your concentration will slip and your opponent may be working especially hard to beat you.

9. **Study the Rules of Golf**. The Rules of Golf can be complicated and difficult to truly understand, but by knowing the rules, you know all your options and this can help you save strokes. Jack Nicklaus, for example, used to read the Rules of Golf cover-to-cover before the start of every season. It's especially important to understand how the rules differ in medal- and match-play situations.

10. **Never give up**. It's a simple truth that in match play, it's never over until it's over. You may pull off a miracle shot or your opponent may surprise you and miss a relatively simple shot and let you back in the hole—or even the match. Golf is simply too difficult and unpredictable to ever take anything for granted.

Some Tips for Team Play

Again, just as most weekend golfers compete in some form of match play, it's also true that they usually team with a partner in their matches. There are no absolute rules about what make a good partnership—a lot simply comes down to two personalities that happen to get along, and their games benefit from that congeniality. That said, however, there are some guidelines that will help produce more successful partnerships.

1. **Opposites attract**. If you tend to be long but somewhat wild off the tee, you'll benefit from pairing with a player who, while not quite as long off the tee, knows how to keep the ball in play.

2. **Safety first**. Whenever possible, get a ball safely in play or on the green. This allows the other member of the team to take a calculated gamble and try to hit a long drive or shoot at a dangerous pin placement.

3. **Pair with a putter who has a similar style**. There are basically two styles of putters: those who like to take an aggressive, charging approach and those who prefer to lag the ball to the hole. Two examples would be Tiger Woods, who is a charger, and Juli Inkster, who lags her putts. Because of their differing styles, it would be very difficult for them to help read one another's putts as partners. A better approach is to find a partner who shares your approach to putting. That said, it's not required or always a good idea to read greens for each other.

4. **Find a kindred spirit**. One of golf's most successful pairings was Ben Hogan and Jimmy Demaret, although the two men couldn't have been more different in terms of personality. Hogan was a quiet, shy man while Demaret was gregarious. Their partnership succeeded for just that reason. Hogan enjoyed Demaret's conversation and it helped him relax, while Demaret always seemed to pick up the level of his game when paired with the quieter Hogan. The foundation for their success, however, came down to the fact that they respected each other as people and as players.

5. **Skip the apologies**. Paul Runyan, a two-time winner of the PGA Championship and a member of the World Golf Hall of Fame, enjoyed great success when he teamed with Horton Smith. According to Runyan, the secret to their success was simple: "On the first tee, we'd shake hands and both of us would apologize in advance for any error or poor shot. That would be the only time we'd apologize in the course of the match. There was no need for any further apologies. We both understood that the other fellow was trying his hardest."

17

Games People Play

Let's make this clear right from the start: The PGA of America does not condone gambling on golf games in any way, shape or manner. That said, we understand that almost for as long as people have been playing golf, they've been willing to put a little something on the outcome of their matches—even if it's only bragging rights.

The reason for this goes well beyond whatever is on the line at the end of the day. For a huge majority of golfers, it increases the enjoyment of the competition and helps them focus their attention on the game, as two-time PGA Champion Paul Runyan explains:

"I don't care if we play for marbles or matchsticks, just as long as we play for something," Runyan has frequently said. "Playing with nothing on the line is like going for a walk in the woods. It's pretty and it's nice exercise, but it's not competition."

In this chapter, we'll explain some of the most popular games you can play. Some may already be familiar to you, but others may be new and will, we hope, add to your enjoyment. This is particularly true if you happen to be a beginning golfer.

If you do elect to bet money or valuables on the outcome of your matches, we offer this word of warning: Don't get in over your head. The point of golf is to have fun—and golf stops being fun when the stakes get too high.

One other word of warning: The United States Golf Association takes a dim view of gambling. While the USGA does not object to wagering among individuals or teams as long as that wagering is limited to the participants, the Rules of Golf prohibit amateurs from competing for prize money. To that end, the USGA opposes types of gambling such as calcuttas, auction pools, pari-mutuels or other organized events that encourage people to bet on players other than themselves or their partner(s). Players participating in such events without waiving their right to cash prizes are deemed to be playing for prize money and may be at risk of having their amateur status revoked.

Unless otherwise noted, most of these games can be played either with handicaps or in a straight gross-score format.

Arnies A point is won by a player who manages to make par or better on a hole without ever hitting a shot into the fairway. Named after Arnold Palmer, in recognition of his legendary ability to scramble out of trouble.

Automatics An agreement between players or teams that when one entity falls a predetermined number of holes down in a match (usually two) a new match begins while the existing match continues in place. For example, if the automatic kicks in when a player or team falls 2 down, this is referred to as an Automatic Two-Down.

Basket A series of side competitions that offer a possible six points per hole: one point each for: closest to the pin in regulation; low ball, fewest putts (or combined putts when played in a team format); birdies; and two points for low team total. If a team wins all six points, they've won a basketful (hence the name), and the point totals are doubled.

Beach Bum A side wager in which a player who fails to successfully play from a bunker must pay an agreed-upon amount to his fellow players for every failed attempt.

Best-Ball A match in which a player plays against the best-ball of two or more other players. This can also be played as a team match, when one team matches its best-ball against the best-ball of the other team. When played as part of the Ryder Cup Matches or Walker Cup Matches, this is known as a fourball competition, and is also occasionally known as a better-ball format.

Best-Drive A foursome match in which all four players drive, and then each team picks the best drive and finishes the hole in an alternate-shot format.

Bingle-Bangle-Bungle A competition in which three points are at stake on each hole. One point is awarded to the player who hits the green first. A second point goes to the player whose ball is closest to the hole once all players have reached the green. The third point goes to the player whose ball is the first into the hole. All putting is determined by which ball is farthest from the hole. On par 3s, no point is awarded to the player who hits the green first. Instead, points go to the two players whose balls are closest to the hole once everyone in the match reaches the green. This is a particularly good game to play if your group is made up of players with a wide disparity in handicaps.

Birdies A game where players receive points for birdies. Sometimes one point is awarded for a net birdie and two for a gross birdie.

Bloodbath A form of foursomes play in which each golfer drives, but the opponents get to select which ball must be played by their opposing team.

Break the Bank This is about as straightforward as a game can get. At the conclusion of the round, each player pays every other player a predetermined amount per stroke. When the dust clears, the player with the lowest score wins most of the marbles.

Bridge This is a team competition. On the first tee, a coin toss decides which team gets to offer a bid. The bid they offer is a prediction of what their combined score will be on that hole. Upon receiving the opening bid from Team A, the opposing team (Team B) has the option of accepting the bid as is; accepting the bid but doubling the bet; or placing a lower bid of their own, in which case Team A has the same three options. Whatever the agreed-upon wager bid is, it doubles for every stroke above or below the winning bid. In other words, if Team A controls the bid (of, say, $1) and shoots a combined total of one stroke lower than the total bid, they win $1. If they beat their bid by two strokes, they win $2. Exceeding the bid by three strokes wins $4 and so on. The opposite holds true if they fail to equal their bid. If their score matches their bid, the hole is tied (or pushed) and the teams have the option of carrying the bet over to the next hole.

Carryovers An agreement between players or teams that when a hole is tied, the bet carries over to the next hole, and continues to do so until a hole is won.

Chicago A handicap formula in which players are awarded a set number of points based on their handicap. For example, a 1-handicapper gets 38 points, a 2-handicapper 37, etc. Players are then awarded additional points according to their score on each hole. A bogey earns one point; a par two; a birdie four; eight for an eagle and 16 for a double eagle. The player who wins the most points in excess of his or her original quota is the winner.

Double-Ups This game can get a little complicated, but it does add an element of risk and excitement to a match. Playing at full handicaps, each player or team determines how much each hole is worth, say $1. At any time during the time the hole is being played, either side may double the bet. The opposition can either accept the doubled bet or concede the hole, but once a doubled bet is accepted, it cannot be redoubled by the team originating the double until the opposition has elected to double the bet because their situation has improved.

Fairway and Greens This is a game that Ben Hogan favored in practice rounds, for obvious reasons. Each player gets a point for hitting a fairway and a point for hitting a green in regulation. The winner can be determined on a per-point basis, which almost always reduces the amount of anyone's losses, or as a winner-take-all.

Flags A side game where points are awarded for tee shots on par 3s that come to rest inside the measure of the flagsticks (or pins, hence the name).

Foursomes A match-play format in which two-player teams play one ball each. This format is often referred to as "alternate shot." Team members decide which player will drive on odd-numbered holes and which will drive on even-numbered holes, based on the strengths and weaknesses of their individual games. Players alternate hitting shots until play is finished on a hole. This format is a popular element of international team competitions.

Freebies An agreement prior to the start of play that allows each player a predetermined number of replays or "freebies" in the course of the round. The only stipulation is that once players elect to use one of their freebies, they must play that ball, even if it ends up in a worse position than the original shot. In some competitions, especially charitable events, players are allowed to purchase an unlimited number of freebies per round, with the proceeds going to the charity or common fund.

Garbage (or Junk) A collective term for any side competitions such as greenies, sandies, birdies, etc.

Got'cha A game in which each player has the right to make his or her opponent replay up to four shots per round.

Greenies A side competition in which a player (or team) is rewarded for hitting the closest shot to the green on a par 3.

Hawk This is a game played by a foursome of golfers. Prior to teeing off on the first hole, players establish a 1-2-3-4 hitting order they will follow throughout the round. Whoever has the honor drives first on that hole. After all players have hit, the player with the honor decides which player will be his or her partner on that hole, or if he chooses, he can stand alone against the other three players. In that case, should he win, he collects three points. Otherwise, the hawk and his partner (or their opponents) win a point each. The player with the least number of points after 16 holes assumes the honor on the 17th tee, and the same rule follows after 17 holes.

Highs and Lows This is a team game in which two points are at stake on each hole. One point is awarded for the lowest aggregate team score. The other point goes to the team whose individual high score is lower than the individual high score of the opposing team. In case of ties, the points carry over to the next hole.

Hogans Named after Ben Hogan, this side competition rewards the player who hits the fairway and then hits the green in regulation, whether on a par 4 or par 5. Some people favor making a Hogan twice as valuable as other side bets.

Low Ball/Low Total A team competition in which a point is awarded for the low individual score on a hole and a second point is awarded to the team with the lowest combined score on the same hole. In the case of a tie, the points carry over to the next hole.

Nassau This is the most popular form of both team and individual competition. Basically, three points are at stake in the match: one for the front nine, one for the back nine and one for the overall 18, although in some variations of the game, double points are awarded for the overall 18. (This form of nassau favors the better players, since while they may lose one nine, it's unlikely they will lose the 18-hole match.)

Nicklaus Named after you-know-who, it awards a point to the player with the longest drive in the fairway on par 4s and par 5s.

Nines This is a good game for a threesome. Nine points are available on each hole: five for low score, three for the next lowest and one for the highest score on the hole. In the case of a tie, the points are totaled and then divided equally. For example, if two players tie for low score, the total would equal eight points, and each player would earn four points.

Pinehurst This is a team competition in which both team members drive on every hole, then play their next shot from their partner's ball. After playing their second shots, the team selects the ball in the best position and plays an alternate-shot format from that point.

Sandies A point awarded to a player who gets up and down from a greenside bunker. A variation of the game also provides a point to a player who makes a par from a fairway bunker and two points to a player who makes par after driving into a fairway bunker and then getting up and down from a greenside bunker.

Scramble A popular format in pro-am competition since it keeps every player in the game and speeds up play. Each player drives and then the team's designated captain selects the ball in the best position and each team member plays from within a foot or so of that spot, continuing the process until the hole is completed. There are several variations of this format. In one, the team is required to use each player's drive a set number of times, usually four. This increases the pressure and also injects an element of strategy, particularly over the closing holes. Yet another element calls for each team to have an A, B, C and D player based upon their handicaps. The "A" player tees from the championship tee markers; the "B" player hits from the middle markers and so on. If the course has just three sets of markers, the "B" and "C" players tee from the middle markers and the "D" player plays from the forward tees.

Sixes A format in which four players switch partners after the sixth and 12th holes. One point is awarded to the winners of each six-hole match.

Six, Six and Six A team game in which formats change after every six holes. The first six holes are played as a four-ball (or best-ball). The next six are played as foursomes (alternate shot), and in the final six, each person plays his or her own ball and the winner of the hole is the team with the lowest combined score.

Skins Another popular format, largely because of the televised Skins Games. A point is awarded to the player with the low score on each hole. If the hole is tied, the skin carries over to the next hole and continues to do so until someone wins a hole and all the combined skins. In a variation of this format, the value of the skins increase as the round progresses.

Snake A game in which the first player to three-putt gets the "Snake" and must keep it until a fellow player three-putts, at which point, they get the Snake. The player who has the Snake must pay fellow players for each hole he or she keeps it. In a variation of this game, the player who has the Snake at the end of each nine pays doubled points.

Stableford A competition in which points are awarded based on the score for each hole. Typically, the point breakdown is: bogey (1), par (2), birdie (3), eagle (4) and double eagle (5). The player with the highest total points is the winner. A modified version of this game serves as the format for The International on the PGA Tour.

Strings A game in which each player receives a length of string prior to teeing off at the beginning of the round, typically five to 10 feet. Players can use all or part of that string to move their ball without penalty in the course of the round. For example, if you face a difficult three-foot putt for par, you can use three feet of string and make your birdie. The challenge is not wasting your string early in the round . . . or having any string left at the close of the round.

Three-Ball A threesomes competition in which players compete against their fellow players while playing their own ball.

Threesomes A match in which one person plays his or her own ball and the other two players team and play alternate shots.

Vegas This is a somewhat complicated four-ball game but it can be a fun change of pace. Each team records their score, lowest first. For example, if John makes a 4 and his wife, Anne, makes a 6, their team score is 46. If their opponents both make 5s, their team score is 55. The low team score is then subtracted from the higher team score, in this case John and Anne win 11 points. The match is settled, either on a per point basis at the end of each nine or as an 18-hole match, or for a predetermined amount.

Watson A side competition in which a player gets a point for holing a shot from off the green. The name comes from Tom Watson's pitch into the hole on the 71st hole of the 1982 U.S. Open at Pebble Beach.

Wolf This is a threesomes game in which the player with the middle-length drive on a par 4 or par 5, or who is the second-closest to the pin on the par 3s, becomes the "Wolf." His or her score on the hole is doubled, and if it is lower than the combined score of the other two players, the Wolf wins a point.

Woodsie A point is awarded to a player who hits a tree and still makes a par. The ball must hit the tree and not simply fly through the leaves. If a player hits two different trees and still makes a par, it's a double-Woodsie, worth two points.

Worst-Ball If time isn't of the essence this team game can really teach you how to scramble. Every player drives, but the team must play its second shot from the ball that is in the worst position. This continues until the team holes out, and the team with the lowest score wins a point.

18

A Day on the Course

Golf can be a very intimidating game for anyone, let alone beginners. Not only are the elements of the swing and the short game difficult to master, but the subtleties of the game can be mystifying for people who are just taking it up.

With that in mind, we thought it might be helpful to devote a chapter to what people can expect during a round of golf, from beginning to end.

When you arrive at the course, inquire whether caddies are available. If they are, we suggest supporting the program by taking a caddie. It's not that we have anything against golf cars, particularly for people with injuries or ailments who might not otherwise be able to enjoy the game. But typically, caddie programs have been an excellent way for young people to earn some money *and* be exposed to a sport that they can enjoy and that might help shape their character. A good caddie can make the round more enjoyable by being good company and giving you hints that might lower your score. A caddie can provide information on yardage, club selection, reading the greens and the layout of the course. However, if you do take a car, pay careful attention, follow direction signs and avoid areas around the greens and roped off areas.

Upon your arrival, it's a good idea to ask if restrooms and beverage carts are located on the course, where telephones are located, and if there are local rules such as the requirement that golf cars be driven to and from the ball on a 90-degree angle from the carpath. You should also ask how the course is marked, where yardages to the green are marked and if any part of the course is under repair.

Try to arrive soon enough to give yourself time to warm up properly. It's important to do some stretching exercises before you begin hitting balls, since this will help guard against any injuries. If time allows, work your way through the bag, beginning with the short irons, moving onto the middle and long irons and then the woods. It's often a good idea to finish warming up by hitting a few soft wedge shots before heading for the practice green and hitting a few putts. If you do not have time to do this, make sure to hit at least a few balls with the club you plan to use for your opening drive. Keep in mind that very often, the practice green will not match the speed of the greens on the course—and remember, the point of all this is to hit just enough shots to warm up. Don't hit hundreds of balls and leave your game on the practice tee.

On the first tee, check the scorecard to learn any local rules. Local rules

Repairing a ball mark

apply only to the specific course you are playing and are designed to enhance your golf experience at that course. If your playing companions suggest a match, it's a good idea to make sure everyone is comfortable with the stakes. Also, make sure to place an identifying mark on your ball and inform the other players the type and number of the ball you are playing.

One of the biggest challenges facing golf today is slow play, so as a golfer it is your responsibility to play at an acceptable pace. Slow play is when your group is not keeping up with the pace of play of the group in front of you. There are several things you can do to help keep pace.

First, walk at a reasonable speed between shots. You don't have to race, but don't treat it as a leisurely stroll through the park. Begin planning your next shot as you approach the ball by studying the strength and direction of the wind. If you are unfamiliar with the course, ask your caddie or a playing companion if there is any hidden trouble around the green or any local knowledge that might be helpful. Finally, when you reach your ball, check the lie, select your club, visualize your swing and shot, and then play your shot. From the time you select your club until you actually hit your shot, you should take no more than 30 to 45 seconds. The important point is that you be ready to play when it is your turn. If, for some reason, you aren't ready to play when it is your turn, encourage one of your fellow players to play.

As a player, you have a responsibility for maintaining the course in the

Before teeing off, check the scorecard for local rules that affect the course you're playing.

Most clubs have dress codes. It's always a good idea to check in advance.

Marking the ball

best possible condition. This is an important part of the game's tradition, and it is also a courtesy to your fellow players.

With that in mind, it is important that you replace your divots. In most conditions, this means fitting the divot back into position and then stepping on it firmly. If you are playing a course with Bermuda-grass fairways (which is the grass on most courses in southern climates), the turf tends to explode on impact, making it difficult, if not impossible, to replace the divot. In this case, you have two options: You can use the toe of your shoe to kick in the turf around the edges of the divot. You probably won't be able to completely fill the divot, but Bermuda grass grows very quickly, so the damage will be short-term. Many courses put containers of a soil/seed mixture on their golf cars and tees. If this is the case, simply fill in the divot with the mixture.

If you hit your approach shot into a greenside bunker and do not have a caddie to rake the sand after you play, take a rake into the bunker with you—remembering that you should always enter the bunker from the low side, at the point nearest to the ball. Whenever possible, avoid walking on the steep face of a bunker. After hitting your shot, rake the area you played from, as well as all your footprints and any others within reach.

There are two schools of thought on where rakes should be left—either in or nearby the bunker. Those who favor leaving rakes inside the bunker argue that this prevents a rake from stopping a ball from running into the sand. Most courses prefer that rakes be left outside the bunker, so ask for the club's policy. In fact, many courses equip their golf cars with rakes so the question of where to leave them isn't an issue.

Just as you should replace your divots, it's equally important to repair any pitch marks or indentations caused by the ball hitting the green. The key word here is "any," since far too many golfers neglect this element of the game, causing damage to the greens. Fixing a pitch mark is easy: Using either a tee or a tool designed for the job, simply work your way around the outside of the mark, gently lifting out the compressed soil until it is level with the putting surface. Once you have done this, tap the area with your putter until the surface is level. Don't neglect spike marks or other damage done by spikes. Use your putter to gently smooth them out—just remember that while the Rules of Golf allow you to repair pitch marks on your putting line, you cannot repair spike marks on your putting line until after you have putted. Repairing spike damage and pitch marks is a courtesy to your fellow players—and ultimately helps reduce maintenance costs.

When you are on the green, it is important that you take special care not to step on your fellow players' putting lines—the imaginary line that connects the ball to the hole—so be aware of the position of everyone's

Tending the flagstick. Hold the flag so it doesn't flutter. Hold it at arm's length so your shadow doesn't fall across the hole or putting line.

Loosen the flagstick at the bottom so it pulls straight up.

ball. If your ball is on a player's line, volunteer to mark the ball. If the position of your mark interferes with that player's putt, volunteer to move the mark following a specific procedure. First mark your ball, either with a plastic marker or a small, thin, dark coin such as an old penny. After you have marked your ball, place your putter down at a 90-degree angle with the heel touching your marker. Once you have done this, move the marker from the heel to the toe of your putter. Reverse the procedure to return the ball to its original position. Failing to follow this procedure or failing to properly replace the ball is a violation of the Rules of Golf and will result in a one-stroke penalty or the loss of the hole in match play.

Also, when on the green, take special care not to stand where you might distract a fellow player and don't move or make any noise when another player is preparing to putt. If you don't have a caddie and are asked to tend the flagstick, make sure you aren't standing on anyone's line. Hold the flagstick at arm's length so the flag doesn't flutter in the breeze, and make sure your shadow doesn't fall across the hole or line. Loosen the bottom of the flagstick so it doesn't stick when you try and remove it by pulling it straight up after the other player has putted. The flagstick should be removed right after the player has hit the ball. If you lay down the flagstick, lay it off the green to prevent doing any damage to the green. Generally, the player closest to the hole will tend the flagstick.

If you have carried extra clubs onto the green, lay them in a spot where you'll be exiting the green as you head for the next tee. This will help

Fixing your divot. Most courses will provide a soil/seed mixture on golf cars for filling in your divots.

ensure that you don't forget the clubs and have to run back for them, slowing play.

One final thought: After everyone has putted out, immediately walk to the next tee. Don't linger on the green filling in your scorecards or hitting extra putts, since this also slows down play and is discourteous to the players waiting in the groups behind you.

If you hit a tee shot into the woods and suspect that it might be either lost or out-of-bounds, the Rules of Golf allow you to play a second or provisional ball. You then have five minutes from the time you reach the spot where you suspect the ball landed to find the ball. If it is not found within that five-minute period, you must declare it lost and play your provisional ball with a one-stroke penalty. If, however, you play the provisional ball and subsequently find your original ball, you must continue to play the provisional ball. The key point to remember is that if you suspect your ball might be lost or out-of-bounds, play a provisional. Don't delay play by walking all the way back to the tee.

It should also go without saying that if one of your fellow players hits a shot into trouble, you have an obligation to follow the flight of the ball and help in the search.

For safety's sake, never hit when there's a chance you might be able to reach the group ahead of you, and anytime you hit a shot that you think even has a remote chance of hitting any other players, yell "fore" immediately, and make a point of apologizing to any players your ball lands near. If you hear someone yell "fore," turn your back in the direction of the person issuing the warning, and cover your head as completely as possible, especially the areas of your temples and your neck. As a rule, an errant shot won't do any serious damage unless it strikes your head—but that can result in serious injury.

Golf can be a very frustrating, even maddening game. Bobby Jones once said that it is "very often a game that cannot be endured with a club in your hands," and as a youngster he had a reputation for throwing clubs that once earned him a letter of reprimand from the United States Golf Association.

Displays of frustration are one thing, but outbursts of temper are quite another. Yelling, screaming, throwing clubs or otherwise making a fool of yourself are unacceptable and, in some cases, dangerous to yourself and others. Not only will it have a negative effect on your scoring, but you may find yourself having a tough time getting a game, so try to stay under control at all times.

As a player, you also have a responsibility to learn and understand the Rules of Golf. They can be confusing, but it's important that you follow them to the best of your ability. Five of the most common Rules are those that deal with out-of-bounds, lost balls, unplayable lies, carpaths and water hazards.

One other point about the Rules: If you find yourself playing in a tournament, you have an obligation—even a responsibility—to the rest of the field to see that the Rules are followed completely. Happily, cheating (or overlooking the Rules) is extremely rare. At every level of the game, players pride themselves in the fact that golf is a self-policing game, witness this story about Bobby Jones.

Jones was playing in the 1925 U.S. Open at Worcester (Mass.) Country Club. As he prepared to play a shot from the deep rough, he noticed that the ball moved when he addressed it. Jones called a one-stroke penalty on himself, and was forced into a playoff with Willie Macfarlane, who went on to win.

Later, when a reporter praised Jones for his sportsmanship, the great champion bristled.

"There's only one way to play the game and that's by the Rules," he said. "You might as well praise a man for not robbing a bank."

If you have the unfortunate experience of seeing someone violate the Rules, you have an obligation—however unpleasant—to point out the violation as politely as possible. If the player protests his or her innocence, don't make a big deal about it. Simply refer the matter to the tournament committee for their resolution.

Moving on, if your group stops for refreshments, either at the turn (the end of nine holes) or following the round, volunteer to pay and offer to buy drinks for the caddies. Bear in mind that at some courses, groups that stop at the turn lose their turn in the order of play. If everyone in the foursome offers to pay, a good solution is to flip a coin to decide who will pay. Whoever pays at the turn, however, should not be expected to pay for refreshments at the end of the round.

Finally, at the end of the round, shake hands with your fellow players, congratulate the winners, console the losers, and thank them for their company. At the end of the day, the great pleasure of the game is the time you get to spend with your friends—whether old friends or new friends you just made through the game.

19
Getting Youths Started in the Game

Golf is truly the game for a lifetime and it is a perfect way for families to spend time together. But it's important to keep in mind that golf can be an intimidating and sometimes frustrating sport for youngsters. As PGA Professionals have learned over the generations, there may not be one right way for youths to learn to play and love the game, but there are plenty of things adults can do wrong—all the best intentions notwithstanding— that can dampen a child's enthusiasm.

In this section, we'll try to offer some "Do's and Don'ts" that can help make learning the game more fun for kids and adults alike.

For starters, The PGA of America's PGA Foundation has raised tens of millions of dollars since its inception in 1954, with more than $20 million spent in the past 10 years. That money has been used to fund a variety of services and programs to help encourage the growth of junior golf. Among the most popular programs are Clubs for Kids (which helps get clubs into the hands of youngsters who might not otherwise be exposed to the game), the National Junior PGA Championship and PGA Junior Series, National Golf Day, the National Golf Marathon and the Junior Medalist Teaching Program. In addition, The PGA of America is involved with the PGA Golf in Schools program, Kids on Course (in conjunction with local Police Athletic Leagues), The First Tee and Golf for the Disabled. Through the National Minority College Golf Championship, The PGA of America helps provide 20 college scholarships annually. The PGA of America also works closely with the Urban Youth Golf Program in Louisville and offers a

The PGA of America has a large commitment to helping junior golfers discover the joys of the game.

*Teaching juniors the proper funda-
mentals will help ensure they
grow to love the game.*

Practicing is a lot more fun when you have friends along to learn the game with you.

variety of publications and videos such as "First Swing," a summary of the Rules of Golf and others.

Keep Things Fun

If there is one simple rule when it comes to helping youngsters get started in playing golf, it's that it is a game and games are supposed to be fun for youngsters—and for adults, for that matter.

Keeping practice fun and simple will go a long way toward developing an enthusiastic golfer.

As you begin to introduce a youngster to golf, the best guideline is to follow his or her lead. Let youngsters tell you what they want to do and when they are ready to call it a day. Some kids will prefer to hit balls for a while and then head for the swimming pool or soccer practice. Others will want to head for the course at the crack of dawn and play until the last light of day. Neither approach is right or wrong.

One approach might be to invite your child to join you for a few holes. If they want to try a few putts or hit a couple of shots, great. If, in the beginning, they want to enjoy just spending some time with you, that's great, too. When you get older, and your children are grown, it's simple times like these that you'll treasure.

It's also important to let your child set his or her own goals. If you set arbitrary goals, they may be too ambitious and that will only frustrate the child. No matter what goals a child sets, however, the key is for an adult to be encouraging and supportive. Witness this story about President John F. Kennedy.

After his first televised debate with Vice President Richard Nixon in the 1960 presidential election, Kennedy received a congratulatory phone call from his powerful and influential father, Joe. After he hung up, Kennedy said to a friend: "You know, if I had fallen flat on my face, Dad would have called and said, 'Jack, that was the greatest fall in history. I'm proud of you.'"

It's also important to keep in mind that your kids look up to you and will follow your example. It's no accident that the parent who sits in the stands screaming at the umpires, coaches, his or her child, or even other players will probably be the parent with a child who does the same thing. With that in mind, it's important not only to keep your temper in check, but also to teach your child early on about the etiquette and rules of the game. This is especially important when children begin playing by themselves or with friends and will be held accountable for their actions—and playing privileges—by adults.

For young golfers, success is often measured in small accomplishments that can lead to great things.

Make an Investment in Lessons and Equipment

It's certainly true that many of golf's greatest champions have been self-taught. Lee Trevino is probably the best example. And it's also true that some fantastic players had fairly rudimentary equipment when they started out.

"My brothers and me made our first clubs," Sam Snead told a writer. "We'd get a limb off a swamp maple and whittle it down so it had a really pretty head on it. You could hit a ball pretty good with it. After a while, we found ourselves some old clubheads and stuck them on the end of a buggy whip. Oh, you could hit 'em a mile with those things. Of course, they broke pretty easily so you had to spend a lot of time chasing after the club-heads. They'd sometimes go as far as the balls. One day my brother Homer and I were skipping church on Sunday and I sent a mashie head right through one of the church windows. We ran like the blazes up into the hills. We never did get caught, but I felt so bad about it that years later I bought a new organ for the church to try and make up for it."

While your child may indeed have the talent to become another Trevino or Snead, the odds of success will be greatly improved if you get him or her started properly by learning the fundamentals from a PGA Professional, either with individual or group lessons.

The simple fact is that without a grounding in the proper fundamentals, the game will be infinitely harder—and more frustrating—for your child to learn. Take it from Arnold Palmer.

"My father was the professional at Latrobe [Pa.] Country Club and the one thing he stressed to me over and over was the importance of a good grip," Palmer has frequently said. "He was constantly checking to see how I had my hands placed on the club. He knew that everything stemmed from how you grip the club."

Even if you are an accomplished player, it's best to have your children take lessons from a trained professional, not only because they understand the game inside and out, but because a teaching pro has the experience, time and patience to work with a child. Also, there will be less pressure to please and succeed if the child is working with a PGA Professional rather than a parent. That's just human nature.

Another reason to have your child learn from a Professional is that, given the time pressures of today's life, the Professional will have more opportunity to observe the youngster's progress. It's important to remember that when learning to play golf, very often every step forward is met with a temporary step back. The Professional can trace your child's progress and suggest remedies to correct any problems.

Years ago, kids taking up the game were usually handed a few cut-down clubs and a handful of balls. The problem with these clubs was that they were too heavy, especially for smaller children. This created all sorts of swing flaws as children tried to fashion a swing that would allow them to some-how make contact.

Today, manufacturers have developed clubs specifically designed for youngsters. The heads are lighter, the shafts are more flexible, and the grips are thinner so small hands fit properly on the club. Not only do these clubs make the game easier for a child, but they also give him or her the sense of ownership that comes with having your own clubs instead of Mom or Dad's castoffs. As the child grows bigger and stronger, it is easy for your PGA Professional to provide equipment that fits properly.

Golf equipment isn't cheap. It can be a significant investment and that may place added pressure on a child. If he or she knows that Mom and Dad spent several hundred dollars on equipment, it could have an intimidating effect on the child—especially if, in a moment of frustration, the parent brings it up as a way of coercing the child to practice. That's a bad idea for every imaginable reason.

Bear in mind that a junior set doesn't have to include 14 clubs. Usually, for a child who is just starting out, a fairway wood, 3-, 5-, 7- and 9-irons, a sand wedge (that's not too heavy) and a putter will get the job done.

That said, how does a parent know it's time for additional equipment? The answer is that children will let you know, not necessarily by asking—

although they undoubtedly will—but by their enthusiasm. And notice we said enthusiasm and not scores. If a child clearly is smitten by the game and your Professional believes it's time to complete the set, by all means do it. But to hold out a few additional clubs as a reward for a lower score, or some other subjective standard, may be counterproductive. Remember that in golf, very often the journey is more important—and ultimately more rewarding—than the goal itself.

The Joys—and Dangers—of Competition

Just as all children learn in different ways and at different speeds, so too do all children have different feelings about competition. Some just love to compete at anything and everything. That's just their nature. Others are more reticent and may be attracted to golf for any number of reasons that have nothing to do with competition. For those children, being pushed into competitive golf can be disastrous.

While it's a good idea to offer children an opportunity to compete, it's important that when they show an interest, they are steered to the appropriate level of competition. It doesn't do anyone any good to enter a youngster into a match or flight where he or she doesn't have a prayer of being competitive.

When a child does begin to compete, it's vitally important that adults be supportive and not critical. If a child loses, he or she will feel badly enough without having to listen to a parent list all the things the child did wrong. Take the case of Patty Berg.

When Patty was 15, she entered the Minneapolis Ladies Championship. She shot a 122 in the qualifying round and was placed in the last flight. Her opponent was an older woman who beat her, 10 and 8. Berg was crushed, and when she got home her father, whom she adored, tried to console her.

"Don't feel too bad, Patty," he said. "You aren't used to playing 36 holes. You probably just got tired."

"Daddy, it was just 18 holes," she said.

"Oh, dear," said her father. "Did anything go right?"

"I remembered to pay my caddie and he seemed very pleased," she said.

"Well, there you go, Patty," he said. "Good job."

Patty Berg went on to become a Hall of Fame golfer, in no small part, because she had a great deal of love and support from her family.

20
The Dangers of Lightning

Golf is fun but there is nothing funny about lightning. There's an old joke that goes "Sam Snead is only afraid of three things: Ben Hogan, downhill putts and lightning." Snead would never admit to the first, even if it were true, he might admit that the second never thrilled him, but will happily concede that when storm clouds blew in, he headed for the clubhouse.

So should you.

Weather detection systems are infinitely more advanced today than they were even just a few years ago, and the result is that hundreds—possibly thousands—of lives have been saved by early warning alerts on the golf course.

Still, for all the advances in science and meteorology, the simple rules of common sense can go a long way toward protecting you from the dangers of lightning.

First, keep an eye on the horizon. If you see dark clouds or towering thunderheads, or hear thunder booming in the distance, start figuring how long it will take you to reach shelter, preferably the golf shop or clubhouse.

There's an old rule of thumb that says that when you spot a flash of lightning, begin counting "one thousand one, one thousand two, one thousand three . . ." and so on until you hear the thunder. Each second indicates the number of miles from the storm to you. Like any rule of thumb, this is imperfect, because storms advance at varying degrees of speed. Still, it's a pretty good guide.

As the storm approaches, the absolute first priority is to find shelter—and the bigger the shelter the better.

By the same token, a golf car may offer some minimal protection, but an enclosed vehicle like an automobile or truck is far superior. The old notion that a car's rubber tires will protect you is wrong. The safety afforded by a vehicle is that if it's struck by lightning, the metal shell dissipates the force of the lightning, reducing its impact.

Another general rule of thumb is that any solitary object such as a building or tree will act as a lightning rod, so never seek shelter under a lone tree. If trees are your only option, seek out a heavily wooded area and find shelter under a clump of smaller trees, preferably in a low area.

Bear in mind that water conducts electricity, so while you want to find the lowest possible area, never head for a creek bed. And while you may be tremendously attached to your clubs, remember that metal conducts electricity as well. It's a good idea to leave the clubs and come back for them once the storm passes.

If worse comes to worst and you're caught in an exposed area and cannot reach shelter, your best recourse is to make yourself as small and low a target as possible. That is especially critical if you feel your hair begin to literally stand on end. This is a sign that the air is charged with electricity and lightning could strike at any moment. Immediately get away from any metal objects and lie as flat to the ground as possible. If you can reach a bunker that is not filling with water, that's even better.

What to Do If Lightning Strikes

The first step to take when you encounter a victim of lightning is, if possible, send for professional help, either a doctor, emergency medical technician, police or fire department personnel or anyone trained in cardiopulmonary resuscitation (CPR).

Next, determine if the victim has a heartbeat by feeling for the jugular vein along either side of the neck. If no heartbeat can be detected, the first priority is to try and restart the heart by placing both hands over the sternum (breastbone) and pushing firmly every two seconds, replicating a normal pulse.

Once there is a heartbeat, the next priority is to restore breathing. In order to prevent brain damage, breathing must be restored within roughly the first five minutes. If he or she isn't breathing, lay the victim on his or her back, gently tilt the head back to open the airway, pinch off the nostrils to prevent air from escaping, and insert your thumb over the tongue to keep it from blocking the air passage. Then place your mouth over the victim's mouth completely and begin mouth-to-mouth resuscitation, providing a strong blast of air roughly every five seconds.

This CPR can literally be a lifesaver, but the chances of success are greatly improved if it's performed by an individual who has taken a CPR course, which is usually offered by a local chapter of the American Red Cross or at a local hospital.

Once the victim has a heartbeat and is breathing, gently examine the victim to determine the point where the lightning either entered or exited the body. Depending on the severity of the lightning strike, these entry and exit injuries will be either first- or second-degree burns and, if possible, should be lightly covered with a clean cloth. Do not press the cloth into the wound. Also, look for other burn areas on parts of the body where a ring, watch, belt buckle or other metal objects were worn.

Finally, bear in mind that even if the victim is breathing and has a strong, regular heartbeat, there's a strong risk of shock. The victim should be covered to help maintain a constant body temperature until professional medical assistance can be provided.

21

How to Be a
Good Guest

One of the joys of golf is visiting other courses and meeting new people, but there are certain codes and customs to keep in mind. The most obvious rule is to act the way you'd like a guest to act at your club or course. With that in mind, here are 10 Rules for Being a Good Guest.

Giving your host a moderately priced gift is a nice gesture.

1. **Take Ben Hogan's advice**. The old Seminole Pro-Am was one of the most popular tournaments in the 1940s and '50s, drawing the top touring professionals to the Donald Ross masterpiece in south Florida. One year, however, the tournament was marred by controversy when a young professional criticized the course in a local paper. Ben Hogan, who counted Seminole as his favorite course, took the player aside and taught him the facts of life.

   "You listen to me," he said sternly. "You are a guest at every single course you play. You need the members more than they need you, so you should count your blessings every time you tee it up. If you can't bring yourself to say something nice about a course, just say 'It's the best course of its type I've ever seen' and leave it at that. You won't be lying and you'll be long gone before anyone tries to figure out exactly what you meant."

2. **Get to the course on time**. There's no better way to get off on the wrong foot with your host than to show up late. You must make it a top priority to show up on time or, even better, 15 minutes or so early. You'll go a long way toward doing this if you get accurate directions ahead of time. If, however, you find you're going to be late, you had better call the golf shop—and have a good excuse.

3. **Know the dress code**. Most clubs and courses have dress codes, so it's a good idea to check with your host or call the golf shop and find out what types of clothing are acceptable. For example, most courses will accept shorts but they must be knee-length. Also, the majority of courses also require a shirt with a collar. It's always best to check in advance.

4. **Mind your temper**. No matter how poorly you play or how frustrated you become, it's crucial that you keep your temper in check. If you don't, you'll not only embarrass yourself, but worse, your host.

5. **Offer to pick up a tab**. At many private clubs, cash transactions aren't allowed, but you should still offer to buy drinks and a snack at the turn, buy lunch or the first round of post-game drinks, or pay for the caddie or the car rental. If you belong to a local club, bear in mind that clubs often have reciprocal charge privileges.

6. **Bring a gift**. Is there a hot new golf book that everyone is talking about? Or maybe a new ball that everyone is clamoring to play? If so, it's a nice gesture to bring a modestly priced thank-you gift for your host.

7. **Watch your pace of play**. Slow play is the plague of golf. There's probably no better way of ensuring you won't be invited back than by playing at a glacial pace. Be ready to play when it's your turn and pick up if you're hopelessly out of a hole.

8. **Avoid politics, religion and sex**. There are plenty of safe topics for discussion without treading into the minefields of politics, religion and sex. The last thing you want to do is offend your host or your host's friends. Stick to the weather.

9. **Keep the betting modest**. It should be a simple matter of common sense, but if your host and your host's friends propose betting on the match, follow their lead when it comes to the size of the wager—and make sure you have enough cash to cover any losses.

10. **Don't bring up business**. Even if your host is your best client—or best potential client—don't discuss business unless your host initiates the conversation. As in so many areas on this list, if you follow your host's lead, you'll generally do just fine.

How to Be a Gracious Host

First and foremost, your responsibility as a host is to try and ensure that your guest feels relaxed and comfortable, since playing a new course with new people can be an unnerving experience—particularly if your guest is not an accomplished

Tell your guests any information about the course that may be helpful.

player. Here are 10 suggestions that can help you put your guest at east and make the day more fun for everyone involved.

1. **Provide clear and accurate directions**. Nothing will get the day off to a rockier start than having your guest get lost and arrive late and frazzled. Several days before the round, provide your guest with clear, accurate directions and, if possible, provide a map and include the golf shop's phone number. Also, keep in mind that there are Internet sites that can provide exact directions and maps to your course from anywhere in the country.

2. **Explain the dress code**. The more information you can provide for your guest, the less intimidated your guest will be. That's certainly the case when it comes to what clothing is acceptable at your club or course. You don't have to pick out the wardrobe for the day, but knowing what's acceptable and unacceptable will go a long way toward making your guest comfortable. Very often clubs will even have the dress code printed on a card you can provide to your guest.

3. **Arrive early**. If at all possible, suggest an appropriate time to meet and be there to greet your guest when he or she arrives. See that your guest's clubs are taken to the golf shop and then take your guest to the locker room so he or she can change. It's also a good idea to arrange for the attendant to have a locker available, and make sure you tip the attendant ahead of time.

4. **Allow time to warm up**. Even if you're a player who doesn't believe in warming up prior to your round (and shame on you for that), allow enough time for your guest to loosen up and hit a few putts. This is a particularly good idea if you plan to be your guest's partner.

5. **Tell your guest about the other players**. It will be a big help if you tell your guest something about the other players in your foursome: what kind of players they are; what they like and don't like; what they do for a living, etc. This will help avoid any faux pas. It might be a helpful touch to write down the other players' names for your guest. It's also a good idea to tell the other players a little bit about your guest, for just the same reason.

6. **Share your home course knowledge**. Before teeing off, make sure to give your guest any information about the course that may be helpful. For example, if the greens generally slope from back to front, remind your guest that it's always important to leave your approach shots below the hole. The same holds true if putts generally break away from any mountains or toward any water. Also, make sure to mention any interesting club traditions or history.

7. **Don't bet the ranch**. Everyone has a different comfort level when it comes to betting. What may seem like small change to you and your friends may be a suffocating amount of money for your guest. Not only will a big bet ruin your guest's fun, it will probably ruin their game as well.

8. **Car or caddie?** Some people like to walk while others simply must take a golf car. Try to find out before the round what your guest prefers and try to be accommodating.

9. **Share the cost**. Most people will offer to pay for part of the day, whether

it's lunch, drinks, snacks or the cost of a caddie or golf car. By letting your guest help cover the cost, you'll make him or her feel more like a friend and less like a guest.

10. **Spend time together after the round**. Finally, if at all possible, plan your day so you have time for a sandwich or a drink after your round. This indicates that you really did enjoy the round.

22

Talking the Talk

One reason many beginning golfers find the game confusing—even intimidating—is that golf seems to have a language all its own. This is particularly true when it comes to the technical terms used in areas like instruction, architecture and equipment. Also, another element of confusion stems from the fact that in golf, one word can have several meanings. A textbook example is the word "grip." You grip (hold) the club with an overlapping grip (the way you arrange your hands) on the grip (the part of the club where the hands are placed).

Is it any wonder beginning golfers—not to mention golfers from non-English-speaking nations—find the terminology of the game more than a little baffling?

To help clear up any confusion, we thought it would be helpful to devote an entire chapter to the terminology of golf. That way, even if you can't quite walk the walk just yet, you'll at least be able to talk the talk. When appropriate, we've used the word in a sentence to help clarify its proper usage.

Acceleration The steady increase in speed most often associated with the hands, arms or club. (Tiger Woods has tremendous acceleration through the hitting area.)

Address The act of setting up the body and club to the ball when preparing to hit a shot. (Every golfer could profit from studying Jack Nicklaus's address position.) When used in the context of the Rules of Golf, it refers to the point when the player has taken a stance and grounded his or her club. (The ball moved after he addressed it, resulting in a one-stroke penalty.)

Aiming The act of aligning the clubface to the target. (She had a problem aiming the club properly all day and missed several shots to the right of her target.)

Alignment The position of the body in relation to the initial target. (One reason she plays so well is that her alignment is so consistent from one shot to the next.)

Angle of Approach (or Attack) A term that describes the relative angle at which the clubhead approaches the ball at impact which, in turn, helps determine the distance and trajectory the ball travels. (He hit the ball with a sharply descending angle of attack, which caused the ball to fly high enough to carry over the tall trees.)

Approach A shot hit toward the green (His approach shot to the 17th hole came up short of the green) or toward the hole (Sam Snead was a great approach putter).

Axis Generally refers to a straight line (the spine) that the upper body rotates around in the course of the golf swing. (One reason for her consistent ball-striking is that her axis remains in a constant position throughout the swing.)

Backspin The rotational movement or spin of the ball produced by contact with the clubface. The greater the backspin, the higher the ball will fly and the more it will spin, and therefore stop or even spin backward on impact with the turf. (The ball had so much backspin that when it hit the green it spun back into the water hazard.)

Backswing The motion that involves the club and every element of the body in taking the club away from the ball and setting it in a position from which the club can be delivered to the ball at impact. (John Daly has an unusually long backswing that causes the club to go past parallel at the top of the swing.)

Balance The proper distribution of weight both at address and throughout the swing. (Tom Watson's swing has always been characterized by perfect balance.)

Balata A rubberlike substance used as a cover material for golf balls. Pure balata is rarely, if ever, used today. Instead, manufacturers use blends or synthetic material. Many players prefer balata or balatalike covers because balata provides a softer feel and can provide increased spin. (Most of the players in the championship played with balata-covered balls.)

Baseball Grip A grip in which all 10 fingers are placed on the grip of the club. (Bob Rosburg was a very successful player who used a baseball grip.)

Birdie A score of one under par on a hole. (Her birdie on the 10th hole was a turning point in the match.)

Bladed Shot Often referred to as a "skulled" shot, it occurs when the top half of the ball is struck with the bottom portion of an iron, resulting in a low-running shot. (She bladed her approach shot but the ball ran onto the green and set up her putt for a birdie.)

Block A swing in which the rotation of the forearms is delayed or prevented throughout the hitting area, generally producing a shot that flies to the right of the target. (With a pond guarding the left side of the green, Ernie Els blocked his approach shot to the right of the flag.)

Bobbing The act of raising and lowering (or lowering and raising) the swing center in the course of the swing. (Because of an inconsistent knee flex in her swing, her bobbing led to inconsistent ball-striking.)

Bogey A score of one over par on a hole. (The bogey on 18 cost him the championship.)

Borrow The amount of break a player allows for when hitting a breaking putt. (One of the confusing factors for young players at Augusta National is learning how much they have to borrow on their putts.)

Bowed The position of the wrists at the top of the backswing in which the top wrist is bent slightly inward. (For many years, Tom Weiskopf had a bowed wrist at the top of his backswing.)

Break The amount a putt will curve to the side because of the slope, grain and wind that affect the movement of the ball. (The swale in the middle of the green produced a tremendous break on Palmer's putt.)

Bump and Run A pitch shot around the green in which the player hits the ball into a slope to deaden its speed before it settles on the green and rolls toward the hole. (The mounds and swales at Pinehurst No. 2 resulted in many players hitting bump-and-run shots during the Open.)

Bunker A hollow comprised of sand or grass or both that exists as an obstacle and, in some cases, a hazard. (The greens at Winged Foot were protected by deep bunkers.)

Caddie A person hired to carry clubs and provide other assistance. (A good caddie can be worth several strokes a round.)

Calcutta An auction in which people bid on players or teams in a tournament. (For many years, calcuttas were a regular event at many popular tournaments.)

Cambered Sole A rounding of the sole of the club to reduce drag. A four-way cambered sole is one that is rounded at every edge of a wood. (The 5-wood had a cambered sole to help it slide through the deep rough.)

Carry The distance a ball will fly in the air, usually to clear a hazard or safely reach a target. (Many of the holes at Pine Valley require a substantial carry over waste areas.)

Carryover When a hole is tied in a match and the bet is carried over to the next hole. (He won the 10th hole as well as the carryover.)

Casting An uncocking of the wrists prematurely on the downswing, resulting in a loss of power and control. Also known as "hitting from the top." (Smith had a tendency to swing at and not through the ball, which caused him to cast the club from the top of the swing.)

Cavity-back A type of iron in which a portion of the back of the clubhead is hollowed out and the weight distributed around the outside edges of the clubhead. (The cavity-back irons were far more forgiving than his old blades.)

Center of Gravity That point in the human body, in the pelvic area, where the body's weight and mass are equally balanced. (Ian Woosnam has a lower center of gravity than the much-taller Nick Faldo.)

Center of Rotation The axis or swing center that the body winds and unwinds around during the swing. (A stable center of rotation is an important element in solid ball-striking.)

Centrifugal Force The action in a rotating body that tends to move mass away from the center. It is the force you feel in the downswing that pulls the clubhead outward and downward, extending the arms and encouraging you to take a circular path. (Tiger Woods' swing creates powerful centrifugal force.)

Chicken Wing A swing flaw in which the lead elbow bends at an angle pointed away from the body, usually resulting in a blocked or pushed shot. (Once Jack's PGA Professional saw him hit, he knew the cause of Jack's loss of power was his chicken wing position at impact.)

Chip and Run A low-running shot played around the greens where the ball spends more time on the ground than in the air. (She saved par with a beautiful chip and run that ended inches from the hole.)

Choke A derogatory term describing poor play that results from nervousness. (Early in his career, some critics claimed Tom Watson choked under pressure.)

Choke Down The act of gripping down on the shaft, which is generally believed to provide greater control. (She choked down on a 7-iron and hit a beautiful pitch to save par.)

Chunk A poor shot caused by hitting the turf well behind the ball, resulting in a fat shot. (The defending champion's defense ended when he chunked his tee shot on the par-3 16th and hit the ball into the pond guarding the green.)

Cleek A fairway wood with the approximate loft of a 4-wood that produces high shots that land softly. (He played a beautiful shot with his cleek that almost rolled into the cup.)

Closed Clubface The position formed when the toe of the club is closer to the ball than the heel, either at address or impact, which causes the clubface to point to the left of the target line. (Her closed clubface resulted in her missing several approach shots to the left of the green.)

Closed Clubface (swing) A position during the swing in which the clubface is angled to the left of the target line or swing plane, generally resulting in shots hit to the left of the target. (When they looked at a videotape of his swing, his PGA Professional pointed to his closed clubface at the top of the backswing as the reason he hit his drive into the left rough.)

Closed Grip Generally referred to as a strong grip because both hands are turned away from the target. (PGA Tour pro Ed Fiori was nicknamed "Grip" because of his closed grip.)

Closed Stance A stance where the rear foot is pulled back away from the target line. (Her closed stance allowed her to hit a gentle draw off the tee.)

Closed-to-Open A swing in which the clubhead is closed on the backswing but then manipulated into an open position on the downswing. (Miller Barber was a very effective player, even though he had a closed-to-open swing.)

Cocked Wrists A description of the hinging motion of the wrists during the backswing in which the hands are turned clockwise. Ideally, the wrists are fully cocked at the beginning of the downswing. (He cocked his wrists early in the backswing to hit a high, soft shot over the bunker.)

Coefficient of Restitution (COR) The relationship of the clubhead speed at impact to the velocity of the ball after it has been struck. This measure is affected by the clubhead and ball material. (Testing showed that the new ball had a very high coefficient of restitution.)

Coil The turning of the body during the backswing. (Her ability to fully coil on the backswing resulted in tremendous power.)

Come Over the Top A motion beginning the downswing that sends the club outside the ideal plane (swing path) and delivers the clubhead from outside the target line at impact. This is sometimes known as an outside-to-inside swing. (Sam Snead came over the top slightly, which he felt produced more powerful shots.)

Compression A measure of the relative hardness of a golf ball ranging from 100 (hardest) to 80 (softest). (Like most powerful players, he preferred a 100-compression ball.)

Connection A description of a swing in which all the various body parts work harmoniously to produce a solid, fluid motion. (Many players focus on connection as a key element in the golf swing.)

Conservation of Angular Momentum (COAM) A law of physics that allows the player to produce large amounts of kinetic energy. As the body shifts his or her weight and turns toward the target in the forward swing, the mass (arms and club) is pulled away from the center into an extended position by centrifugal force. By temporarily resisting that pull as well as the temptation to assist the hit by releasing too early, one maintains the angle formed between the club's shaft and the left arm and conserves the energy until a more advantageous moment. This has been referred to as a "delayed hit," a "late hit," "connection," "lag loading," "the keystone," or COAM, but when performed correctly may simply be called "good timing."

Croquet Style A putting stance popularized by Sam Snead in which the player stands aside the ball, facing the hole, holds the club with a widely split grip, and strikes the ball with a croquet-type stroke. A similar style, in which the player faced the hole with the ball positioned between the feet, was banned by the United States Golf Association. (A croquet-style putting stroke is popular among players who suffer from the "Yips.")

Cross-Handed A grip in which the target (or lead) hand is placed below the trail hand (in other words, a grip that is the opposite of the traditional grips). (Bruce Lietzke used a cross-handed grip when putting and was very successful.)

Cupped Wrist A position in which the target (or top) hand is hinged outward at the top of the backswing. (Her cupped wrist caused the club to be pointed to the left of the target at the top of her swing.)

Cuppy Lie A lie in which the ball is sitting down slightly, usually in a small depression. (He had a difficult shot because he had to play from a cuppy lie in the fairway.)

Cut Shot A shot played with a slightly open clubface and a swing path that travels out to in. The result is a soft fade that produces additional backspin and causes the ball to stop quickly on the green. (Lee Trevino was known for his ability to play beautiful cut shots.)

Dead Hands A shot in which the hands remain relatively passive in the hitting area, resulting in a shot that flies a shorter distance than it normally would. (He dead-handed a 5-iron on the par 3, which confused his fellow players.)

Decelerate A decreasing of the clubhead speed in the hitting area. (Jones decelerated on his putt, and left it short of the hole.)

Deep-Faced Driver A driver with greater-than-standard height on its face. (His PGA Professional suggested trying a deep-faced driver.)

Delayed Hit A golf term used to describe the Conservation of Angular Momentum.

Divot The turf displaced when the club strikes the ball on a descending path. (Her divot flew into the pond.) It also refers to the hole left after play. (Her ball landed in an old divot, making her next shot difficult.)

Dormie The point in match play when a player is up in a match by the same number of holes that remain. (When Lanny Wadkins had his opponent dormie 3, it seemed as if the Americans would win the Ryder Cup.)

Double Bogey A score of 2-over-par on a hole. (The double bogey ended her hopes of defending her title.)

Double Eagle A score of 3-under-par on a hole. (Gene Sarazen's double eagle at Augusta National is one of the most famous shots in golf history.)

Doubles When a caddie carries two sets of clubs. (Carrying doubles was hard work in the hot weather, but he never complained.)

Downswing The swing forward from the top of the backswing. (The clubhead accelerated smoothly on the downswing.)

Draw A shot that flies slightly from right to left for right-handed players. (She hit a draw into the green that stopped two feet from the hole.)

Driving Range Another term for a practice area. Also known as a golf range, practice range or learning center. (Watson headed for the driving range following his round.)

Duck Hook A shot that flies sharply from right to left for right-handed players. It is usually hit unintentionally, since it is difficult to control. (He hit a duck hook from the tee and the ball flew out-of-bounds.)

Dynamic Balance Transferring the focus of weight appropriately during the golf swing while maintaining body control. (Sue worked with her PGA Professional on improving the dynamic balance of her swing.)

Eagle A score of 2-under-par on a hole. (His eagle on the 17th hole assured his victory.)

Early Hit When a player prematurely releases the cocking of the wrists on the downswing, resulting in a loss of power at impact. This is also known as "casting from the top." (Her tendency to make an early hit made her one of the shortest hitters in the field.)

Effective Loft The actual loft on a club at impact as opposed to the loft built into the club. Effective loft is determined by, among other things, the lie and the position of the hands relative to the ball at impact. (The uphill lie added effective loft to the club.)

Explosion A shot played from a sand bunker, usually when the ball has buried or settled down into the sand. (He played a spectacular explosion shot from the bunker to save par.)

Extension The width of the swing as measured by the target arm on the backswing and the trail arm on the follow-through. (Tiger Woods has beautiful extension in his swing.)

Fade A shot that flies slightly from left to right. (She hit a gentle fade from the tee and never missed a fairway in the final round.)

Fanning An exaggerated opening of the clubface as the backswing begins. (He fanned the club open on the backswing and hit mostly slices.)

Fat Shot A description of a shot when the clubhead strikes the turf behind the ball, resulting in poor contact and a shot that comes up well short of the target. (She hit a fat shot from the tee on the par 3, and as the ball sank from sight in the pond, so did her chances of victory.)

Flange A portion of the sole of a club such as a sand wedge or putter. (The wedge's wide flange made it an effective club from the deep, powdery sand.)

Flat Swing A swing that is more horizontal and less vertical in plane than is typical. (Because he had a flat swing, he had to guard against hooking the ball.)

Flip Shot A shot, usually played with a wedge, that involves a wristy swing designed to hit the ball a short distance but with a lot of height. (He hit a flip shot over the bunker, landing the ball near the hole.)

Floater A ball struck from the deep grass that comes out slowly and travels a shorter distance because of the heavy cushioning effect of the grass between the ball and the clubface. (Gail caught a floater from the rough and hit her approach shot into the pond.)

Flop Shot Similar to a flip shot except that it involves a long, slower swing. (Phil Mickelson is a master at playing the flop shot.)

Fluffy Lie A lie in which the ball rests atop the longish grass. This can be a tricky lie because the tendency is to swing the clubhead under the ball, reducing the distance it carries. (The ball came to rest in a fluffy lie near the green, but he played an excellent shot and won the hole.)

Fly The distance the ball carries (He can fly the ball 280 yards with his driver) or a shot that carries over the intended target (She flew the green with her approach shot and made a bogey).

Flyer A shot from the rough or in wet conditions that reduces the amount of backspin on the ball, causing it to fly lower and farther than it might under normal conditions. (She caught a flyer from the light rough and hit her approach shot over the green.)

Follow-through That part of the swing that occurs after the ball has been struck. (His powerful follow-through was a result of his long backswing.)

Footwork The coordinated action of the lower body during the golf swing. (Tom Watson has some of the best footwork of any player in history.)

Forward Press A slight movement of the hands and arms (and occasionally the legs) that initiates the golf swing. (A good forward press helps relieve tension in the golf swing.)

Forward Swing The downward motion of the hands, arms and club from the top of the backswing to impact. Another term for downswing. (Ben Hogan began his forward swing with a lateral shifting of his left hip toward the target.)

Fried Egg The slang term for a buried lie in the sand. (When Nancy Lopez reached the bunker she saw she was facing a fried egg lie.)

Golf Range A facility where people can practice full swing and, in some cases, their short game. (In Japan, golf ranges are very popular because the number of golf courses is limited.)

Grain The direction which the blades of grass grow, which is of primary importance on the greens (particularly Bermuda-grass greens) as this can affect how much and in which direction a putt breaks. (Sam Snead won many tournaments in Florida because he was so adept at reading the grain in the greens.)

Grand Slam The Modern (or Professional) Grand Slam describes winning the four professional major championships—the PGA Championship, the Masters and the United States and British Opens—in a calendar year. The Career Grand Slam describes winning each of these events once in a career. Only Gene Sarazen, Ben Hogan, Gary Player, Jack Nicklaus and Tiger Woods have accomplished this. No one has ever won the Modern Grand Slam. In 1930, Bobby Jones won the U.S. and British Amateurs and Opens, a feat which was termed the Grand Slam and has never been duplicated. The 28-year-old Jones retired from competitive golf that year. In addition, The PGA of America's "Grand Slam of Golf" is a late-season event that features the winners of that year's four Professional major championships.

Greenkeeper An older, outdated term for the course superintendent. (He was the greenkeeper at Merion for many years.)

Grip (equipment) That part of the golf club where the hands are placed. (After John's disappointing round, his PGA Professional suggested that he have his grips replaced.)

Grip (hands) The placing and positioning of the hands on the club. The various types include the Vardon or overlapping, the interlocking and the 10-finger or baseball grip. (The Vardon grip is the most popular grip today.) There is also the reverse-overlapping grip, in which the index finger of the left or top hand overlaps the smallest finger of the right or bottom hand. This is primarily used in putting, although some players use this grip when chipping the ball.

Groove (equipment) The horizontal scoring lines on the face of the club that help impart spin on the ball. (Before teeing off on the par-3 12th, Jack Nicklaus cleaned out the grooves of his 8-iron with a tee.)

Groove (swing) A description of a swing that consistently follows the same path, time after time. (In his post-round interview, Curtis Strange said his swing was in the groove all day, resulting in a 65.)

Ground When referred to in the Rules of Golf, it means the point when the club touches the ground (or water) prior to playing the shot. (It is against the Rules of Golf to ground your club in a hazard.)

Group Lesson A teaching session in which several pupils work with one or more PGA Professionals. This type of lesson is particularly effective for beginners, especially juniors. (The PGA of America offered group lessons for youngsters as part of the city's summer recreation program.)

Half Shot A shot played with an abbreviated swing and reduced swing speed. This shot is often played when trying to keep the ball out of a strong wind. (With so much at stake, Amy Alcott played a half shot to the final green and made a comfortable par.)

Heel The part of the clubhead nearest the hosel. (Fuzzy Zoeller addresses the ball off the heel of his driver.) A shot hit off the heel is said to be "heeled."

Heel and Toe Weighted A club design where weight is distributed toward the heel and toe of a club, usually an iron, to reduce the effect of mis-hits. (When he played with heel-and-toe-weighted irons, his scores improved.)

High Side The side of the hole that a putt breaks from. (He missed the putt on the high side of the hole.)

Hitter A player who favors a forceful, aggressive style of swing. (Arnold Palmer has been a hitter of the ball throughout his career.)

Hooding The act of placing the hands ahead of the ball, both at address and impact, which tends to reduce the effective loft of the club. (Because he was trying to hit his shot under the tree limbs, Tom Kite hooded a 6-iron and ran the ball onto the green.)

Hook A shot that curves sharply from right to left for right-handed players. (When playing the par-5 13th at Augusta National, many players try to hit a sweeping hook from the tee.)

Hosel The part of the club connecting the shaft to the clubhead. (When the PGA Professional studied Tom's 5-iron, she saw that it was bent at the hosel.)

Impact The moment in the swing when the club strikes the ball. (Betsy's feet slipped at impact, resulting in a poor drive.)

Inside-to-In A description of the swing path that, all things being equal, will produce the greatest percentage of solid, straight and on-target shots. It refers to a path in which the clubhead travels from inside the target line, to impact, and then back inside the target line. (Once she developed an inside-to-in swing, her ball-striking improved dramatically.)

Inside-to-Out A swing path in which the clubhead approaches the ball from inside the target line and, after contact, continues to the outside of the target line before turning back to the inside of the target line. (Every so often, his inside-to-out swing path resulted in shots that missed the target to the right.)

Intended Line of Flight The direction a player plans for the ball to begin in after impact. (Because she planned to hit a hook from the tee, her intended line of flight was at the right-hand fairway bunker.)

Iron Byron A testing device modeled after Byron Nelson's swing. It is used to test clubs and balls.

Kinesiology The scientific study of man's movement and the movements of implements or equipment that he might use in exercise, sport or other forms of physical activity.

Kinetic Energy The form of energy associated with the speed of an object. Its equation is $KE = 1/2 \ mv2$; or kinetic energy $= 1/2$ mass $\times$ velocity squared. (It is obvious from the formula that increasing clubhead velocity has more potential for producing distance than increasing the clubhead weight.)

Lag A shot (usually a pitch, chip or putt) designed to finish short of the target. (Since the green was severely sloped from back to front, he hit a lag putt that stopped just short of the hole.)

Lateral Slide or Shift A movement early in the forward swing in which the hips begin to slide to the target and rotate while, at the same time, weight begins to shift from the trail side to the target side. The timing of this motion is crucial to a proper swing. (The commentators were impressed by the young player's lateral shift.)

Lay Off When the swing plane flattens out at the top of the backswing, it causes the club to point to the side of the target and the face to close. (His PGA Professional watched him hit a few balls and then told him that he was getting the club laid off at the top of his backswing.)

Learning Center A complete practice and instruction facility, which may or may not be on the site of a golf course. (While there was no golf course nearby, she was able to work on her game at the local learning center.)

Level-Par A term describing a score of even par. (Jones was level-par after the first round of the Open.)

Lever System The skeletal system is composed of numerous bones which, in mechanical terms, act as levers. The two primary levers in the golf swing are (1) the target arm, comprised of the radius and ulna of the lower arm and the humerus in the upper arm, and (2) the club when the target wrist becomes cocked.

Lie As it relates to the ball, the position of the ball when it has come to rest. (He hit his drive into the rough, but luckily had a good lie.) As it relates to the club, it is the angle of the sole of the club relative to the shaft. (He liked the sand wedge but the lie was too flat.)

Lights-Out A slang term describing an outstanding round or stretch of holes. (She played lights-out after the turn.)

Line The intended path of the ball, usually referred to in the context of putting. (She judged the line perfectly and made the putt.)

Line of Flight The actual path of the ball. (There was a grandstand in his line of flight, so the Rules official allowed him to take a drop without penalty.)

Links The term for a course built on linksland, which is land reclaimed from the ocean. It is not just another term for a golf course. (The Old Course at St. Andrews is the most famous links in the world.)

Lob Shot A short, high shot, usually played with a wedge, designed to land softly. (He played a delicate lob shot over the bunker and saved his par.)

Loft The degree of angle on the clubface, with the least loft on a putter and the most on a sand wedge. (Tom Kite popularized the sand wedge with 60 degrees of loft.) It also describes the act of hitting a shot. (Kite lofted his approach over the pond.)

Long Irons The 1- to 4-irons. (The long irons are often difficult for people to hit, so PGA Professionals often recommend replacing them with fairway woods.)

Looking Up The act of prematurely lifting your head to follow the flight of the ball, which also raises the swing center and can result in erratic ball-striking. (Once she stopped looking up, her scoring improved dramatically.)

Loop The shape of the swing when the backswing and forward swing are in different planes. (Jim Furyk has a distinct loop in his swing but his swing is very effective.) Loop also refers to a round of golf. (The caddie finished his morning loop and then went right back out without eating lunch.)

Loosened Grip Any time a player opens his fingers and loses control of the club. When this happens at the top of the backswing, it is often referred to as "playing the flute." (Once he made the grip changes his PGA Professional suggested, his problem with a loosened grip was corrected.)

Mechanics The components of a golf swing or putting stroke. (Nick Faldo constantly works on the mechanics of his swing.)

Middle Irons The 5- to 7-irons. (He was very accurate with his middle irons, which helped set up a lot of birdies.)

Mulligan The custom of hitting a second ball—without penalty—on a hole, usually the 1st tee. (Mulligans are not allowed according to the Rules of Golf.)

Nassau A competition in which points are awarded for winning the front nine, back nine and overall 18. (Nassaus are the most popular form of betting game.)

Off-Green Putting When a player elects to putt from off the green rather than chip. (She favored off-green putting because she lacked confidence in her chipping and pitching.)

Offset A measure of the distance between the leading edge of the hosel and the leading edge of the clubface. (The added offset on his new irons helped reduce his slicing.)

One-Piece Takeaway Sometimes called the "modern" takeaway, it describes the beginning of the backswing when the hands, arms and wrists move away from the ball, maintaining the same relationship they had at address. (Sam Snead is credited with developing the one-piece take-away.)

Open Clubface When, either at address or during the swing, the heel of the clubhead is leading the toe, causing the clubface to point to the side of the target. (An open clubface caused him to hit his approach shot to the side of the green.)

Open Grip Also referred to as a weak grip, it is when the hands are turned counterclockwise on the club. (His open grip made it difficult for him to hook the ball.)

Open Stance When the target (or lead) foot is pulled back farther from the target line than the trail (or rear) foot. This stance generally helps promote a left-to-right ball flight for right-handed golfers. (Since she played from an open stance, it was easy for her to fade the ball around the large tree.)

Open-to-Closed A description of the movement of the clubface when a player fans it open on the backswing and then closes it at impact. (When his timing was correct, his open-to-closed swing produced wonderful shots.)

Outside-to-In A description of a swing path when the clubhead approaches the ball from outside the target line and then continues to the inside of that line following impact. (His outside-to-in swing path allowed him to hit his approach shot very near the pin, which was cut on the right side of the green.)

Overclub To pick the wrong club, usually for an approach shot, causing the ball to go over the green. (He overclubbed his approach to the 18th green, and his ball came to rest in a shrub.)

Pace The speed of the golf swing (He had a beautiful pace to his swing) or the speed of the greens (The greens at the PGA Championship had a quick pace, which the better putters favored).

Paddle Grip A putting grip with a flat surface where the thumbs rest. (Ben Crenshaw's old putter had a paddle grip.)

Par The score an accomplished player is expected to make on a hole, either a 3, 4 or 5. (The 12th hole at Augusta National is one of the most famous par 3s in golf.)

Path The direction the club travels during the swing or the putting stroke. This is best observed from an overhead view. (When they studied the videotapes in the learning center, they saw that she had a pronounced outside-to-in swing path.)

Pendulum Stroke In putting, a stroke that moves the clubhead back and forth on a constant line, without deviation. (His pendulum stroke made him a very effective putter.)

Pinch Shot A shot played around the green in which a player strikes the ball with a crisp, clean descending blow. (She pinched the ball off a perfect lie and holed the shot.)

Pistol Grip A grip, usually on a putter, that is built up under the left or top hand. (He had a pistol grip placed on his new putter.)

Pitch-and-Run A shot from around the green, usually with a middle or short iron, where the ball carries in the air for a short distance before running toward the hole. (She played a beautiful pitch-and-run to within a foot of the hole.)

Pivot The rotation of the body around a relatively fixed point, usually the spine. (Throughout Fred Couples's career, people have marveled at his full pivot.)

Plugged Lie The condition when the ball comes to rest in its own pitch mark, usually in a bunker or soft turf. (The ball plugged in the bunker, resulting in a difficult shot.)

Plumb-bob A method many players use to help them determine the amount a putt will break. It involves positioning oneself behind the ball and holding the putter vertically so it covers the ball. In theory, the shaft of the putter will indicate the amount the ball will break. It does not, however, measure the speed of the green, which is an important element in reading a putt. (Ryder Cup Captain Curtis Strange often plumb-bobs his putts.)

Pre-Shot Routine The actions a player takes from the time a club is selected until the player begins the swing. (Her pre-shot routine never varied when she was playing her best golf.)

Press To try and hit the ball harder than usual. (He thought he could carry the trees and so he pressed with his driver.) This also describes an extra effort to play well. (When he bogeyed the first two holes, he began to press.) In betting terms, it's an additional bet made after a player falls behind in a match. (When he fell 2 down in his match, he pressed.)

Private Lesson Generally speaking, when a PGA Professional gives a lesson to a single pupil. (After losing in the club championship, she had a private lesson with her PGA Professional.)

Pronation An inward rotation of the hands toward the body's centerline when standing in a palms-facing-forward position. (The term was inaccurately used for many years to describe the rotation of both hands through the impact area. In fact, one hand, the right, was pronating while the left was supinating. Obviously, it is impossible to pronate both hands through the shot.)

Pulled Hook A shot that begins to the side of the target line and continues to curve even farther away. (He hit a pulled hook off the 18th tee in the final round, but luckily the ball stayed in bounds.)

Pulled Shot A relatively straight shot that begins to the side of the target and doesn't curve back. (She pulled her shot and ended up in the left-hand bunker.)

Pulled Slice A shot that starts well to the side of the target but curves back to the side. (He hit a pulled slice that landed safely on the green.)

Punch Shot A low-flying shot played with an abbreviated backswing and finish. The key to the shot is having the hands slightly ahead of the clubhead at impact, which reduces the effective loft of the club. (With the winds howling off the ocean, she played a beautiful punch shot into the green.)

Pushed Hook A shot that begins to the side of the target but curves back to the target. (Under the pressure of the final round, he hit a pushed hook from the tee of the 17th hole.)

Pushed Shot A shot that starts to the side of the target and never curves back. (He pushed his tee shot into the right rough.)

Pushed Slice A shot that starts to the side of the target and curves farther away. (His pushed slice on the first hole flew out-of-bounds, setting the tone for the match.)

Radius The distance between the center of the swing arc (the left or forward shoulder) and the hands on the grip. (Because of his unusually long arms, his swing had a large radius.)

Raised Swing Center Elevating the central area in the body (somewhere between the top of the spine and the center of the neck) around which rotation takes place. What the novice frequently refers to as "looking up" and which results in a swing that is too high.

Rap To hit a putt with a short, firm stroke. (PGA Champion Gene Sarazen liked to rap his putts.)

Reading the Green (or Putt) The entire process involved in judging the break and path of a putt. (Her caddie, Tom, was a genius at reading a green.)

Recover To successfully hit a shot from a poor location. (Throughout his career, Arnold Palmer was known for his ability to boldly recover from trouble.)

Release The act of freely returning the clubhead squarely to the ball at impact, producing a powerful shot. (Tiger Woods has a textbook release of the club at impact.)

Reverse Weight Shift A swing flaw in which the weight moves forward on the backswing instead of to the back leg. (His reverse weight shift caused him to be a poor driver of the ball.)

Rhythm The coordination of movement during the golf swing or putting stroke. (For generations, Sam Snead's golf swing has been the model of perfect rhythm.)

Road Hole The par-4 17th hole at the Old Course at St. Andrews, one of the most famous and difficult holes in the world. (His approach on the Road Hole missed the green and cost him the British Open.)

Round Robin A tournament format in which players or a team play a variety of other teams, the winner being the player or team that accumulates the highest number of points. (The two brothers always teamed in the club's Fall Round Robin.)

Scoring Clubs The driver, putter and sand wedge. (He devoted much of his practice to the scoring clubs.)

Scramble To recover from trouble (Seve Ballesteros could scramble with the best of them) or a popular form of team play in which the team members pick the ball in the best position and everyone plays from that spot (The member-guest was played in a scramble format).

Semiprivate Lesson An instruction format where a limited number of pupils work with a Professional. (When the triplets wanted to take up golf, their parents arranged for them to take semiprivate lessons with their PGA Professional.)

Separation When any of the various body parts and/or the club move either faster or slower than the other elements of the swing. (He worked very hard to prevent his arms from separating on the downswing.)

Setup The process of addressing the ball, so that the club and body are properly aimed and aligned. (Since his setup was so good, he could occasionally recover from the slight errors in his swing.)

Shank When the ball is struck on the hosel of the club, usually sending it shooting off to the right. (He hit a shank on his approach to the eighth hole, and the ball almost struck his caddie.)

Shape To curve a shot to fit the situation. (His ability to shape a shot really impressed the older players.) The word is also used to describe the flight of the ball. (The usual shape of his shots was a fade.)

Short Game Those shots played on and around the green, including putting, chipping and pitching, and bunker shots. (To go along with his power, Tiger Woods has a phenomenal short game.)

Short Irons The 8- and 9-irons and the pitching wedge. The sand wedge is considered a scoring or specialty club. (He wanted flatter-than-standard lies on his short irons.)

Shut A position in the swing when the clubface is closed relative to the target line. (The cause of his poor driving was a shut clubface at the top of the backswing.)

Sky A high, short shot caused by the clubhead striking the underside of the ball. Also known as a "pop-up." (He skied his tee shot and the ball barely reached the fairway.)

Slice A ball that curves from left to right to a greater degree than a fade. (His game was plagued by a terrible slice that he developed as a youngster.)

Smothered Hook A low right-to-left shot that dives quickly to the ground. The cause is an extremely closed clubface. (He hit a smothered hook from the tee, and the ball splashed into a nearby pond.)

Sole When referring to equipment, it is the bottom of a club. (The sole of his wedge had become rusty over the winter.) When referring to the swing, it is the point when the sole of the club touches the ground at address. (When he soled his club, the ball moved and he called a penalty on himself.)

Sole-Weighted A design, usually for fairway woods, that incorporates additional weight along the sole of the club. This makes it easier to get the ball into the air and is also effective from the rough. (Many players in the PGA Championship had sole-weighted clubs in their bags because of the deep rough.)

Splash Shot A shot played from a good lie in the bunker. The club "splashes" through the sand, throwing the ball into the air. (He splashed the ball out of the bunker, landing the ball within a foot of the hole.)

Spoon A term for a 3-wood that is seldom used today. (He reached the par 5 with a driver and a spoon.)

Spot Another term for marking the ball on the green so it might be lifted. (He put a spot on his ball so he could clean it before putting.)

Spot-Putting Using an intermediate target such as a discolored blade of grass or an old ball mark as a means of aiming a putt. (Once he began spot-putting, his scores began to improve.)

Square A term frequently used in golf. It can be used to describe a stance (His feet, hips and shoulders were all square to the target line) or the clubface (His club was perfectly square to the target line) or to describe contact with the ball (The key to greater driving distance is making square contact). It can also refer to the status of a match. (They were all square [tied] at the turn.)

Stance The position of the feet at address. (He played most shots from an open stance.)

Steer An attempt to guide the flight of the ball that usually results in a loss of distance. (He tried to steer the ball off the first tee, but wound up hitting a weak push into the rough.)

Straight-faced The description of a club with very little loft, such as a driving iron, or a driver that lacks the standard bulge and roll. (Because of the strong winds, he often drove with a straight-faced iron.)

Stroke Play Also known as medal play, it is a form of competition based on the cumulative number of strokes taken, either over one round or several. (Most professional tournaments are stroke-play events.)

Strong Grip A term used to describe a grip in which the hands are turned counterclockwise on the grip. It does not connote a stronger-than-normal grip pressure. (PGA Champion Paul Azinger has a strong grip.)

Supination An outward rotation of the hands (thumbs turning out) away from the body's centerline when standing in a palms-facing-the-body position. In the golf swing it is the trail-hand rotation motion on the backswing and the target hand's rotation on the forward swing.

Swaying An exaggerated lateral movement of the body on either the backswing, forward swing or both, which results in inconsistent shotmaking. (His PGA Professional suggested a drill to correct his swaying.)

Sweet Spot The point on the clubface where, if it is struck with an object, the clubface will not torque or twist to either side. (To find the sweet spot on his putter, he held the grip with his thumb and forefinger and let it hang vertically. Then he tapped the face of the putter with the eraser-end of a pencil until the putterhead moved back without any torquing or twisting.)

Swing Arc The entire path the clubhead makes in the course of a swing. It is a combination of the swing's width and length. (His swing arc resulted in tremendous clubhead speed.)

Swing Center A point, usually near the base of the neck and the top of the spine, around which the arms and upper body rotate during the swing. (Since his swing center remained constant throughout the swing, he was a very consistent ball-striker.)

Swinger A player whose swing is based on timing and rhythm, as opposed to a "hitter," whose swing is based on sheer power. (Gene Littler is a textbook example of a swinger.)

Swing Plane An imaginary surface that describes the path and angle of the club during the swing. (As a rule, tall players tend to have a more upright swing plane than shorter players.)

Swingweight A measure of the effective weight of a club. (His driver had a D-8 swingweight, which is heavier than standard.)

Swingweight Scale A device for measuring swingweight. (Every PGA Professional knows how to use a swingweight scale.)

Takeaway The movement of the club at the start of the backswing. (Her slow takeaway set the pace for her entire swing.)

Target Line An imaginary (often visualized) line drawn behind and through the ball to the point a player is aiming at. If the player is planning to curve the ball, this point is the initial—not the ultimate—target. (Jack Nicklaus visualizes his target line before every shot.)

Tee Box The area where players tee to start a hole. (Robert Trent Jones designed long tee boxes.)

Tempo The speed of the swing (not necessarily the clubhead speed). (Ernie Els has a beautiful tempo.)

Texas Wedge A term describing a shot played with a putter from well off the green. It is a good shot for players who lack confidence in their chipping and pitching, or in extremely windy conditions. (Under tournament pressure, he often played a Texas wedge, rather than risk chipping the ball.)

Three-Quarter Shot A shot played with a shortened backswing and lessened arm speed. (With the winds blowing off the ocean, he played a three-quarter shot into the 15th green.)

Tier A rise or level in a green or tee. (It was important to land your approach shot on the proper tier.)

Timing The sequence of motions within the golf swing. (Her timing was so good that it made up for her minor swing faults.)

Toed Shot Any shot hit off the toe of the club. (Facing a fast, downhill putt, he toed his approach putt and left it short of the hole.)

Topped Shot A low, bouncing shot caused by the bottom of the club striking the top half of the ball. (He topped his drive on the first tee and never regained his composure.)

Touch A player's sense of feel, generally around the greens. (Ben Crenshaw has always had a great touch.)

Trajectory The height and angle the ball travels when struck. (Great players are able to control the trajectory of their shots.)

Transition The change of direction in the swing, from the backswing to the forward swing. (It's very important to make a smooth transition in your swing.)

Uncock The release or straightening of the wrists during the downswing. (She uncocked her wrists prematurely, causing her to lose power in her swing.)

Upright A steeper-than-normal swing plane. (His upright swing helped him escape from the rough.) Upright also refers to a club's lie in which the shaft is placed at a steeper-than-standard angle. (His PGA Professional suggested upright lies in his long irons.)

Vector A quantity or measure related to force that has both magnitude and direction. An important factor in determining the distance and direction a ball travels.

Visualization A mental image of a swing or shot or even an entire round. (Once she began visualizing her shots, her scoring improved dramatically.)

Waggle A motion or several motions designed to keep a player relaxed at address and help establish a smooth pace in the takeaway and swing. (His father told him to try to copy Sam Snead's waggle.)

Weak Grip A term describing a grip in which the hands are turned to the left for a right-handed player. (When Ben Hogan weakened his grip, he began fading the ball.)

Whiff A complete miss. Also known as an "air ball." (He was so nervous that he whiffed his drive.)

Yips A condition, generally believed to be psychological, which causes a player to lose control of his hands and club. In Great Britain, the condition is referred to as the "Twitchies." This generally occurs when putting or in the short game, but it can also afflict people hitting a tee shot. (Bernhard Langer has fought the yips for much of his professional career.)

Index

The PGA Manual of Golf by Rick Martino with Don Wade
Note: Page numbers in italics refer to illustrations.